ALIGNING PAY and <u>*RESULTS*</u>

ALIGNING PAY and RESULTS

Compensation Strategies That Work From the Boardroom to the Shop Floor

Howard Risher, Editor
Senior Fellow, Center for Human Resources, Wharton School

AMACOM
American Management Association
New York • Atlanta • Boston • Chicago • Kansas City • San Francisco • Washington, D.C.
Brussels • Mexico City • Tokyo • Toronto

PUBLISHED IN COOPERATION WITH **ACA** AMERICAN COMPENSATION ASSOCIATION

Special discounts on bulk quantities of AMACOM books are
available to corporations, professional associations,
and other organizations.
For details contact Special Sales Department,
AMACOM, an imprint of AMA Publications,
a division of American Management Association,
1601 Broadway, New York, NY 10019
Tel. 212-903-8316   Fax. 212-903-8083

This publication is designed to provide accurate and authoritative
information in regard to the subject matter covered. It is sold with
the understanding that the publisher is not engaged in rendering
legal, accounting, or other professional service. If legal advice or
other expert assistance is required, the services of a competent professional person should be sought.

Library of Congress Cataloging-in-Publication Data

Aligning pay and results : compensation strategies that work from the
     boardroom to the shop floor / Howard Risher, editor.
          p.   cm.
     Includes bibliographical references and index.
     ISBN 0-8144-0458-8
     1. Compensation management.   2. Wages and labor productivity.
3. Wage payment systems.   4. Executives—Salaries, etc.   I. Risher,
Howard.   II. American Management Association.
     HF5549.5.C67A355   1999
     658.3'22—dc21   99-25896
                                                              CIP

Printing number

10 9 8 7 6 5 4 3 2 1

Contents

===== · ∎ · =====

Preface

This book brings together a group of prominent consultants to focus on one of the most important trends in the management of people: the use of compensation as a reward for achieving organizational goals. The phrase *linking pay to performance* is widely used in discussing compensation programs where payouts are contingent on reaching specific performance goals. Contingent compensation has been common, if not universal, for executives and managers, but it has been rare below the management level until the past few years.

The traditional compensation model has its origins in the owner-management thinking that dominated the first half of the twentieth century. That model reserved the rewards of business success for the owners. Over the last half of the century, the group of participating executives was gradually expanded, but below the executive level, incentive plans (other than sales commission plans) were rare. That is now changing rapidly.

In the emerging compensation model, incentives are an integral component, reflecting the belief that every employee can and should be expected to contribute to the company's success. The new pay systems are often referred to as gain-sharing plans, although other phrases—*goal sharing, success sharing,* and *achievement sharing* are examples—readily communicate the intent of these plans. Incentive plans are now being designed for all job levels and occupations. In hospitals, for example, it is common to find group incentives where patient satisfaction is one of the criteria used to determine payouts. Gain-sharing plans have also surfaced in government.

The new incentive plans reflect the heightened interest and new thinking in measuring performance. Performance measurement has become a routine issue at all levels and an integral element of the performance management process. Linking the measurement process to the reward system is a natural extension of this thinking.

At every level, from the boardroom to the shop floor, incentives are being designed to align the financial interests of plan participants with measures that are related to the success of the organization. Financil measures still dominate, but the array of nonfinancial measures—everything from process measures to employee skill development—is indicative of a more sophisticated way of looking at indicators of organizational health.

The program design problem is basically the same at the executive level as it is for shop floor employees. Someone has to decide what level of performance or results is expected, and that in turn is linked to planned payout levels. It thus requires an understanding of how incentives fit an organization and the working relationships of the people who will participate in the program. That rides on an understanding of both the business dynamics and the human dynamics. Incentives are effectively the fuel that drives the machine.

Base salary management has also been affected by the concern with improved performance. The new ideas in wage and salary management—skill-based pay and competency-based pay—link increases to the behaviors and abilities that contribute to results. The traditional merit pay policy was intended as a reward for last year's performance; the new concepts shift the focus to the individual's value into the future. The intent is to provide an incentive for employees to assume greater responsibility for developing the skills and competencies that will make them more valuable.

The use of incentives is not new. Profit sharing is now over one hundred years old, gain sharing was conceived in the 1930s, and executive incentives and stock ownership arrangements have been part of executive compensation since the end of World War II. What is new is the reliance on incentives as a flexible management tool that needs to be molded to the situation and changing organization priorities. The new plans represent a more aggressive use of reward opportunities at all levels to provide a focus for employee efforts. There is a clear expectation that linking pay to performance will enhance the organization's prospects for continued success.

This book is intended as a resource for readers who are considering changes in a compensation program. There was a time in the not-too-distant past when every pay program looked very much like every other pay program. New pay programs in that era were purposely based on methods that were defensible because some number of companies were doing the same thing. That house of cards has effectively crashed. Companies now want to be sure a new pay program meets defined organizational needs. That requires creative problem solving. This book was developed to meet that need.

Overview of the Contents

My objective as editor was to assemble a team of authors that includes the premier consultants in the country. Each author has been asked to develop a chapter on a subject that is a focus of his or her consulting practice. They have individually and through their firms been leaders in developing the ideas discussed in their chapters. A number of the authors have books of their own that cover the subject in greater depth. No single consulting firm has the breadth of expertise represented in the team of authors. That makes this book a unique resource.

My introductory chapter looks at the changes in the way work is organized and managed. In combination, the changes are the often mentioned new work paradigm. The intent is clear: to raise the bar of performance. The use of incentives is one of the tools to accomplish that.

Chapter 2 is a personalized account of the lessons learned by an in-house expert, Edward Sullivan, who has spent most of his career as an internal compensation consultant for DuPont. That corporation has had a decade of experience with variable-pay systems and recently announced a plan to develop and install incentive plans covering all DuPont employees worldwide. The introduction of these plans represents a significant change in compensation strategy for DuPont, and line managers have resisted it at times. Chapter 2 is an overview of what Ed learned.

Section I looks at traditional incentive plans. Executive and management incentives are well established but they are still evolving.

- In Chapter 3 Richard Bannister and Bill Gentry, senior consultants with Towers Perrin, develop a framework for designing annual management incentive plans. The basic plan concepts have not changed, but the performance measures have, and they now cover the use of several new concepts.

- Chapter 4, by Jude Rich, chairman of Sibson & Company, focuses on another important trend, the use of economic value or the creation of shareholder value, as the basis for typically longer-term incentives.

- In Chapter 5 Eric Marquardt, a senior consultant with the Compensation Resource Group, looks at the use of company stock in compensation programs. Executive stock ownership (and other equity ownership opportunities), along with broad-based options, are now significant components of the program at all levels.

- Pearl Meyer, president of Pearl Meyer & Partners, explores the trends in directors' compensation in Chapter 6. These programs have also undergone a dramatic change away from simple fee arrangements for attending meetings to opportunities to acquire stock in the companies they serve.

In Section II we switch to the new concepts in wage and salary management. There is a widely shared recognition that the traditional pay program model does not fit the new work paradigm.

- Jim Kochanski, a senior consultant with Sibson, has jointly authored Chapter 7 with me on competency-based pay.

- Chapter 8, by Marc Wallace and Fred Crandall, cofounders of the Center for Workforce Effectiveness, looks at competency-based and skill-based pay as incentives for employees to enhance their competence and add new skills. With both concepts, the focus of base pay management shifts from the value of the job to the value of the individual.

Section III explores the new ideas in the use of incentives for employees below the executive level. The experience with these plans represents a new direction for industry and one of the most important trends in the management of people.

■ In Chapter 9 Tom Wilson, president of the Wilson Group, explores the broad area of group incentive plans. The phrase *gain sharing* is often used to refer to these plans, but the original understanding of that phrase has been broadened to include any incentive in which a group of employees are eligible to share equally in a bonus pool that depends on one or more performance measures relevant to the group. Group incentives have been linked to performance at every level, from the company to the plant, and even to work groups within a plant.

■ Steve Gross, the compensation practice director for William Mercer, looks in Chapter 10 at the more specific problem of team-based pay. Team pay involves the introduction of a new pay system, including changes in the management of base salaries as well as an incentive plan linked to team performance. Team pay violates the one-program-for-everyone thinking that has dominated compensation planning. For companies that are comfortable with this change in philosophy, it opens the door to the introduction of different and separate programs for different teams.

■ Chapter 11 by Neil Coleman, a senior consultant at Organization Resources Counselors, looks at these problems in a global context. Other societies do not view employee compensation and incentives in the same way as we in the United States do. At the same time, companies like DuPont are working to implement incentives worldwide. The chapter provides an overview of how to extend this thinking so it is successful in other cultures.

■ Rick Anthony, president of the Solutions Network, discusses in Chapter 12 the overriding issue of how to communicate changes in compensation programs to employees. Change is always difficult to accept, especially when it affects an employee's future earnings. Since the increased reliance on incentives is a new strategy to most employees below the management level, there is commonly some skepticism and hesitancy. At the same time, new pay systems are intended to affect employee motivation and their behavior in desired ways. That makes it essential for them to understand and accept the changes. In today's world of aggressive marketing and advertising, the selling of these new ideas cannot be accomplished with simple announcements.

Chapter 13 concludes the book with a look at the role of compensation, specifically its role as an incentive in driving desired organizational changes and reaching higher levels of performance. In an environment where employees do not trust management, pay cannot effectively play this role. But in the right circumstances and with compatible people management practices, pay can be a powerful tool that energizes the workforce. The opportunity to take part in a successful enterprise and to benefit from that organization's success has been an important element in the history of the United States. The high level of interest in linking pay to performance is consistent with that history and takes advantage of an important source of motivation.

1

Aligning Pay and Results

· ■ ·

Howard Risher
a senior fellow in the Center for Human Resources,
Wharton School, University of Pennsylvania

The way that work is organized and managed is in an ongoing revolution triggered by technological breakthroughs and the mounting pressure of global competition. Everything is moving and changing faster and faster. In response, corporations have been forced to find ways to become more competitive. The pressures to keep up with fast-changing technology and to improve performance are driving employers in every sector to change the way they operate. Corporations will never be the same again.

In this environment the traditional ways of defining jobs and work systems are being rapidly transformed. The ideas that have come together to create a new work paradigm seemed radical and experimental only a few years ago.

At the heart of the traditional work management model is the principle best expressed as "paying an adequate wage." That belief system got started in the factories of the 1930s when the Great Depression had lowered wage levels and triggered the labor-management confrontation that continued to World War II. The pay systems that evolved out of this era reflected a solidly entrenched belief that a few senior executives were responsible for making all of the important organization decisions and therefore were the only individuals who should reap the financial rewards of corporate success.

As recently as the early 1990s, the only people who could expect to participate in incentive plans or to be eligible for stock ownership opportunities were senior executives. Sales personnel have been paid in part on commission, but that is also an old tradition. Compensation planning focused on creating programs for the small group of professional managers and executives who replaced the entrepreneur founders. The goal was to create incentives to make these corporate leaders act as though they were owners.

That philosophy stands in direct contrast to the new work paradigm with its emphasis on worker empowerment. Now we recognize that people at all levels can and should be expected to play a bigger role in achieving organizational goals. We also understand that the old "us-versus-them" mind-set is an impediment to the improvement that all corporations need. In the new paradigm, everyone is expected to pitch in and work together to achieve corporate goals.

The transition from the old to the new has proved to be difficult to realize. People are always more comfortable with old ideas and established behaviors. Increasingly, though, employers have come to realize that traditional pay systems are part of the problem; a sense of entitlement is common, and pay program design is locked in a past era. Annual pay increases have been virtually automatic, with the cost of living a more important consideration than performance. Anyone who works hard enough to stay out of trouble can expect an increase. Our so-called merit increases have provided little, if any, incentive to change behavior and improve performance and, in fact, they reinforce the old behaviors over and over.

A rapidly growing number of companies have begun to introduce incentive plans where pay is linked to performance. This is happening at every organizational level and in every industry, including the public sector. The clear intent is to use the power of money as a motivator to reward employees for improving performance. Although that tool has always been available to management, traditionally it was reserved for management pay programs. Employees in the typical company have been treated as a cost that had to be minimized. The new plans that link pay to performance represent a radical shift in thinking that is the keystone of a new employer-employee relationship.

Solid evidence shows that people will commit to the achievement of organizational goals when they feel their efforts and their contributions are appropriately recognized and rewarded. Cash payments are certainly not the only type of rewards, but those payments are the most easily managed across an organization. When employees are rewarded for accomplishing specific goals or results, it is more likely that the goals will be accomplished. Conversely when the importance of goals is not reinforced with the reward system, meeting goals is less likely.

The linkage between performance and rewards—pay-for-performance—has become an important strategic issue at all organizational levels. The reward system changes that are now being installed at many corporations represent a basic fundamental philosophical change in the relationship between employees and their employers. The intent with the new plans is to provide a shared focus and commitment and to encourage everyone to work toward the organization's success.

Profit Sharing: The Traditional Pay-for-Performance Model

Profit sharing is by far the oldest approach to reward employees for good performance, with origins going back to the mid-nineteenth century. It is simple and straightforward—a portion of the profits is distributed among employees—and it can be a highly effective incentive. Surveys show that it is still the most common pay-for-performance approach. It has served as the foundation for incentive plans for both executives and hourly workers.

In the typical profit-sharing plan, payouts are contingent on operating above some minimum level of profitability. The focus on profits is an obvious one for owners and gives everyone a shared goal. Typically a funding formula stipulates the percentage of profits in excess of the threshold that will be paid out to plan participants.

That concept can work effectively when an organization is small and employees feel that their efforts have an impact on profits. But as companies grow and establish multiple work locations across the country and the rest of the world, workers can begin to lose their sense of direct connection to the profits of the company. They may also realize that factors outside their control, such as the demand for the company's products or accounting decisions, may have as much or more impact on profits than their efforts.

3

Profit sharing is the foundation for executive incentive plans. The threshold is usually is defined as a percentage return on assets or stockholders' equity—the minimum acceptable return to investors. Payouts are then determined by a formula that designates the percentage of the excess profits that will be paid to participants. Executive plans based on this concept go back at least as far as the 1930s and developed in companies where the owners, the majority stockholders, were no longer the primary executives responsible for day-to-day operations. Until recently the participants in these plans were typically limited to senior executives, perhaps 1 percent of a company's workforce.

Even at the executive level, however, there are problems with incentives based on profit sharing. One of the most fundamental issues is that a company's financial results are independent of and driven by economic forces different from executive pay levels. When an executive incentive plan is first designed and adopted, a formula is commonly devised to generate the "right" amount of money to compensate the participants. That amount is based on determining the desired payouts at specified levels of profitability and then backing into a formula that generates the desired incentive pool.

From that point on, however, a company's financial results inevitably grow or decline at a rate that is unrelated to the number of executives and their salaries. If the company prospers, the incentive pool can become much bigger than it should be within a few years, and the company's directors may become reluctant to pay out all of the money in the pool. Conversely, if organizational performance deteriorates and profits do not exceed the threshold for several years, the company's inability to make incentive payouts could cause the better executives to leave for other companies that offer them the promise of higher compensation. When problems like this arise, there is a tendency to reconsider the formula, which affects the plan's credibility.

Similar credibility problems affect broad-based profit-sharing plans, which include virtually all employees (in contrast to executive plans). At lower levels, the understanding of accounting details and the calculations to determine payouts may be limited so the success of a plan often depends on employees' trust in management. When formulas need to be gerrymandered, for the same reasons that affect executive plans, employees will continue to accept the payouts but may be suspicious of the company's motives in changing any change in the formula. This can quickly become a source of tension and a morale problem.

Merit Pay as a Reward for Performance

Traditionally rewards for sustained good performance have been limited to annual merit wage or salary increases. That is commonly understood to be an increase that depends on an appraisal of an employee's performance and in concept is independent of increases in living costs, the other common rationale for pay increases. Merit pay has been a virtually universal practice for managers and professionals in corporate America, and often for all employees. That pattern has not changed in any significant way for several decades. The word *meritocracy* is sometimes used to refer to the culture of the United States, and that philosophy clearly carries over to the typical corporate culture.

Merit pay is not prevalent in the public sector. Significantly, however, a growing number of state and local public employers are moving to merit increase policies. Surveys show that it is not the dominant practice in health care, higher education, or not-for-profit organizations, although it is gradually gaining acceptance in those areas. It is also rare to find merit pay policies in workplaces governed by collective bargaining agreements.

In a corporate environment, the alternatives to merit pay— automatic step increases or across-the-board increases—are alien to the value system. It is hard to imagine a corporate CEO who would publicly proclaim his support for any salary increase alternative other than merit pay. The general agreement is that hard work and outstanding results deserve to be recognized in our society. Conversely, there is generally no organizational support for granting increases to poor performers, although supervisors often have trouble denying increases to the few individuals who are identified as marginal performers.

Despite this, the reality is that merit pay has had more than a few critics. W. Edwards Deming, the quality management guru, was perhaps the most prominent. Performance appraisal was one of his "deadly diseases."[1] He argued strongly and persuasively that rewarding individual performance is a mistake.

Merit pay is no longer a hot button in the human resources literature, nor is it a topic that receives any attention at conferences. These polices are simply taken for granted. Professional human resources associations, such as the American Compensation Association, offer training courses that address merit increase policies, but only briefly. These policies are now routine and for the most part applied consistently across corporate America.

At the same time, the research evidence confirms that employees want to have their performance recognized and rewarded. From a management perspective, every employer needs to know who is considered to be a star performer and who is having performance problems. Any salary increase practice that ignores these differences is sending the message that performance is not a management priority.

As a source of motivation, merit pay is probably not very effective. When the average pay increase is 4 to 4.5 percent (the pattern in the 1990s), even the best performers may be granted only an 8 percent increase. For an employee earning $30,000 or so, that means an extra $25 a week, before taxes. And since marginal workers often receive at least a 2 percent increase, the money available in a budget pool for the star performers is limited.

When inflation soared in the 1970s and early 1980s, the differences between the increases granted to good performers and those granted to poor performers were even less. And when inflation reached double digits, the "keep them whole" thinking (which means pay increases should be large enough to enable employees to maintain the same level of purchasing power) that evolved from the cost-of-living (COLA) allowance or clauses common in labor agreements meant everyone could expect at least an inflationary increase. This experience contributed to a sense of entitlement that is still seen as a problem.

The typical merit pay policy is often referred to as a zero-sum game in that the budget is treated as a fixed sum that supervisors have to allocate among subordinates. The pressure to give at least a minimum increase to even poor performers means that less money is available for the best performers. That is attributable to the practice of showing the amount available as a single line item in the budget.

That situation can be rectified by establishing a separate budgeted amount, such as 2 percent of payroll, that is available for special, supplemental increases for a limited number of superstars, perhaps 15 to 20 percent of the workforce. This simple change makes it easier for supervisors to give above-average increases to the best performers.

There are clearly problems with the way merit pay has been handled in a traditional wage and salary program, problems widely recognized and acknowledged by human resources experts. Line executives also understand that the traditional model for compensating employees is not meeting their organizational needs. It is in part the recognition of those problems that sparked the current high level of interest in finding more effective incentives for improved performance.

Scientific Management and Piece-Rate Incentive Systems

The exception to merit-based increase practices has been the so-called piece-rate incentive systems developed initially for jobs where the quantity of output is a key issue. With a piece-rate pay system, each employee's earnings depend on a measure of productivity. These systems date to the beginning of this century and to the work of Frederick W. Taylor and his principles of scientific management. His thinking became the standard for the organization and management of work across the world. He argued that jobs and work systems should be organized according to "scientific" principles that would guarantee efficiency and optimal production.

Taylor's approach results in jobs designed to be simple, standardized, and highly specialized. Analysts study the tasks that have to be performed and break the worker's efforts down into work units—one of the early Taylor disciples coined the word *therbligs* to refer to those units—that could be documented and managed. Once the work has been broken down to this level of specificity, the information provides a basis for determining supposedly optimal productivity levels. When a job is analyzed and work activities standardized, workers can be trained and become productive quickly. This has been a basic premise of industrial engineering since the 1920s.

To complement and reinforce this approach to work management, incentive systems were developed that paid workers for each piece or unit of output—the so-called piece-rate incentive systems. The idea was that each individual's compensation would be directly tied to his or her productivity. The worker who produces one hundred widgets earns twice the pay as the worker who produces fifty. Piece-rate systems were quickly adopted in the factories of the Depression era and flourished after World War II.

Piece-rate pay practices can be effective incentives that lead to increases in productivity. They also lead to poor quality and assorted other production problems. Since workers are rewarded for the quantity of their output, the message the reward system sends is that nothing else matters, regardless of what a shop foreman might tell them. Piece-rate systems also may trigger tension among workers. When an employee works at a pace that far exceeds the level of output that is the norm among other workers, it demonstrates that the production standards might be too low, and workers quickly learn that this can lead to new, higher standards for everyone.

Piece-rate systems rely exclusively on extrinsic motivation. In the early twentieth-century work environment, intrinsic satisfaction and motivation were hardly considerations. In the workplace, workers were simply cogs in the wheel of production. Management focused on how employees moved their arms and legs, and generally ignored what was going on in their minds.

In one of those summer jobs that many college students experience, I learned firsthand why piece-rate systems fell out of favor. I worked in a tire factory in the mid-1960s where truck tires were assembled in several stages, with industrial engineered production standards at each stage. Each worker had a specified level of output for an eight-hour shift. As a novice, after five weeks I was able to finish the required work in roughly five hours. When we finished, we were allowed to sit around and read, play cards, or do anything else that kept us out of trouble. If they had allowed me to go home when I finished, I probably could have met the production standard in less time. There were a couple of workers who met their standard in as little as three and a half hours. Something was obviously wrong even to a nineteen-year-old kid.

More important than the piece-rate system was the environment it produced and the relationship between the foreman and the workers. This was a union shop, and the pay rates were relatively high. Many of the workers had started in these jobs after they finished military service and had worked in the plant for twenty or more years. In today's world, they might have gone to college. They knew as much or more about building truck tires as anyone in management and could probably have resolved most production problems, but no one ever asked them. There was a classic us-versus-them culture that the foremen seemed to share. They said as little as necessary to the workers, and their interactions were often limited to points of contention. Everything focused on meeting the production standards and otherwise avoiding problems. The waste of that knowledge was in no one's best interest.

Although piece-rate systems have fallen out of favor in many industries, some vestiges still remain in manufacturing operations as well as other production-oriented operations, such as data entry. Any time a reward system is linked solely to the quantity of output, the chances that quality may suffer are high. "You get what you reward" is an old adage. From a different perspective, the fact that piece-rate systems focus on individual performance is clearly out of sync with current work management thinking. (Team and group incentives can be linked to productivity, but it is difficult to establish industrial engineered standards.)

A basic problem was and is the view of workers and their capabilities that is the foundation for scientific management. In 1890 more than a few workers could not read or write; some could not speak English; many had never worked in a factory setting. Work was often harsh. Taylor's principles made sense in that environment and served the world well for most of this century. His principles evidence low expectations of workers; they were not expected to think. And that is now antithetical to the sea change to worker empowerment and the new expectation that every worker contributes to the success of the organization.

Pay-for-Performance as a Management Tool

· ■ ·

Despite the importance of money as a motivator, organizations have been reluctant to rely too heavily on the incentive impact of money. Somehow the acknowledgment that money is so important to people is contrary to other cultural values. The widely shared belief in our society that "there are more important" aspects of life has come together with the traditional reluctance of investors to share the financial rewards with workers. There was a time in the not-too-distant past when a common compensation strategy was to pay employees as little as possible. Both reasons argue against the use of money as a motivator.

Influential "experts" have argued that employers should rely primarily on intrinsic motivation—the satisfaction that one can gain from the work itself. The writings of W. Edwards Deming suggest that he believed that intrinsic satisfaction is the best source of motivation. Significantly many of the individuals who make this argument are lucky enough to work in jobs where intrinsic satisfaction is important.

In some jobs, however, intrinsic satisfaction is not possible. More important, intrinsic satisfaction is inherent in the work itself, and it is unrealistic to expect every job incumbent to derive the same satisfaction and motivation from his or her job. It is also true that the motivation to perform a job in a way that is satisfying is not always in the organization's best interest. Nurses, for example, may not be working to meet hospital goals when they provide the highest level of personal care for patients.

We have learned that intrinsic satisfaction can be a powerful source of motivation. In fact, that is one of the primary outcomes of the new work paradigm with its emphasis on empowerment. The challenge is to channel that motivation to accomplish goals that are important to the organization. That is so important to workers that they often react negatively if they are prevented from realizing intrinsic satisfaction.

The experience with quality management and reengineering has helped to prompt the new thinking about the role of reward systems. Those initiatives were kicked off with high expectations and with little or no concern for the impact of people management policies and programs. If anything, there was a disdain or disregard for those policies.

The advocates for these ideas appeared to assume that everyone would get on their respective bandwagons. They assumed the practices they advocated would have obvious value, and that alone would be enough to prompt people to accept the new ideas.

Those practices, however, have produced only modest results, and consequently the support for quality management and reengineering has faded. There are those who now contend that it was a mistake to ignore the need for a people management strategy that focuses on gaining worker buy-in and commitment. One simple change would have been to refocus pay systems to reward employees for quality or for the improvements anticipated from reengineering. Again the adage, "You get what you pay for," applies. It is apparent in hindsight that these initiatives would have been more successful if they had been reinforced by prospective rewards linked to desired outcomes, even if that was not addressed in Deming's philosophy or Michael Hammer's argument for reengineering.

Another trend over the past decade or so has been the pressure to reduce or control costs, is a focal issue in a broader trend to improve operating results. Employers have slashed costs whenever possible in an attempt to remain competitive. Those concerns came together with a growing realization that employees can influence day-to-day results to trigger a mushrooming interest in gain sharing as a tool to help accomplish management's goals. In contrast to profit sharing with its somewhat fuzzy link to employee efforts, the payouts from a gain-sharing plan can be explicitly tied to measures or results that employees can control or influence.

Gain sharing has been around for a long time—it was introduced in the 1930s by a union leader, Joe Scanlon—but until the past few years, it has been little more than a curiosity concept. A few companies tried it with success, and those organizations were often cited in the business press. Lincoln Electric, a manufacturing firm based in Cleveland, is perhaps the best known of those organizations. The payouts from its gain-sharing plan commonly exceed the typical worker's base salary.

A classic gain-sharing plan is based on the comparison of labor costs over a specified period with the levels in a base period. If the costs are lower, which is interpreted as an increase in worker efficiency or productivity, the savings or gains are shared with employees; typically the savings are split fifty-fifty between the company and its employees. Research has shown that companies have saved roughly three or four dollars for every dollar paid to employees. Gain sharing is similar to profit sharing but is not dependent on profitability. That difference makes it feasible to establish plans at the plant level where profitability is generally hard to determine. Gain-sharing plans are commonly self-funded in the sense that there is no added cost.

In the past few years, the phrase *gain sharing* has been used to refer to a new generation of group incentive plans with payouts tied to a broad range of other performance criteria. Those criteria include but are not limited to customer satisfaction, safety, and quality. For example, hospitals frequently have gain-sharing plans where one of the measures is patient satisfaction. This newer generation of plans may not be self-funded, but they are based solidly on the assumption that the criteria are important to the organization's performance and worth rewarding.

These new plans represent a break with the after-the-fact profit-sharing tradition. In contrast to the philosophy of profit sharing, where the payouts are defined only after profits are determined, the new generation of plans specifies the payouts in advance and are based on meeting specific goals or accomplishing specified tasks. This is analogous to the old donkey-and-carrot story where the carrot is hung on a string in front of the animal's eyes. Everyone knows what he or she can expect. The plans are not necessarily self-funded, although reducing costs may be one of the performance goals.

The latest group incentive plans are based on the belief that pay can be used explicitly as a reward system and as a tool to improve performance. Moreover, as program planners broaden their thinking beyond the profit-sharing philosophy, the door opens to reward systems designed for specific work groups or operations. Profit sharing, in contrast, is predicated on an "everyone shares equally" philosophy. The traditional thinking makes internal equity an important priority and reflects a concern that workers who are excluded from a plan might become contentious.

This new orientation is important also because it represents another break from the past. Traditionally employee compensation programs have been the domain of the human resources function, with all of the legal concerns with fairness and the assumption that employees should be treated equally. That background prompted what in hindsight was an unsubstantiated conviction that employees had to be paid under an umbrella pay system, which covers everything including disparate jobs and employees. The new reality treats incentive systems as a management tool that can be designed specifically to fit small groups of workers.

This perspective is reinforced by the exploding interest in teams and the evidence that employees are more likely to become effective team members if they are rewarded for team results. The important issue is that every team is different and that an incentive system that works well for one team may not be the best answer for another one. As we move to team-based pay systems, it becomes that much more logical to design specific reward systems for other groups. That trend portends a very different employee compensation philosophy from the one used in the past.

As we move into this new era, problems and a level of discomfort will be inevitable. The model for salary management has been surprisingly static since at least the 1960s. Employees have had few reasons to think about the way they were compensated other than to speculate about next year's increased budget.

To some degree, the critics have been correct in arguing that pay systems can do more harm than good. That is, traditional pay systems have frequently been a disincentive rather than an incentive. Now we are counting on the new generation of pay systems to influence employee behavior and boost organizational performance. That will require a period of adjustment and transition; the changes are not going to be completed over night.

If the recent trends are indicative of the future, every employee in a few years will be a participant in one or more incentive plans, with payouts tied to the achievement of results that the organization deems important. Organizations will install multiple incentive plans linked to specific operational goals and outcomes. Some employees may participate in two or possibly more incentive systems tied to performance at different levels (e.g., corporate profit sharing and a specific plan tied to customer satisfaction).

Developing a Work Management Strategy to Improve Performance

· ■ ·

Traditional pay systems reflected a work paradigm that originated in the 1930s when labor strife was common. Both labor and management worked under the assumption that, to paraphrase Marx, there was an inherent conflict. One of the overriding goals of management was control, and that meant workers had to do what they were told. Industrial engineers analyzed jobs, documented work duties, and established production standards. They then relied on job evaluation systems—some companies still use a system developed in the 1930s for members of the National Metal Trades Association (NMTA)—to determine appropriate wage levels. Workers had virtually no discretion and actually needed little because jobs and organizations were essentially static. This paradigm was based on a mechanistic view of organizations: the goal of the organization was to become a well-oiled machine.

That world began to change in the 1980s. Deming was one of the first to argue that workers should be more involved in and accountable for decisions that affect quality and customer satisfaction. Although Deming certainly was not focused on people management issues, he effectively opened the door to worker empowerment. The belief that workers have something to contribute other than their muscles was still radical in many organizations. The total quality management (TQM) movement may have faded, but Deming's thinking has changed the work paradigm forever.

With the old paradigm, workers were not responsible for much more than showing up on time, meeting at least minimal performance standards, and staying out of trouble. Work has been seen as undesirable, again attributable to Marx, so limiting the time spent on the job and the mental commitment to it was a reasonable goal. Decisions were made at the highest levels that justified only a minimal sense of responsibility below the management level. In that environment, it made sense to limit pay-for-performance schemes to the few people accountable for results.

Employers also failed to take advantage of the full range of capabilities that workers brought to the job. Jobs have been defined narrowly to make it easier to recruit, train, and make new employees productive. Moreover, there have been either explicit or implicit sanctions discouraging employees from performing duties not listed on their job description. More than a few jobs are tedious and routine to the point that a worker can slide through the day without confronting a single challenging situation. Even the most sophisticated professional jobs have moments when the incumbent is bored and unchallenged. My guess is the typical worker probably uses at most half of his or her capabilities.

Solid research evidence shows that workforce productivity can be increased at least 30 to 40 percent with a different work management paradigm. The research, conducted by Barry Macy at the Texas Center for Quality and Productivity, was based on analyses that started with roughly 300 productivity studies conducted between 1960 and 1990.[2] Macy identified a list of almost sixty "action levers," defined to include equipment, organizational changes, and human resource practices, that are related to employee productivity. Quality management is an example of the levers on his list. Gain sharing is another.

The big increases in productivity are realized when several of the levers are used as an integrated strategy. One of the problems is and has been that organizations have jumped on the bandwagon for one of the levers, treated it as a fad, and focused on it in isolation. That helps to explain the failure of TQM and reengineering. In combination, the levers are elements of a work paradigm that is very different from the traditional work management model. For example, quality management would have been a more powerful lever if it had been connected with a supportive reward system. Macy's research confirms what is intuitively apparent: the problem is complicated, but the potential for improvement easily justifies a commitment to change the way work is organized and managed.

Using Rewards to Drive Improved Performance

Changes in the reward system have to be a component of any strategy to improve performance. Not too many years ago, the standard argument was that changes in a pay system should follow any significant organizational changes. The idea was to allow the organization to settle down before tinkering with the pay system. That, however, runs the risk that the changes will never be fully accepted, as with TQM. When employees continue to be rewarded for old behaviors, they are likely to continue behaving in the same way. For that reason, possible changes in the reward system need to be addressed in developing the change strategy.

For the same reasons, a change in the pay system will affect employees and their behavior and cannot be treated in isolation. Employees will naturally react to the change and will be interested (and anxious) about how the change will affect them. The possibility will be a hot button on the in-house grapevine long before any changes are rolled out. Their reactions can and should be considered fully. As a consultant, I have heard several client executives use the word *bloodletting* in referring to their prior experience with changes in wage and salary programs. There was a time not too long ago that the planning for a new compensation program focused on the numbers—a continuation of the industrial engineering orientation—and was done with a high level of secrecy. That era has ended.

Now, as an early planning step, project leaders need to decide what they want to accomplish as an outcome of the program changes. If there are desired behavioral changes, such as greater sensitivity to customer satisfaction, then that needs to be articulated and agreement reached on how to assess that outcome. If incentives are included in the program changes, the proposed system needs to be tested at the full range of anticipated performance and payouts.

This work needs to be considered as part of the planned paradigm. Any new pay system has to be compatible with and support the paradigm. For example, traditional job evaluation systems commonly are keyed to the hierarchy of jobs and in reality reinforce the importance of the hierarchy. If a company is trying to move to a flatter, more flexible, and more responsive organization, it will be important to modify or eliminate the job evaluation system. Similarly, if the intent is to create a team environment, it is important to measure and reward team performance.

A new model for compensation programs is emerging, with incentives as an important element. There are also important changes in the logic and methods of salary management. Traditional salary management thinking was developed in a different era and is compatible with the traditional work paradigm. Traditional salary programs are now an impediment to change.

Wage and salary management has focused on tightly defined jobs. In fact, if any aspect of the job is changed, it could justify a change in the job's supposed value. In concept, whenever job duties change, the textbooks would have someone from the human resources staff initiate the process to see that the job description is rewritten and the job re-evaluated. Few organizations are able to justify the staff resources to stay on top of this bureaucratic process.

Perhaps more important, traditional salary programs send a message to employees that is out of sync with the way organizations and work are changing. Point factor job evaluation systems, for example, generate points that are an explicit index of where each job ranks in the hierarchy. Everyone knows that their pay and importance depend on how their points slot them in the hierarchy. Moreover, more than a few evaluation systems rely on budget responsibility or staff size to determine a job's value—at a time when a goal of almost every organization is to reduce budgets and staff size! All of this is commonly controlled by "personnel police," who spend a lot of time arguing with managers and job incumbents about why their claims that a job should have a higher salary are not valid.

These programs were conceived in the 1930s and the changes since then have been minor. The NMTA job evaluation is still important. Edward N. Hay, the founder of Hay Management Consultants, was writing articles about his new system in the late 1940s. In the mid-1980s companies started using computers to generate job evaluation answers, but the technology only speeded up the process and facilitated record keeping. The conceptual framework and decision logic were unchanged.

Now we are moving away from this thinking. One of the hottest concepts in salary management has become *broad banding*, which reduces the importance of the hierarchy and the time required to manage the pay program. (See the Introduction to Chapters 7 and 8 for more information on this concept.) Banding introduces new flexibility and effectively delegates much of the responsibility for salary decisions to line managers. All of the old control mechanisms are thrown out or reduced to minimal importance.

Within a broad-band framework, the old thinking about the measurement of job value is no longer meaningful. Everyone in a band is for practical purposes equal in importance, which makes it easier for them to work together. When a job is redefined, it is unlikely that this change will be a reason to move it to another band. The flexibility means that less time and energy are spent on the machinations that traditionally have been required to reevaluate jobs. Banding also reduces the importance of the claimed differences that affect job value. This means job duties can change as the organization responds to its customers and to its product or service markets, and those changes do not trigger a bureaucratic response. There are too many more important issues for employees to worry about than how their job is evaluated relative to others.

In the new model, the focus is on the value of the individual and his or her capabilities. The more an employee can do, the more valuable that person is. At the hourly level, there is a high level of interest in skill-based pay. At the professional level, where cognitive abilities are a key, the new model for managing salaries is competency-based pay. Both concepts focus on the individual's capabilities. The differences are to a degree semantic, but skills are commonly important to manual jobs; the value of a professional or manager does not depend solely on skills.

Both skill- and competency-based pay are explicitly intended as an incentive for employees to enhance their value and their capabilities. The concepts are compatible with the learning organization philosophy and the common desire of employees to grow in their jobs. Employees who take the initiative to add new capabilities are rewarded with pay increases.

Performance or results in this new model are rewarded primarily with incentive payments based on team or group performance. Those rewards will be tied to performance criteria that are important to the organization's future. Smaller companies too will have rewards that give employees a share in the company's success. Those incentive plans are not new, but their importance is dramatically increased.

The focus on the future is an important change in philosophy. The traditional merit increase policy is linked to last year's performance. Similarly, profit sharing and the classic gain-sharing plans are tied to last year's results. The new compensation model shifts the focus to the future and is designed and managed to support future business plans.

Another change in philosophy is the willingness to introduce specific incentive plans for small work groups. Profit sharing started out as an umbrella plan that covered everyone. Gain-sharing plans commonly cover everyone working in a work site. As soon as we start thinking about team-based pay systems, the door opens to multiple plans, each designed for a small group. Each plan may be tied to a set of common organizational goals, but the specific measures and planned payouts may be different for different teams.

The final component of the model will be the opportunity to invest in and own company stock. Those opportunities will never be available in every company, but there is solid evidence that broad-based stock options, such as those granted by Pepsi, or similar stock ownership plans will be more important in the future (see Eric Marquardt's discussion in Chapter 5). This is consistent with the increasing willingness of people at all levels to invest in mutual funds and other alternatives for building personal capital. If we want employees to commit to the success of the company, then it is decidedly advantageous for them to have a stake in its future.

Perhaps the most striking change in the new model is the shift to a philosophy that emphasizes inclusion rather than exclusion. In the traditional model, the focus was executive compensation, and everyone other than that small group was excluded from the club that enjoyed the benefits of company success. This focus can be traced back to the time when owners ran their companies. Profit sharing was commonly all-inclusive, but those plans were a distinct minority. Now a central theme of the new paradigm is the realization that the company stands to benefit when everyone is committed to its success. One of the overriding goals of the new compensation model is to bring people together with a shared commitment to company success. That goal was never evident in the design of a traditional compensation program.

Notes

· ■ ·

1. W. Edwards Deming, *Out of Crises,* Cambridge, MA, MIT Center for Advanced Engineering Studies, 1982. (For discussion of Deming's "deadly diseases" see Chapter 3.)
2. B.A. Macy and H. Izum. "Organizational Change, Design, and Work Innovation: A Metanalysis of 131 North American Field Studies, 1961–1991," As stated in R. Woodman and W. Pasmore, Editors, *Research In Organizational Change and Development* (Greenwhich, CT: JAI Press, 1993), Vol. 7, pp. 235–311.

2

Moving to a Pay-for-Performance Strategy
Lessons From the Trenches

· ■ ·

Edward Sullivan
corporate compensation consultant, DuPont, retired

[Editor's Comment: In 1988 the DuPont Company, one of the ten largest American corporations and one of the larger global corporations, announced the implementation of a variable compensation plan for all its employees in its fibers division, the largest business unit. The plan was called Achievement Sharing and would affect all of the division's 20,000 employees. After two years of high-profile attention in the business press, the plan was discontinued.

Many experts have speculated as to why the plan was not continued. The general consensus was that the concept was too far ahead of its time considering the historical emphasis on base salary in the DuPont culture. Employees were simply not ready to live with the risk. Furthermore, the size of the business unit was so large that the employees did not see the connection between their efforts, the overall division business results, and their share of the variable compensation payout.

Since that time DuPont has piloted over sixty variable-performance compensation plans. Recently its CEO, Charles Holliday, announced that starting in 1999, all of the corporation's business units should be ready to roll out variable compensation plans covering all employees worldwide. DuPont is thus one of the largest corporations to announce its commitment to using compensation as a tool at all levels to drive performance.

The author of this chapter, Ed Sullivan, was involved in the planning for all but a few of these plans and shares here the collective learning of his experience. In his role as corporate consultant at DuPont, he was also afforded an opportunity to interact with hundreds of executives in many of America's more prominent corporations as they looked at variable compensation.]

[Author's comment: Professional conduct and confidentiality demand that individuals and companies contributing not be identified. Credit for all of the experiences must be given to the many hundreds of individuals within DuPont and the men and women in human resources professions as well as corporate leaders who have shared their successes and failures in this trend to align individual objectives with corporate goals with more than words.]

In the early 1980s I, along with one of our top marketing managers, was asked by top management to visit over thirty major American corporations. The purpose was to determine how to reinforce competitive performance with various forms of incentives. These companies shared with us their various reward systems, leadership styles, recognition efforts, and reinforcement of the intrinsic values people have for doing things they felt were significant. Our most significant discovery was the surprising variation in the forms of alternative compensation plans on the drawing boards for the 1990s.

Over sixty companies eventually participated in the effort. The word of our initiative spread, and interest in our findings resulted in companies' requesting to participate in our vision of where compensation strategies were headed. It became obvious that a change in compensation strategy was already well underway, and a rapidly growing number of companies had already adopted basic profit- and gain-sharing plans.

Predictions were that the use of variable compensation would begin in the early 1990s and become a way of life by the end of this century. The result would reduce fixed costs as percentage of product cost and, more significant, reinforce desired individual behavior and subsequent business results.

Since then the number of companies that have adopted variable-compensation plans, which provide for sharing financial success with employees, has mushroomed, yielding solid evidence that this is an important new strategy for American corporations. Certainly there have been failures along the way, attributable to flaws in concepts, plan design, plan communication, and plan management. For the most part, these initiatives have been trial and error, and what proved to be a successful game plan for one company could easily fail in another.

There have also been a number of notable success stories. By reflecting on some of the reasons for successes and failures here, I hope I can illuminate the path ahead for a new generation of variable-compensation systems that will benefit employees and stockholders alike. (Eventually the benefits of the new plans will carry over to our customers and society in general). Performance-based pay is here to stay and will continue to grow.

Opening the Door to Pay for Performance

If you are one of the diminishing number of corporate leaders who have not considered the option of paying out a portion of your compensation investment to support better performance by your human assets, it is now time to get over that hurdle. The predictions of the 1980s have become reality and only the beginning of a sea change that will be critical in the workplace of the future. Successful companies are seeking and finding creative compensation alternatives that reinforce competitive results and help people, from the highest levels to the lowest, feel better about themselves and their jobs.

Despite convincing evidence showing a significant return on investment for variable-pay systems, many companies continue to limit participation in these plans to executives and managers. These same organizations rely on base salary only for nonmanagers. That model served industry well for several decades, but it has become obvious that we need better performance from people below the management level. Until there is a major shift in their thinking, these organizations will miss out on the opportunity to reinforce the behaviors they need for sustained competitive advantage. The evidence shows clearly that employers that change their pay systems are opening the door to a powerful tool that can help them make the quantum leap they need for business success. In the words of a CEO of a major corporation, "My job is constantly balancing the interests of investors and employees." Another CEO put it somewhat differently: "My job is to find a way to let both investors and employees know that what we are doing is in the best interests of both." They see pay-for-performance as a vehicle to help accomplish this.

Getting Started

The first step that leaders are taking is to answer a basic question, "Are employees a cost or an investment?" The latter is a position that all leaders seem duty bound to profess, although it has only been in the past couple of years that their people decisions have reflected this belief. If employees are an investment, then we should be able to expect an adequate return on compensation dollars.

Learning about some real-world experiences that others have had may help you develop a new compensation philosophy and beliefs. That shift in thinking could facilitate a significant improvement in the return on the funds spent as compensation.

The second step for leaders may be to correct misguided notions, including these:

- The misrepresentation of the excellent works of W. Edwards Deming to justify policies and practices that fail to differentiate in compensation
- Oversimplification of Frederick Herzberg's classic studies on motivation for self-serving reasons to argue that "money really doesn't change behavior"

Statements by Deming, Herzberg, and Abraham Maslow have been frequently cited by those who are uncomfortable with the use of money to motivate employees. Yet if you revisit Maslow's "hierarchy of needs" from bottom to top, you will find money nestled there, although not explicitly mentioned, at every level. None of these "experts" said pay is not a powerful incentive; at worst, they cautioned readers to proceed carefully.

I have addressed several large conferences on the fallacy of the statement, "We are okay; on average we pay better than our competitors do." Many of us have smugly gone along paying more (as high in a few cases as the upper decile of all industry) without coming close to reaching performance levels commensurate with that investment. Some leaders and human resources professionals still use this "pay more base salary only" logic, but it is increasingly difficult to justify this policy when there is pressure to shift from fixed to variable costs.

A growing number of the Fortune 500 companies have caught up to the smaller companies that pioneered creative plans. It is easier for smaller, single-industry companies to anticipate, define, and reward the desired behavior. Larger companies have to overcome the bureaucrats and the dinosaurs and the more complex challenges facing bigger, diversified, and global operations.

Avoiding the Potholes

The companies that have tried but failed to overcome resistance to change and the obstacles mentioned have continued with base salaries only. In many instances, this was undoubtedly a sound decision, rather than implementing a costly plan that many perceived as divisive or too costly. Here are some of the real issues DuPont and other companies have had to overcome in order to reinforce behavior that results in improved business performance:

- Defining what is exceptional business achievement that is attributable to sustained employee commitment and high performance
- Determining the mix of incentive plans that will maximize the return on the compensation investment

- Determining the percentage of the financial gain that should be shared with employees and the percentage of base salaries that will maximize compensation investment
- Replacing the focus on internal equity and internal interests with a focus on external business performance
- Avoiding the tendency to fall back on simplistic answers and the "overuse" of profit sharing in lieu of line-of-sight results-based plans (These are performance measures that are under control of an employee or group of employees. Profit sharing is *not* within line-of-sight.)
- Finding the most effective balance of top-down and bottom-up compensation incentives
- Avoiding the copying of another company's plans or having someone else design a plan rather than designing a pay system to support the company's business needs and culture

Referring to variable compensation, a CEO of one of the world's largest companies repeatedly stated, "We know it's the right thing to do, but we don't know how to do it." Another CEO said, "It is the right thing to do. Find a way, and if you need help let me know, but I am confident we can do this."

CEOs from other companies have been as committed to incentive compensation, but ran into continued resistance from isolated business units for a variety of reasons:

- Objections to potential internal inequities
- Fear of overpaying
- Inability to set realistic goals
- Discomfort with any form of incentive for nonmanagement employees
- Resistance from employees who thought there was more to lose than to gain

A progressive human resources vice president in a dynamic and progressive U.S. company ran into collective bargaining obstacles; employees in this organization lost an opportunity to share in the company's success, and the company lost a significant opportunity to enhance its competitive advantage. In other companies, morale dropped seriously as employees became disenchanted. They were told, "It is as a result of your efforts that we have been successful," yet from the employees' perspective, the investors and top executives became wealthier while employees lost jobs and saw cutbacks in opportunities for pay increases.

The signs held up and leaflets distributed at one company read, "You want our loyalty; we lose jobs and you want us to contribute more; stop the greed—share the success." Management's simplistic response to this was, "We can provide the opportunity to earn more only if you share the risk like we do." That attitude only served to increase the resentment. Those who believe in variable compensation, including forward-looking leaders in small, medium, and large companies, are overcoming obstacles mentioned earlier in this chapter by this four-step process:

1. Defining more clearly what the business objectives are
2. Determining what is needed to get there
3. Defining what people can do to make it happen
4. Defining what needed behavior change can be reinforced with money

There is a changing contract between employer and employee. As sure as the evolution of human relationships has moved from savagery, to slavery, to servitude, and then to paternalism, it will evolve to participation and sharing in an employer's success. Sharing in the growth and profitability of an organization is truly an outgrowth of the standoff between socialism and capitalism, and reflects a philosophy that can be accepted throughout the world.

Learning to Live With Pay-for-Performance
· ■ ·

All major surveys from the nation's industrial associations and consulting firms show a massive shift from base salary only to a compensation mix of four elements:

- *Base salary,* the "commodity element"
- *Short-term incentives,* based on specific line-of-sight financial

and operational metrics with payout frequencies between one month and one year

- *Longer-term incentives,* based on three- to five-year performance objectives and milestones with payouts at the end of the performance period
- *Business value growth incentives,* using various forms of stock option and equity sharing alternatives

The mix and the percentage of total compensation of these components differ from one industry to another and certainly by the role the individual plays in the organization.

Many business leaders and professionals still struggle with the concept, for several good reasons:

- The effort and the risks can be significant.
- The philosophy underlying plans that enable employees to share in a business's success is contrary to management's shared beliefs.
- The corporate culture is outdated, and is led by corporate dinosaurs who wish to finish their years peaceably and not have to cope with the necessary changes, which will surely be stressful.
- Knowledgeable professionals and the newer, more enlightened, and energetic leaders have little influence in the decision-making process.

In our visits to the companies participating in our study we focused on two generic types of plans: profit sharing and gain sharing. Both have advantages, and both also have limitations.

Profit sharing is considered the easiest, simplest plan concept and offers the path of least resistance. You prepare a formula, tell everyone what the potential sharing will look like, providing the business does well, and virtually everyone comes away pleased.

Well, not so fast. Did the company get a return on its investment? Many CEOs and human resources executives have reported the development of an entitlement mentality and also that a new plan does not always trigger a change in employee behavior. If there is a disconnect between the individual's contribution and the business results, employees will certainly enjoy the payouts, but it is unlikely that they will be motivated by the plan. Although many companies have a profit-sharing plan and say it is okay, most have realized that a profit plan alone is not the answer to increased productivity or financial performance.

Several major corporations have reported that their initial move into variable plans using profit sharing was satisfactory but now plan to develop an integrated plan incorporating both a profit-sharing element and a results-based element such as gain or goal sharing. They are making the change to strengthen the ties between employees efforts and the plan payouts.

Gain sharing is a better reinforcer of desired behavior, yet it also has its limitations:

- The goals need to be redefined within one to three years, and that means continuing work to establish meaningful goals.
- Payouts could occur without the business's meeting its profit objective.
- Reducing labor costs is normally not the only performance goal.
- Goals are often set too low, and the plan becomes cost additive (that is, costs go up rather than down).

Failure to resolve these limitations can end up increasing the company's overall costs. While gain sharing has worked well for many companies in reducing costs, improving yield, and improving quality, other organizations have failed. These plans are not as easy to put together as profit sharing and in fact can result in a need for significant annual maintenance.

EMPLOYEE INVOLVEMENT IS IMPORTANT FOR PLAN SUCCESS

In the December 26, 1996, edition of *The Wall Street Journal*, the lead story, "Dodging Doom," about Pratt & Whitney's Maine plant reflected how the successful use of results sharing met the critical objectives: "no schedule problems, cut costs, regroup machines and reduce the amount of time machines were out of service." The new pay system was developed with involvement by twenty-two employees from the factory floor and offices.

The idea that employees at that level would have been asked to play a role in designing a pay system would have been heresy a decade ago but now is commonplace. Employee involvement has been the key to success in almost every effort of the sixty or more plans I have worked on and almost every one of the hundreds of successes reported by other companies.

The two following failures reflect the tendency of management to perceive gain sharing as a cost only and consequently often end up often with no gain, more work, and diminished morale.

THERE SHOULD BE A CLEAR LINK BETWEEN PAYOUTS AND RESULTS

The pilot program for a new gain-sharing plan in one of a company's manufacturing plants had no payout, despite the fact that the facility far exceeded its objectives. The parent company refused to allow the payout.

The 300 plant employees worked harder and better, but because of poor systems and flawed business decisions, the company as a whole did not reach its profit objectives. The plan design did not permit any payout unless the company exceeded its profit objectives. The employees were saying, "Look how much worse the business results would have been if we hadn't exceeded expectations.' " Employee morale and that plant's performance dropped dramatically in the next quarter.

Other business units learned from this and permitted their plants to pay bonuses when they surpassed their objectives, independent of the larger business unit's performance.

Actually most companies incorporate a larger business unit profit threshold that must be met before any of its subunits receive a variable payout. The argument is that if we lose competitive war, we all lose. This threshold or minimum performance must be carefully managed to avoid undermining the potential impact of the plan in smaller, subordinate units.

EMPLOYEES NEED TO FEEL THE PLAN IS FAIR

The wisdom of the responsible business unit vice president prevailed, and the plan implemented had a maximum payout of 3 percent of base salary. The employees knew they could far exceed their current cost cutting, quality, and on-time delivery objectives, but did just enough to earn the 3 percent maximum. Comments on the floor ran something like this: "You say we are partners, and we are the key to our unit's financial success. The financial gain to the company could be up to $20 million if we really 'had at it,' but why try harder when you will share such a small portion of the financial gain?"

EMPLOYEES WANT TO BENEFIT FROM IMPROVED PERFORMANCE

A company reported that operators and maintenance people asked whether they could share in some of the savings if they achieved an improvement in the manufacturing process. Plant management said yes, but the corporate compensation people said no. The organization hired an outside consultant at a high fee to make job improvements rather than pay employees more than current rates. As you might imagine, there were some serious long-term labor relations repercussions.

The following case reflects one of the most disappointing situations I have witnessed; sadly, it is not uncommon for units that are new to results sharing.

PERFORMANCE GOALS SHOULD REPRESENT REAL GAINS

Months after a gain-sharing plan was installed, management at one of our plant sites related how they belatedly discovered that the goals set were so low that they had added 5 percent to the compensation costs but had targeted no real gain. The site management decided it was unwise to go back to their people and their management and increase the goals. They ended up desperately working extra hours in futile attempts to reduce costs to compensate for the underestimated goals.

Another company reported it had set utilization goals in excess of mechanical maximums that were physically impossible to achieve, and the plan became a laughing matter. Efforts to design a replacement plan were met with humorous comments of a nature that said a lot about employee trust of the site management.

A team incentive is exemplified by a business that was building a new plant and wanted to have it up and running by a given date. Hitting the target date was worth a great deal financially to the company. Beating that target date and breaking into the market before competitors is worth X dollars per month and that makes the pot larger; beyond the target date, the value and the pot decline, or there may even be no payout. Similar plans have been successful in R&D functions, information systems, and marketing units.

One problem with gain sharing, says the CEO of a top U.S. corporation (who is not in favor of these plans), is that these plans all ride on different metrics, so there can be an endless period of negotiating goals. He contends that eventually a business unit will produce only what it would have anyway and end up paying more. This CEO is not opposed to variable plans, just cautious about their real value.

Another CEO indicated his concern that business unit leaders were too inconsistent in setting objectives. Despite his concern, however, many companies have benefitted from the use of performance plans because they spent more time worrying about business objectives. Money on the table has a surprising effect in keeping behavior focused on the reason the organization is in business.

Other companies found that avoiding all the effort of implementing incentive plans and limiting compensation to high base salaries did in fact reinforce the entitlement mentality. Relying on intrinsic motivation alone resulted in declining competitive performances. In fact, the business found that some employees were happy to be going back to "putting in their time" without the stress and complexity that attend the implementation of incentive compensation plans and the concern with generating payouts.

"Okay," you say, "I've heard all this before, and much has been written on the subject, but what is the bottom line?" The answer is to consider all alternatives, looking closely at how to share the results attributable to improved employee efforts. Program planners can overlook all the rhetoric and go back to basics by answering these four questions:

1. What are our short- and long-term goals?
2. What do we need to do to get there?
3. What specific differences can people make?
4. What behavior changes are needed that can be influenced by financial rewards?

Does a one-size incentive plan fit all? No. The type of variable-pay incentive that will work best depends on the roles people play. The alternatives at different levels in the organization are summarized below.

Group	Performance Measures	Basis for Rewards
Corporate leaders	Economic value added	Stock ownership opportunity
	Balance scorecard	Economic value/ Profit sharing
	Shareholder return	
Business Unit Leaders	Business success of unit	Results sharing
Functional Leaders	Contribution to corporate goals	Milestone awards
Key Contributors		
All other employees	Specific operational results/objectives measured weekly, monthly, or quarterly	Profit/gain sharing Line of sight bonus awards

Global and Regional Considerations

· ■ ·

More and more companies must take into account cultural differences from one region of the world to another. DuPont recently considered some form of incentive for information technology specialists from

33

around the globe. Of four different compensation approaches, the staff in Japan said individual pay incentives would have limited value and some negatives, while those in another Asian country found that individual incentives were highly effective. The people from the European region had less value for one approach than people in both the North and South American regions. The answer was to put all four forms into the global plan and let each region decide what combination and to what extent each form will be used. This solution provides a global plan that can be tailored to the culture of the local region.

Today successful companies are viewing compensation somewhat like a piece of equipment with several levers, each to be used to reinforce a specific purpose and used to the extent that will increase the return on the compensation investment. One or more of the levers might work well in one location but not in others. That makes it important to understand how to operate the equipment in a given situation.

An analogy has been highly effective in presentations to CEOs, design teams, and human resources people from different cultures: looking inside the "cab" of our "equipment" and the levers available to us: (1) base salaries, (2) short-term incentives tied to annual (or periodic) operating results, and (3) longer-term incentives tied to shareholder returns, increases in economic value, or sustained profitability.

The engine is not unlike the impact of our collective resources with a certain capacity. Tapping this capacity can be influenced by which combination of levers used and the results they influence—for example:

- Stock options help to focus on shareholder return.
- Goal-based incentives encourage the achievement of short-term business gains along with the achievement of or portions of long-range goals.
- Profit sharing contributes to an ownership mentality.
- Line-of-sight incentives such as gain sharing linked to metrics relevant to individuals or teams can influence their commitment to achieve specific performance goals.

The degree to which an organization uses each of these options should reflect the role of the employee and the line-of-sight results that the employee affects.

There is a widely shared agreement that pay-for-performance systems should be as simple as possible, yet they need to reflect an appropriate balance of the several forms of compensation. There are jobs where incumbents have limited impact on results, and in those situations a base-pay-only system may be appropriate. But even in those cases, it is advantageous to create an environment where employees act in the best interests of their employer. Opportunities to share in the success of their employer can contribute to that. Developing a truly effective pay-for-performance strategy is not a simple problem to solve.

Different industries and cultures, along with other variables (such as the history of employee-management relations), will determine the optimal investment in compensation expenditures. In the current climate, the challenge boils down to the following issues:

- Who participates in what?
- To what extent?
- Based on what business objectives?
- What amount are we paying out of the value received?

Final Notes About Plan Design

Successful plans have addressed the four basic questions set out earlier in this chapter. An additional design checklist for any type of compensation should include determining answers to the following questions:

1. How much do you have to pay to get what (this is competitive compensation positioning)?
2. How much can you afford to pay at every level of business performance? (Here is where a finance specialist has a role to play.)
3. Generally how do you want to allocate the money (e.g., equally to all employees versus specific team or individual performance incentives)?
4. What specific behaviors do you wish to reinforce, and how do you weigh the relative value or importance of the behaviors?

5. How do you handle the distribution among employees if you decide to differentiate?

One of the elder statesmen in human resources summarizes the transition of a major cultural change in employee and business owner relationships as follows:

Old Deal	New Deal	Future Deal
A fair day's work for a fair day's pay.	More worth and risk for the same pay.	A mutually beneficial opportunity to earn more for better results.

After living through a tendency toward what I call socialistic compensation practices, many of us were amused by a senior vice president of one of DuPont's competitors who, after frustrating efforts to overcome resistance to change, burst out with the statement: "What do you mean it's not the money! It's the money, stupid!" Money *is* important. Even the most hard-nosed and grizzled worker may respond to financial incentives that he or she views as fair and reasonable. When a pay-for-performance system fits the organization, it can be a powerful source of motivation.

The DuPont experience with its Achievement Sharing program in 1988 is probably not surprising in hindsight. Our stockholders, along with many of our managers, did not embrace the idea of sharing financial returns, and our employees were not ready to risk any of what they perceived as part of their future compensation increases. Now, however, the DuPont CEO has launched a companywide strategy to introduce group incentives for all employees. The decade has seen enormous change in the view of employees, their potential contribution, and the most effective way to motivate higher performance. DuPont, along with many other companies, is now ready to make a commitment to new pay strategies with the expectation that changes in these strategies will contribute to improved performance.

Organizations just embarking on the uncertainties of whether to implement some form of a variable-compensation plan should keep in mind that since the mid-1980s, companies have come a long way. There are now thousands of companies where pay-for-performance systems are an important tool, contributing to organization success. These systems often were started as modest pilot studies and then expanded as the company's experience and comfort with the system grew. The track record of successful plans is impressive. There is solid evidence that a well-designed plan can pay off handsomely. In other words, it can be a good investment.

Here are some final guidelines for starting a pilot program:

- Start with small units that are receptive to the concept.
- Let the people in the unit design the plan with the help of experienced resources.
- Define objectives that are perceived as achievable with creativity and extra effort.

By now it should be obvious that these plans are not easily accomplished. Nevertheless, investing in the variable components of compensation money could be a key to company success, and possibly survival, in an increasingly global and fiercely competitive market. The variables—industry, culture difference, workforce composition, leadership styles, labor conditions, government requirements, and tax alternatives, to name a few—are only some of the challenges to consider.

Business leaders; financial, systems, legal and labor relations experts; and human resources specialists all have something to contribute, and all should be asked to approach the topic creatively. Depending on the size of the company and the internal expertise available, external consulting assistance may be needed, but the value of an effective pay-for-performance system should justify the investment.

Another reflection we made, as several of us reviewed the cartons of notes we had accumulated in our meetings with other corporations, was the need to combine academic and theoretical expertise with the real world. There is value in the theoretical and the conceptual, but it has to be combined with the practical experience of workers at every level.

In cultures throughout the world, we are finding different ways to tie compensation to performance, and we are learning from one another. A company's long-term ability to be competitive, grow, and remain a viable entity will depend on maximizing every investment, and compensation is one of the most critical investments.

The key to success is assembling an internal design team that includes a cross-section of the people who will be covered under the new system, as well as a business leader and compensation and financial specialists. In-house human resources staff can provide process guidance, or extensive outside resources are available.

There are indeed many experts to draw on for assistance, including the consultants who have contributed chapters to this book. Pay-for-performance should be an essential part of any leader's strategy to make the company a great organization to work for and a great company for those who are looking to invest their financial resources.

SECTION I

·■·

LINKING EXECUTIVE PAY TO PERFORMANCE

Traditionally corporations maintained two separate but coordinated compensation programs. The program below the executive level was simple and limited to salaries that ostensibly balanced internal equity and external market considerations. At the executive level—typically the top 5 percent of a company—the program combined base pay with annual cash incentives and stock ownership opportunities. Executive programs have been much more closely aligned with prevailing market pay rates. At this level, however, the tax, accounting, and disclosure implications are the dominant concerns. The complexity of these issues has made executive compensation a cottage industry for consultants.

The origins of executive compensation are embedded in the industrial revolution and the evolution from owner executives to professional managers. The earliest executive incentive plans were based on profit-sharing concepts. Payouts were typically calculated with a formula, giving plan participants a percentage of profits, with money going into a fund to be distributed among plan participants. Each year the company's profitability exceeded the threshold or minimum return on investment, the participants received a payout based on the size of the fund, their salary, and their position in the hierarchy.

Since the minimum return was typically close to the risk-free cost of capital, even moderately successful companies could expect to make payouts year after year. For better or worse, the Securities and Exchange Commission did not require companies to disclose much information until the 1970s, so there is not a very good history of how executives fared. There was a strong incentive to reach the threshold level of performance. Since executive salaries and profits were driven by very different economic forces, it was common for profits, and by association the incentive

39

fund, to grow faster than salaries and generate payouts that were almost embarrassing in size.

Has this model been effective? It clearly has stood the test of time. Incentive plans where payouts are tied to profits (or to profitability) have been virtually universal. The model is not without problems, however. The incentive to perform at least at the threshold—the minimum acceptable performance—is obvious. There have been numerous anecdotal stories of year-end accounting games to show needed levels of profitability. The focus on annual profitability reinforces a prominent concern of critics that U.S. companies give too much emphasis to short-term results.

When management by objectives (MBO) became a popular practice, it was adopted as a tool used in determining individual payouts. Those individuals who beat their "MBOs" could expect to receive larger payouts. Since the incentive fund made the determination of individual payouts a zero-sum game, the larger payouts had to be balanced against reduced payouts for executives who failed to achieve their objectives. MBO is intuitively a sound practice, but it can deteriorate into a paper processing exercise that has little to do with day-to-day management. Some companies manage their MBO process extremely well, and the practice is solidly entrenched. Despite the problems, it continues to be widely used in executive compensation.

Stock options have been the primary tool to reward the creation of longer-term shareholder value. With the traditional option program, grants were limited to a smaller group than the incentive plan, and for the most part the stock market generated modest annual gains to supplement the cash compensation package. Stock ownership opportunities have always been included in executive compensation packages, but it was not until the go-go market years in the 1980s and more recently starting in the mid-1990s that large option grants became popular.

When the stock market turned down for several years in the 1970s and options failed to deliver the expected income, companies jumped on new longer-term incentive plans. Performance share plans were the first of the new widely used plan concepts, and these were followed by a variation on this concept: performance unit plans. Both plan concepts were linked to more predictable accounting measures, primarily growth in earnings per share over a three- to five-year period. Tying payouts at least in part to accounting measures reduced the impact of stock market fluctuations and reinforced the importance of longer-term financial performance. These plans were prevalent among larger companies but always secondary to options.

Outside corporate directors, on the other hand, were traditionally paid a retainer for serving as a director and additional fees for attending board meetings and serving on board committees. The lack of a reward for company performance is striking in hindsight. That problem was compounded starting in the 1980s with the addition of retirement benefits based on years of board service. Many directors, of course, own a large number of shares in the company, but it was surprisingly uncommon for companies to grant options to directors until recently.

Chapter 3 by Richard Barrister and William Gentry provides an overview of executive incentive plans. In many respects, executive salary management and incentive plan management is the same today as it was twenty years ago. The difference is in the performance measures used to determine payouts. New ideas like the balanced scorecard and economic profit have been developed and are now used along with more traditional measures. The new measures provide a much more strategic focus.

In Chapter 4, Jude Rich focuses on the creation of shareholder wealth or economic value (EV), a specific long-term metric that looks at the return on capital in excess of the cost of capital. Over the past few years, EV has become a widely used and prominent concept for business planning and financial management. Rich discusses how EV can be used strategically to link executive rewards to the creation of shareholder wealth.

Eric Marquardt discusses the use of stock ownership opportunities in Chapter 5. In the past, it was not uncommon for plan participants to exercise and sell their shares on the same day to reap the rewards but avoid the costs and risk of holding the shares. Now companies want their executives to be owners, and that means requiring them to buy and hold shares for extended periods. Another element of the trend to place greater emphasis on stock ownership is the granting of ownership opportunities to broader employee groups. The goal is the same: to make everyone think like an owner.

In Chapter 6, Pearl Meyer looks at the shift in directors' compensation programs from fixed directors' fees to stock ownership plans. Part of the trend has been to pay fees in shares of company stock rather than cash. The goal in directors' compensation is the same: to make the directors owners. Meyer covers the full gamut of ways that companies are using stock to compensate their directors.

The common thread across the chapters in this section of the book is the increased importance of linking pay to performance. Executive compensation has its critics, but the linkage between pay and performance is clearly stronger today than it was a decade or so ago.

3

Aligning Executive Pay and Company Performance

· ■ ·

Richard J. Bannister, Jr.
a principal in Towers Perrin

William Gentry
a principal in Towers Perrin

S imilar to the star system prevalent in professional sports, competitive pressures have created a "free agent" labor market where successful executives command compensation packages that were unthinkable up until a few years ago. This situation has developed as companies aggressively seek talent they believe will boost performance and contribute to sustained organizational success. Escalating executive compensation packages have focused attention on the link between pay and performance. In the United States, this attention is compounded by regulations that potentially limit the deductibility of compensation in special situations unless the compensation is at risk, or performance based.[1]

In response to internal and external pressures, companies are designing pay programs that deliver a significant portion of pay in the form of performance-based incentives, typically annual bonuses and long-term incentive awards. Bonuses, or short-term incentives, provide executives with reward opportunities for performance over a six-to twelve-month period and are the focus of this chapter. They bridge the gap between the base salaries paid for day-to-day roles and responsibilities and awards paid as long-term performance incentives. Companies should view short-term incentives as an important component of any total rewards strategy.

Articulating a Compensation Philosophy

· ■ ·

Most companies articulate their approach to rewards by developing a formal compensation philosophy. These philosophies or policies provide guiding principles for nearly all aspects of pay, including levels, vehicles, competitive positioning, and how performance will be measured. For example, a company might state its intention to provide executives with highly competitive pay (e.g., at the seventy-fifth percentile of market rates) in order to attract, retain, and motivate executives to achieve goals.

A definitive strategy allows companies to put their compensation philosophies into action using salaries, annual bonuses, and long-term incentives. Collectively, these pay elements are referred to as *total direct compensation* (TDC).

Effective compensation strategy supports business strategy by offering pay programs that are in alignment with special performance objectives. Compensation strategy that is out of alignment with business strategy conveys a mixed message and so can undermine performance by causing confusion and frustration. For example, if a company wants to emphasize short-term priorities associated with a merger, a significant portion of the incentive opportunity should be tied to the successful completion of the merger rather than traditional performance objectives. Potential conflicts can also arise between profit margins and long-term growth or between innovation and financial control.

Effective compensation philosophy and strategy take time to develop. Many issues must be resolved before incentive plans can be designed and implemented. Most important, companies must decide how competitively to pay executives and how best to deliver that pay.

Paying Competitively

One integral element of compensation strategy is the positioning of pay packages relative to competitors. Each element of TDC plays a role.

For example, a company might decide to pay executives base salaries at the midpoint of a competitive range and target the upper end of the range for incentive opportunities. This approach delivers highly competitive pay levels that are largely performance driven without increasing the fixed portion of a company's compensation expense.

Companies refer to several information sources to help them determine appropriate bonus levels. Internal historic data allow companies to compare prior and current reward practices and establish consistent performance standards. External market data can be found in news articles, industry association reports and profiles, search firm and college placement office databases, corporate filings (proxy statements and Form 10-K reports), and salary surveys conducted by academic institutions, government agencies, industry associations, and consulting firms.

Companies should use caution, however, since data represent pay levels at a past point in time. This snapshot can quickly become dated as corporate strategies shift, staffing needs change, labor markets constrict, technologies advance, and competitive pressures intensify. External data can be misleading too. Data comparisons with companies that differ dramatically in terms of market capitalization, assets, or revenues can skew results and lead to pay packages that are higher or lower than actually needed. Matching positions or comparing pay levels is problematic because job titles can be misleading. For example, executives at different companies may share the same job title, but their roles and responsibilities could differ significantly. As a result, it is important to determine if job titles describe similar positions before comparing pay data.

Mixing and Leveraging Pay Elements

Pay mix refers to the balance and blend of fixed versus variable pay, short- versus long-term incentives, cash versus noncash payments, and immediate versus deferred compensation. As shown in Exhibit 3-1, the amount of pay that an executive receives from base salary, annual bonus, and long-term incentive awards can be stated in currency or as a percentage of TDC. In the case shown in Exhibit 3-1, the executive receives 30 percent of TDC in annual bonus (reflecting $30,000 in annual

Exhibit 3-1. Pay Mix and Leverage: Total Direct Contribution of $100,000.

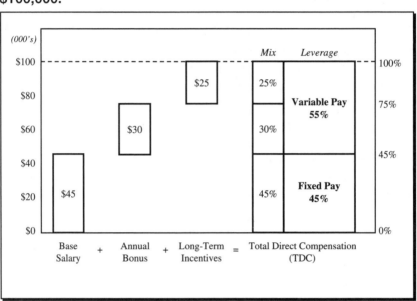

bonus divided by $100,000 in TDC). The remaining balance is earned through base salary (45 percent) and, ultimately, long-term incentive awards (25 percent).

Leverage refers to the ratio between fixed (base salaries) and variable pay (annual bonuses and long-term incentives)—or how much of TDC is at risk, being based on individual, team, or company performance. This ratio allows companies to emphasize performance-based pay by weighting short- and long-term incentive opportunities more heavily than base salaries. In looking again at Exhibit 3-1, we see that the executive receives 45 percent of TDC in fixed pay and 55 percent of TDC in variable pay (reflecting 30 percent annual bonus and 25 percent long-term incentives). The executive's pay package is highly leveraged, with half of TDC contingent on performance. A less leveraged pay package might show 90 percent of TDC paid in fixed compensation and 10 percent paid in variable compensation.

Pay mixes and leverage levels vary widely by position, company, and industry. Why are bonus levels so different? Because market conditions and industry practices are different. For example, a midlevel executive at a consumer products company might receive 20 percent of TDC from annual bonus, while a midlevel executive at a financial services organization might receive 75 percent of TDC from annual bonus. Financial services organizations are known for offering significant bonuses as part of highly leveraged pay packages to retain top producers. Another reason for the discrepancy is that financial services executive might play a direct role in generating a significant amount of revenue, while the executive at the consumer products company might work within a corporate functional area that does not generate revenue. Once organizations decide on the correct mix and leverage, they can start to think about designing their plans.

Designing Short-Term Incentives

Companies use short-term incentive plans and bonus opportunities to motivate executives to achieve optimal performance. The design of these plans varies widely by company and industry, although many share common design features—for example: participation and eligibility, performance measures, performance standards, plan funding arrangements, and payout determination. Collectively, these plan elements determine who participates, how performance is measured and evaluated, and what bonus amounts, if any, executives ultimately receive.

Participation and Eligibility

Participation for executive short-term incentive plans usually is limited to a small percentage of employees in top and middle management ranks. Findings from the 1997 Towers Perrin Annual Incentive Plan Study of over 250 large, publicly owned companies indicate that close to three-quarters of the executive plans cover fewer than 5 percent of employees. Participation at small to medium-size companies can increase to 10 to 20 percent of the employee population since a greater number of these executives generally are in a better position to influence performance.

Companies use varied criteria to establish eligibility, including base salary level, salary grade, position title and reporting relationship, officer status, discretionary approval, or compensation committee approval. As shown in Exhibit 3-2, most companies use more than one criterion, with position title and reporting relationship the most common (used by 48 percent of the companies in the survey). For companies relying on a single criterion, salary grade or position title is most common.

Exhibit 3-2. Companies Reporting Eligibility Criteria for Short-Term Incentives.

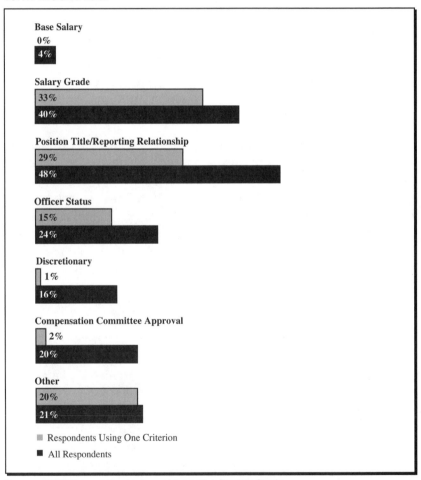

Source: 1997 Towers Perrin Annual Incentive Design Study.

One of the recent trends is to extend participation in short-term incentive plans to cover employees further down in the organization. About 60 percent of study respondents now have short-term plans for employees below the executive ranks. Most try to align these with their executive plans to help focus all employees on the same business goals. Half of the companies use similar performance measures in both plans, and 14 percent offer the same overall structure for both executive and *broad-based plans*, which are available to all or nearly all employees. A mere 16 percent noted no similarities between the two.

Companies broaden participation for short-term incentive plans for many of the same reasons that executives receive short-term incentive opportunities: to recognize contributions made by nonexecutive employees, focus attention on the business goals, help bridge differences between executive and employee pay, and promote a team culture. In essence, short-term incentives reinforce an understanding of the business and accountability for results at all levels.

Broad-based incentive plans often share similar design features. They are usually tied to the financial success of the company (e.g., profit-sharing-type plans) or specific operational goals (e.g., gain-sharing-type plans). Financially based plans typically include all full-time employees and measure performance at the corporate or division level using one or two financial measures. Operationally based plans include nonexecutive employees in production and other supervisory and related support positions. Under these types of plans, performance typically is measured at the business unit or profit center levels with three to five measures that focus on output, productivity, and quality. Participants routinely share in a significant portion of the gain, with awards ranging from 3 to 7 percent of salary.

The success of broad-based plans typically can be tied to three factors. The first factor puts a portion of pay at risk and does not introduce bonus opportunities that are perceived as add-ons to existing pay programs. The second factor deals with the ability to influence measures and the resulting performance outcomes. Employees must understand the link between pay and performance and must be in a position to influence the performance measures that are tied to bonuses. The third factor is the composition of the design team. Plans designed on a top-down basis can be effective, but usually to a lesser degree than those designed by a diverse group of potential recipients. By including non-management employees in the design process, companies encourage communication between staff levels, benefit from the experience of their front-line workers, and provide a means for nonexecutive participants to take ownership for designing the plan and making it work.

Measuring Performance

Short-term plans almost always rely on quantitative measures as a means to assess performance. Data are widely available to calibrate measures and make comparisons with past performance. Quantitative measures, such as those shown in Exhibit 3-3, assess different types

Exhibit 3-3. Prevalence of Financial and Operational Performance Measures.

Financial Measures	Percentage of Companies Using
Earnings per share (EPS)	28%
Net income (NI)	17%
Return on equity (ROE)	16%
Sales	15%
Operating measures	15%
Operating income (OI)	11%
Cash flow	11%
Other financial measures	11%
Pretax income	9%
Return on assets/return on net assets (ROA/RONA)	8%
Customer satisfaction/growth	8%
Expense management	8%
Earnings before interest, taxes (depreciation/amortization) (EBIT/EBITDA)	7%
Economic value added (EVA)	6%
Total shareholder return (TSR)	2%

Source: 1997 Towers Perrin Annual Incentive Design Study.
*Percentages total to more than 100 percent due to multiple responses.

of performance. Many companies rely on traditional accounting-based measures like earnings per share (EPS) and may combine EPS with some individual performance measures. (In general, most plans use two performance measures.) For the CEO, however, use of a single, typically quantifiable measure still dominates, EPS being the most common. For executives who may be in charge of a division, a strategic business unit, or a specific geographic area, performance is often based on results of those particular operations.

The most common accounting-based measures are earnings and income based, such as earnings per share, net income, or operating income. Accounting-based measures are popular since they are readily available and widely understood. These measures also permit external performance comparisons among companies that use these same standards (although accounting standards vary by country).

Accounting-based measures, however, are potentially problematic. They are usually internally focused, linked directly or indirectly to budget (or current financial plans), and therefore are subject to manipulation. Because executives play a major role in setting budgets, they can manipulate performance targets or results to optimize plan payouts. Executives who have reached their goals prior to the end of the performance period would have no monetary incentive to keep pushing. When targets are purposely set too low, the executives' bonus opportunities are never really at risk. Additional criticisms of accounting-based measures are that they fail to capture the quality of earnings, they may not be relevant to business strategy, or they may reward behaviors that are contrary to the interests of the shareholders.

Companies also use other types of quantitative measures (operations-based, market-based, or value-based measures) to assess performance. These include the day-to-day operations of the business, stock price movements for publicly traded companies, or economic performance—areas that accounting-based measures usually overlook.[2]

Operationally based measures assess performance relevant to how a company runs its business. These measures capture performance in strategically important areas like customer satisfaction and growth, expense management, and safety or environment measures. Measuring results is not always easy; good executives understand (and can communicate to their direct reports) how to affect performance in these areas.

Market-based measures can assess performance for publicly traded companies in two ways: (1) stock price growth measures stock appreciation over a set performance period, and (2) total shareholder return measures stock appreciation and captures dividend payments over a set performance period (the total return delivered to stockholders). These measures indicate how equity markets value companies by using past performance as an indicator of future success. When future expectations are promising, stock prices rise; when they are not, stock prices fall.

Value-based measures focus on the criteria that drive the total return to shareholders or increases in total market value. In general, these criteria determine whether companies generate a return on invested capital greater than or equal to the cost of that capital. Types of value-based measures include economic value added (EVA)™, cash flow return on investment (CFROI), economic spread, and total intrinsic value.[3] While EVA is the best known of these measures, value-based measures can be viewed broadly to include any way a company could generate cash flows in excess of its cost of capital and help determine if management is creating or destroying value.[4]

Despite a growing emphasis on value creation, few companies have incorporated the cost of capital, or related value-based standards, into their short-term plans, either implicitly or explicitly. These programs are often expensive in terms of plan design and development, implementation, administration, and management involvement; nevertheless, value-based measures are becoming more common. Companies hope to use these measures to raise awareness that capital comes with a cost and to tie incentives to economic returns and the efficient deployment of capital.

A key consideration in selecting performance measures is *line of sight*, or how clearly employees can see the links between performance and their own behaviors. Employees who understand their role and believe their actions influence success are more motivated to contribute to that success than employees who do not understand how they can have an impact on results.[5]

Companies can ensure line of sight by studying their business processes and understanding the day-to-day responsibilities of their executives. Exhibit 3-4 illustrates how line of sight is applied to various

Exhibit 3-4. Line-of-Sight Illustration.

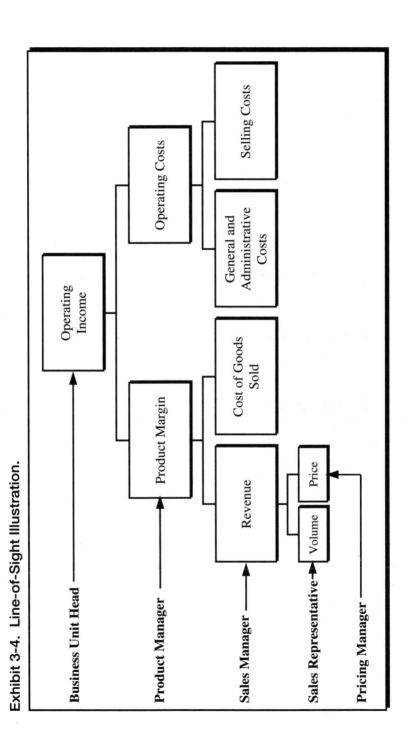

positions in a simplified business unit structure. The business unit head has overall responsibility for the unit's performance, assessed in terms of operating income. Line of sight for the other managers can be tied to the underlying inputs of operating income, such as product margin, revenue, and cost of goods sold.

Identifying the appropriate performance measures is a primary goal in the design of effective incentive plans. Companies can use multiple approaches in identifying these measures. The first is examining business strategy and performance to see what measures arise for consideration, thus identifying the measures that drive company success. Once these are identified, companies can compare them with data that reflect past performance outcomes and project future expectations. Companies can also look to their own or related industries to see what measures their competitors are using.

Reporting capabilities represents a potential problem in selecting performance measures. Companies may want to use measures focusing on specific aspects of operations and find that they lack the financial, reporting, and other relevant internal information systems to capture and report performance data. Additional problems occur when companies select measures that do not reflect line-of-sight considerations. Plans do not provide the proper level of motivation and rewards if participants cannot influence performance. Finally, a potential problem is the number of measures that are selected and included in short-term incentive plans. Plans typically should be limited to a manageable number of performance measures (no more than three to six measures) to ensure that participants are likely to achieve performance objectives since they focus on a smaller number of measures.

Companies may also include qualitative measures in their incentive plans. Qualitative measures provide a means to assess individual performance in areas difficult to quantify, for example: leadership, development of strategic plans, and personal and people development, such as new skills and enhanced competence. Although qualitative measures are not as widely used as quantitative measures, they are useful in reinforcing behaviors and encouraging skill development in areas that influence performance results.

Companies have begun to consider alternative performance measurement and management systems as a means to integrate and align pay and performance programs with strategy, business processes, and capabilities. This approach can be used to establish lines of sight that provide incentive plan participants with a clear understanding of how their actions support strategy and affect performance. This concept is appealing because it promotes the business strategy in a way that everyone can understand.

The Balanced Scorecard

In the early 1990s Robert S. Kaplan and David P. Norton developed a new approach to performance measurement. The Balanced Scorecard™ views a company's strategy from four perspectives: financial, customer, internal business process, and learning and growth.[6] A simplified example of a Balanced Scorecard appears in Exhibit 3-5, which illustrates different performance weightings and measures and how to provide a balanced assessment of performance.

Exhibit 3-5. Example of a Balanced Scorecard.

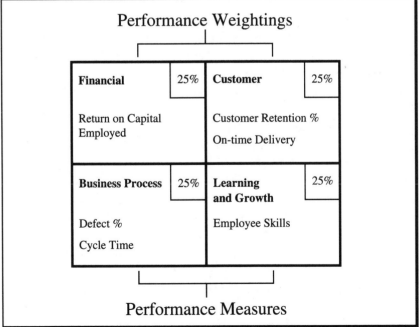

The Balanced Scorecard has evolved as a means to balance both short- and long-term performance objectives with lag/lead performance indicators. The result is a systematic approach that emphasizes strategy development, clarification, and communication, areas traditionally ignored by incentive plans and performance management systems. They had been overlooked or never effectively integrated into the performance measurement and management process.

There is a four-step process for creating a Balanced Scorecard: (1) translating vision and strategy into an easily understandable and executable form, (2) linking rewards to performance, (3) incorporating vision and strategy into the business planning process by setting targets and establishing milestones, and (4) providing continuous feedback and learning opportunities.

The advantage of the Balanced Scorecard is its comprehensive approach to linking pay and performance. Once implemented, the Balanced Scorecard can provide a clear and simple approach to strategy development, clarification, and communication. It ensures that pay and performance systems are aligned with business strategy, and thus provides a better line of sight than a mere review of financial data. It uses both financial and nonfinancial measures, focusing on business unit–level performance and allowing for both lag and lead indicators in the performance management system. Finally, lower-level executives, such as line managers and human resources managers, drive the Balanced Scorecard rather than more senior executives, as in traditional top-down driven plans.

The disadvantages of the Balanced Scorecard stem from an unclear methodology for understanding the interrelationships among the different measures and their linkage to business strategy. Unfortunately for most companies, the process for identifying the measures becomes an exercise in filling out the boxes as opposed to developing measures that are aligned with shareholder value creation and business strategy. The measures therefore can have a limited connection with shareholder value creation and reflect no prioritization of measures and activities, no clear process for linking accountability to activities and measures, and an inability to link appropriate line of sight to each scorecard.

Two additional potential disadvantages could also create problems. Although the Balanced Scorecard communicates a company's vision and strategy to employees, the sheer number of performance measures used can seem overwhelming in terms of line of sight, tracking, and ongoing communications. The other potential disadvantage is that bonus decisions can be viewed as subjective since qualitative measures are used.

The Integrated Scorecard

An alternative approach to linking pay, performance, and strategy is the Integrated Scorecard™ developed by Towers Perrin. Its measurement methodology emphasizes and aligns business strategy and shareholder value. This approach cascades corporate-level objectives down to the individual employee through the use of value trees, which are used to illustrate the linkages that add value to the business. The result is the creation of a line of sight for employees, linking activities and processes to nonfinancial measures and then linking them to the financial drivers of shareholder value.

The Integrated Scorecard is based on a comprehensive measurement framework. It is constructed on a foundation of business strategy that focuses on success drivers, organizational capabilities, and financial impact.

Companies can follow five steps to build Integrated Scorecards:

1. Validate the overall group financial measure based on specific business strategy. This is accomplished with high-level discussions and financial and statistical analysis.

2. Create the financial value tree, which is illustrated in Exhibit 3-6. Here, financial measures are broken down into intermediate drivers to identify the relationship between each driver and overall financial performance.

3. Identify key business strategy success drivers and the associated operational, customer, and employee measures. This may require development of operational measures linked to each activity within the process.

4. Link key measures to specific drivers of financial performance, thus creating line of sight from day-to-day activities to financial performance.

Exhibit 3-6. Example of a Value Tree.

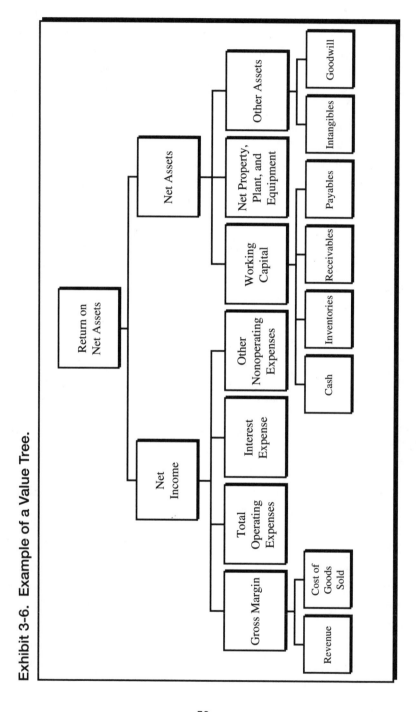

5. Determine high-priority needs and actions based on sensitivity analysis. This analysis determines the financial drivers (and corresponding operational measures) with the greatest impact on shareholder value.

Exhibit 3-7, an example of an Integrated Scorecard, summarizes an annual incentive plan design for a high-level executive, illustrating various aspects of the scorecards in terms of performance areas, measures, targets, actual performance levels, and incremental payouts.

Performance Standards

A key element of performance measurement involves determining target levels for each measure. These become the desired performance standard. Among participants in the 1997 Annual Incentive Plan Design Study, annual budget remains the most common basis for setting a standard, regardless of whether a company uses a single standard or a combination. Exhibit 3-8 shows the various standards. More than half the group (56 percent) combines these approaches, with a common mix being budget, growth, and management and board determination. The remainder of the group uses only one standard.

Ideally, performance standards should incorporate a degree of stretch but should not be impossible to achieve. While most respondents believed they would, or should, make some (minimum) payout most of the time, far fewer (only 13 percent) believed there was much likelihood of providing maximum payouts in a given year.

Performance standards typically fall into three categories. *Absolute performance standards*, the most common, establish target performance in relation to company-specific criteria including budget, prior year performance, or "timeless" standards (the same performance standard is applied each year for determining annual incentives). *Discretionary performance standards* allow management or the board to establish target performance based on an assessment of general business conditions on either an industry-wide or company-specific basis. *Relative performance standards* establish target performance in relation to other companies' performance on the same measure over a defined time period. Relative performance standards can be compelling from the view-

Exhibit 3-7. Example of an Integrated Scorecard.

Integrated Scorecard Summary

Area	Performance Measure	Performance Weighting	Target Performance	Actual Performance	Actual Performance as a % of Target	Payout
Financial performance	Profit growth	33%	5%	6%	120%	120%
	Cash flow growth	33	5	4	80	84
	Revenue growth	33	10	8	80	84
Customer satisfaction and customer value-added	Retention	25	30	25	83	87
	Customer share	25	60	35	58	0
	Market share	25	45	40	89	91
	Feedback	25	20	25	125	125
Operational excellence	Sales effectiveness	25	10	8	80	84
	Defect percentage	25	60	57	95	96
	Cycle time	25	40	45	113	113
	On-time delivery	25	30	33	110	110
Employee satisfaction and commitments	Turnover	33	10	7	70	0
	Training	33	10	2	20	120
	Performance management	33	10	13	130	125

Exhibit 3-8. Types and Prevalence of Performance Standards (Companies Using Only One Standard).

Performance Standard	Description	Percentage Using
Based on budget	Target is the required level of performance in the annual budget	69
Determined by management/board	Target is based on assessment of general business conditions (may be closely tied to budget)	14
Year-over-year growth	Target is based on incremental improvement over last year's performance	7
Peer group performance	Target is defined in relation to other companies' performance on same measure	5
Timeless/absolute standard	Target is based on consistent, year-to-year standard	3
Cost of capital	Target is based on covering organization's cost of capital	2
Achievement of strategic milestone	Target requires achievement of a tangible hurdle (e.g., new product launch)	0

Source: 1997 Towers Perrin Annual Incentive Design Study.

points of management, board members, and shareholders. Peer groups consist of competitors from specific industries, industry subsegments, or existing market composites or indexes. Companies can also use a combination of competitors to create a peer group that reflects performance across multiple industries. As relative performance standards are externally focused, they reduce the ability to manipulate results. These standards also neutralize the factors that are faced by a company's peers, such as the stock market, interest rates, and the economy.

An integral element in establishing and using relative performance standards is data availability. Competitive data must be accurate and readily available in order to develop performance standards that are representative of peer performance. Companies can overcome data availability issues by including only publicly traded companies in peer groups since these companies periodically disclose their performance in corporate filings and communications to analysts and shareholders.

An important consideration in constructing peer groups is the number of companies to select. An ideal group consists of fifteen to thirty companies (groups of this size are manageable), allowing companies to track performance and communicate results throughout the performance period. In addition, a group of this size is large enough to continue to provide accurate performance representation even if several drop from the group during the performance cycle.[8]

Company size is an additional consideration. Common determinants are market capitalization, assets, sales, net income, and number of employees. Ideally, a company should select peers of similar size to allow for accurate performance comparisons. If a large company constructs a peer group consisting of a number of smaller peers, then the performance standard is subject to bias.[9] For example, if net income is the performance standard, a large company could appear to be a high performer relative to its peer group. However, if performance is measured on a return or growth basis, the company's performance might not seem so strong.

Funding Arrangements

Funding arrangements for short-term incentive plans determine the total dollar amounts that participants receive as bonuses. Although the cost of these plans can seem large, annual bonuses are actually a relatively small corporate expenditure. As shown in Exhibit 3-9, annual payouts usually range from a fraction of a percentage to 4 percent of total annual revenues, with the median cost of annual incentives representing one-third of 1 percent of annual revenues and 4.8 percent of annual profits.[10]

Companies usually take one of two approaches to fund bonuses. The first approach is simply to pay bonuses out of cash reserves, working

Exhibit 3-9. Cost of Annual Cash-Based Incentives.

		Revenues (in billions)			
	Total Sample	Under $1B	$1B–$4B	$4B–$8B	Over $8B
Median % of revenue	0.3%	0.7%	0.3%	0.3%	0.2%
Median % of net income	4.8	8.2	4.6	5.1	2.9

Source: Towers Perrin, *CompScan Report on the Cost of Management Incentives* (August 1977), which includes data on over 150 companies from various industries.

capital, or other assets. The second approach is establishing incentive pools from which bonuses are paid. Under the *incentive pool approach*, companies fund incentive plans based on a financially based formula, the sum of all target bonuses, or discretion. *Formula-driven approaches* create incentive pools based on achievement of specific financial objectives, usually an income measure, and are unrelated to target awards. For example, funds in an incentive pool could equal 4 percent of net income. The *sum-of-targets approach* creates an incentive pool based on the aggregate individual target awards under an incentive plan. The *discretionary approach* can use a variety of methods to determine plan funding, including formula-based and sum-of-targets approaches. This approach allows flexibility in determining plan funding in any given year, which can be helpful in cyclical industries or in companies that are experiencing change.

Companies that use incentive pools typically limit the total dollar amounts that go into them by setting maximum funding levels. They rely on several criteria to establish these maximums, including flat dollar amounts, target pool multiples, percentage of income or percentage of income over threshold, or percentage of combined salaries. Another approach is to design incentive pools that do not limit the total dollar amounts. The size of the pool grows as long as improvements in performance are sustained. This way, the levels of the bonuses provided are virtually unlimited.

Companies can also establish a threshold or minimum level of performance that must be achieved before incentive pool funding commences. For example, the plan can be designed to withhold funding until a threshold level of net income or earnings per shares is achieved. In this way, the link between incentive pay and corporate performance is easy to understand and is highly visible. A disadvantage of thresholds is that they can adversely affect performance and motivation levels at the times when companies need them the most. When performance results are behind schedule or well below expectations, participants might be discouraged by the fact that they have little or no chance to receive bonuses regardless of how hard they work. Motivation to improve performance could suffer severely. Therefore, the decision to impose thresholds should be given careful consideration in terms of current performance levels.

Payout Determination

The next step in the design process is to determine how payouts will be calculated. Plan-wide, incentive zones, and payout curves generally illustrate the relationship between pay and performance. *Incentive zones* define the performance ranges over which bonuses will be paid. *Payout curves*, on the other hand, define awards paid at each level of performance. Exhibit 3-10 illustrates a typical incentive zone and payout curve. In the example, bonuses can range from 50 percent to 150 percent of target for performance that ranges from 80 to 120 percent of target. The span between minimum and maximum performance determines the size of the incentive zone, which in this case is 40 percentage points (reflecting the difference between 80 percent and 120 percent). It is also worth noting that the zone is symmetrical since the span from minimum to target is equal to the span from target to maximum. This

Exhibit 3-10. Example of an Incentive Zone and Payout Curve.

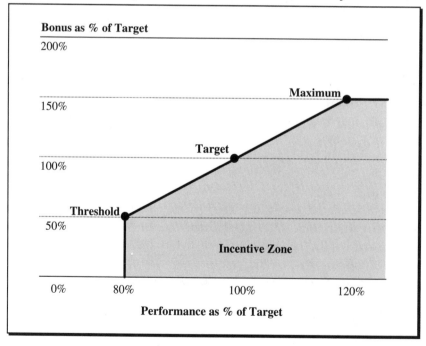

means the relationship between pay and performance remains consistent at each point on the curve.

Exhibit 3-11 illustrates the range of bonus payout opportunities under an EPS-driven plan. Here, no payout would occur unless the company achieved an EPS of at least 94 percent of target performance, or $1.88. At that threshold, a plan participant would receive the minimum bonus payable, roughly 40 percent of target. At the target performance level ($2.00 earnings per share), the target bonus would be payable. And at the upper reaches of performance (up to 108 percent of target or earnings of $2.16 or higher), the participant could expect to receive a bonus two and a half times target (250 percent). Interestingly, the incentive zone is asymmetrical, which is reflected by the kink in the payout curve at target. The kink reflects a change in the slope of the payout curve, with bonus opportunities increasing faster for performance at or above target than below target. The differentiation reflects the difficulty in achieving above-target performance and, as a result, provides higher bonus opportunities.

Unfortunately, incentive zones and payout curves can limit the effectiveness of incentive plan design. If the incentive zones and payout ranges are too narrow, bonus awards will fail to recognize adequately the difference between marginal and superior performance. Ceilings or maximums limit the motivation to push for performance beyond the maximum level. Participants know that performance above this level will not be rewarded, and this may affect their push for success.[11] Finally, the linear relationship of symmetrical incentive zones fails to reflect the importance or difficulty of achieving above-target performance.

Companies can take three steps that may help ensure that incentive zones and payout curves generate desired results. First, ceilings or maximums can, and most likely should, be eliminated. Second, thresholds can be removed or lowered to provide low payouts at low performance levels, thereby keeping participants encouraged to perform consistently during difficult times rather than to give up. Third, companies can change the slope of the payout curve to differentiate between below- and above-target performance. By reducing the slope between threshold and target, companies can decrease bonus levels for performance results that are too easily achieved. On the other hand, the slope

Exhibit 3-11. Example of an EPS-Driven Plan.

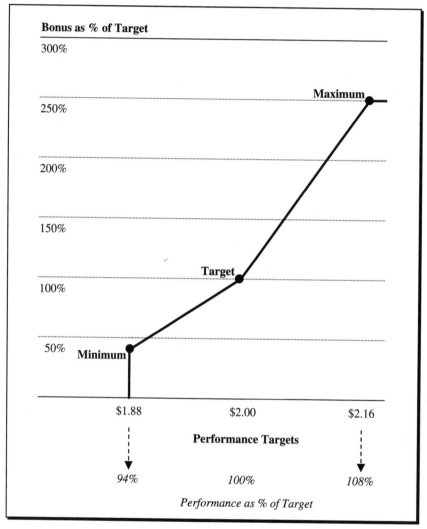

from target to maximum can be increased to provide higher bonus opportunities for outstanding performance levels.

Determining Incentive Awards

· ■ ·

Bonus awards are almost universally delivered in cash. Findings from the 1997 Towers Perrin Annual Incentive Design Study show that 93 percent of respondents deliver entire bonus amounts in cash. The remaining 7 percent of respondents indicate that they deliver anywhere from 50 to 99 percent of bonus in cash and the balance in stock or stock-based awards—either actual or restricted shares, or stock options.

Nearly one-quarter of all respondents have the ability to use stock instead of or with cash, based on either management's discretion or the participant's request. Stock or stock-based award vehicles help increase executive stock ownership levels and help executives meet stock ownership guidelines. Unlike cash bonuses, these award vehicles also help to focus attention on longer-term, value-creating activities. When companies do pay in stock, the awards are generally larger, presumably to offset the greater risk associated with stock and increase the attractiveness of stock as a payout vehicle.

Use of stock or stock-based awards in annual incentive plans can be structured in different ways. Traditional arrangements deliver a portion of an executive's total cash award in the form of stock. An alternative arrangement is to specify that the mix of cash and stock changes as performance improves, with more shares of stock and less cash delivered at higher performance levels. A variation of this arrangement is to provide cash awards up to a certain level. Once this level of performance is achieved, then any additional bonus amounts can be delivered in stock or stock-based awards.

Annual incentive awards are almost always paid at the end of the performance period or shortly after. This allows for timely recognition of performance results and reinforces the link between pay and performance, keeping actual performance levels fresh in the minds of participants. A less common approach is to defer all or a portion of the bonus for one or more years. This approach, like stock or stock-based bonus awards, can be structured to hold participants accountable for performance well beyond the end of the performance period.

Companies that defer bonuses usually set up a bonus bank or other deferral account for part of the award. Bonus banks are relatively easy to develop and use if plans allow for negative bonuses. In years when performance results in a significant bonus payout, a portion of the bonus is paid to the executive, and a portion of the bonus is credited to a participant's account. The account balance and payouts from the account are contingent on future performance. If the participant sustains the performance, he or she earns a portion of the balance in the account in addition to any regular bonus amounts. If the person's performance falters, the target bonus amount is modified by a negative performance factor, which results in a negative bonus. The negative bonus is applied against the participant's bank balance, thus reducing the current bank balance and any future payments from the account.

Deferral arrangements use the same principle as bonus banks, holding participants accountable for performance beyond the end of the bonus period. Unlike cash-based bonus banks, deferral arrangements can tie the value of deferred amounts to the performance of company stock. If short-term performance success comes at the expense of future performance, the value of deferred amounts will fall along with declines in stock price. Alternatively, if short-term performance contributes to performance success in future periods, then the value of deferred amounts will rise along with increases in stock price.

Determining Individual Awards

· ■ ·

Once companies design short-term incentive plans, they should determine award levels for individual plan participants. Effective plan design requires a clear understanding of how performance is measured, how individual participants affect performance, and how individual bonus awards are determined. While specific goal-setting and performance appraisal are beyond the scope of this discussion, they are an integral part of determining individual awards. They communicate performance expectations and provide a rationale for the level of individual bonuses.

Target Bonuses

Most companies determine individual awards by establishing an award opportunity for achieving target performance. They then calibrate the maximum (and minimum) awards in relation to the target. Companies that use bonus targets typically express individual award opportunities as a percentage or multiple of base salary. Alternatively, they may base targets on a salary grade midpoint or use an absolute dollar amount. Also, competitive compensation is usually factored into the target-setting process. This information usually is taken from specific or general industry sources or a defined peer group (perhaps selected by company size). By considering competitors' information, companies ensure that their target bonus opportunities provide the desired level of competitive compensation.

Companies that use targets frequently establish maximum individual award levels, which can be defined as a percentage of base salary or salary grade midpoint or as an absolute dollar amount. The most common method defines maximum awards as a percentage of target.[12] Under this approach, executives are assigned target incentive opportunities at the start of the performance period. These opportunities usually range from a low of 5 percent to 10 percent to a high of 40 percent to 60 percent of base salary. Target bonus opportunities for the highest-level executives are set at the top of the range.

Once established, target bonus opportunities can be adjusted up or down to reflect actual performance results. Adjustments range from 0 percent to 200 percent of target. An executive who receives a base salary of $100,000 per year with a bonus opportunity of 10 percent of base salary has a target bonus opportunity of $10,000. The amount of bonus that the executive ultimately receives ranges from zero to $20,000, reflecting a target bonus opportunity of $10,000 and range of adjustments from 0 percent to 200 percent of target.

The range of adjustments can also be designed to generate negative bonuses, which can be applied against future bonuses. Negative bonuses are generated by expanding the range of adjustments to include negative percentages, or using a range of -50 to 200 percent rather than a range of 0 to 200 percent. If we use the same information as the example above and assume that performance resulted in a -10 percent adjustment to target, then the bonus of -$1,000 (reflecting the target bonus of $10,000 multiplied by the -10 percent adjustment) would be "banked" and applied against future bonuses.

Key Challenges

Companies can draw on a variety of design features to develop effective short-term incentive plans for their executives. The most important is to secure top management's commitment to the plan. If the company leaders demonstrate support for the plan and use it in the planning process, they will validate it in the eyes of other participants. This is an absolute necessity during times of poor performance, when the plan may provide little or no bonus payouts.

Another challenge is to select design features that balance strategy, capabilities, and structure with employee motivation. This challenge is best met by careful consideration and integration of all of the available design options, which entails a commitment of time, energy, and resources. All too often companies attempt to change existing programs or introduce new programs without allowing adequate process time. This time is needed to select design features, model pay and performance outcomes, and educate participants as to how the plan works.

A third challenge is ensuring that plan participants understand the plan. Design issues aside, better communications help improve return on incentive investment and can easily convey performance results. Unfortunately, communications are often overlooked when designing and implementing short-term incentive plans. This leads to gaps between the perceived level of participant understanding and the plan's intended influence on behavior. As shown in Exhibit 3-12, the better the plan is understood, the more it will motivate employee behavior. If companies suspect that communication issues are undermining their plans, they should attempt to determine and amend the level of misunderstanding

Exhibit 3-12. Level of Executive Understanding and Influence on Actions.

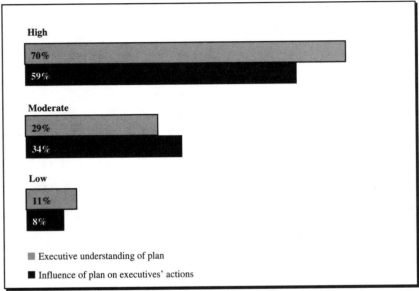

High
70%
59%

Moderate
29%
34%

Low
11%
8%

■ Executive understanding of plan
■ Influence of plan on executives' actions

Source: 1997 Towers Perrin Annual Incentive Design Study.

of participants. This is especially important if the plan design is complex or differs significantly from earlier plans.

Another communications-related issue is the frequency (weekly, monthly, quarterly, or semiannually) that companies communicate results during the performance period. This interval becomes crucial when designs use performance measures not widely available to plan participants. Periodically communicating results will keep employees focused on their performance objectives. The result is an environment where executives are encouraged to discuss results and seek continuous improvement.

Structuring short-term incentives in a way that balances existing long-term performance objectives is another key challenge. This can be accomplished by viewing short-term incentives as part of the total compensation strategy rather than an individual component of pay, thereby providing competitive pay packages that simultaneously support both short- and long-term performance objectives.

A final challenge is to realize when short-term incentive plans need to be modified or replaced. Frequent design modifications can undermine plan effectiveness and confuse participants. Yet companies need to assess continuously how plans are working. By focusing on plan effectiveness, companies ensure that their short-term incentive plans support business strategy, generate the desired performance results, and provide award opportunities and levels that are consistent with the overall compensation philosophy and strategy.

Conclusion

This chapter has discussed how companies can use short-term incentive plans in their total rewards strategies to link pay and performance. We focus on plan design because it determines how effective short-term incentive plans are in guiding behaviors, motivating participants, and helping companies achieve performance objectives.

Designing effective short-term incentive plans is difficult. Companies must develop plans that reflect their strategies and fit within their pay and performance management systems. By working through the topics covered in this chapter, companies will be sure to consider the main design considerations and features common to effective incentive plans. In this way they can improve the chances that their plans will be fundamentally sound and will function as expected.

Case Study: Aligning Annual Executive Incentives to Results

Z Corp is a mid-size public company that is respected within its industry. It experiences few problems in recruiting and retaining employees and is believed to be an enjoyable place to work. Operating performance has been solid, though not spectacular, as the company has achieved budget in each of the past few years. Market performance, however, has declined as Z Corp's stock price appreciation has trailed the rest of the industry.

Z Corp's compensation philosophy is to provide competitive, performance-based pay to its executives. The company provides its executives with a pay package consisting of base salaries, cash bo-

nuses, and stock options. Base salaries target the fiftieth percentile of competitive rates for a select group of industry peers. Cash bonuses and stock option awards can range up to the seventy-fifth percentile of competitive rates, depending on performance.

Management and human resources believed Z Corp's pay packages were competitive and reflected appropriate levels of pay mix and leverage. They believed that the stock option awards adequately addressed the long-term performance of the company's stock. However, both groups also thought that the short-term plan could be improved to reflect the quality and quantity of earnings and performance in relation to peers.

After careful analysis of the short-term incentive plan, management realized the plan was too internally focused. It was designed to measure performance in relation to budget in order to help the company achieve its short-term operating objectives. The plan became outdated as Z Corp focused on relative performance and activities that supported market performance. Management also believed that the cost of capital and the efficient deployment of capital were becoming increasingly important as drivers of market performance.

Management asked human resources to develop a new short-term incentive plan that recognized the quality and quantity of earnings, incorporated the company's cost of capital, reflected the cyclical nature of the industry, and reflected the performance of Z Corp's peers.

Human resources began the design process by deciding which features of the existing plan made sense for the new plan. Participation and eligibility, plan funding, cash bonuses, and the use of target bonuses were to be included in the new plan, while performance measures and standards were design features that needed to be changed.

A key consideration in designing the new plan was determining how to measure performance. Following discussions with the Finance Department, human resources executives selected a return measure based on earnings before interest, taxes, depreciation, and amortization (EBITDA) and beginning gross assets. The measure captured Z Corp's earnings power generated by its gross assets at the beginning of the performance period. The performance measures then would

73

be used to determine the amount of funding available for bonuses under the plan.

The next step was to develop the threshold and maximum performance levels. Threshold performance was determined by multiplying the company's gross assets by its current pretax cost of capital. This way Z Corp needed to earn a return equal to or greater than its cost of capital before plan funding occurred. Maximum performance was determined by multiplying the company's gross assets by a return that represented outstanding EBITDA performance in past years.

1. Threshold & Maximum Levels of EBITDA Calculations	Threshold	Maximum
Beginning Gross Assets (Millions)	$1,200	$1,200
X Current Pre-Tax Cost of Capital or Outstanding Historic EBITDA return	14%	50%
= Threshold and Maximum Performance Level	$168.0	$600.0

Target performance was set at the midpoint of the EBITDA performance zone, or 32 percent.

Human resources decided to expand bonus funding from its current range of 50 to 150 percent of target to 10 percent to 200 percent of target for threshold and maximum EBITDA performance, respectively. The expanded incentive zone was designed to motivate participants to push for continuous improvements once the threshold was achieved.

Human resources used an industry performance modifier to build industry cyclicality into the plan. The performance modifier was based on the industry's median operating margin, defined as EDITDA divided by net sales measured at the end of the year, in relation to the industry's historical operating margin. If the industry's median operating margin exceeded the historical median operating margin, the modifier would increase the performance threshold to reflect the relative strength of the industry. Alternatively, if the industry's median operating margin fell below the historical median, then the modifier would decrease the performance threshold.

2. Industry Performance Modifier Calculation	Result
Historical Industry Operating Margin	18%
÷ Plan Year Median Industry Operating Margin	16%
= Incentive Plan Modifier (16% ÷ 18%)	89%

Once the industry performance modifier was established, it was applied to threshold and maximum EBITDA performance levels.

3. Modified Performance Standards Calculations	Dollar Amount	Return on Gross Assets
Modified EBITDA threshold (89% of $168)	$149.5	12.5%
Modified EBITDA maximum (89% of $600)	$534.0	44.5%
EBITDA that will deliver 100% of target bonus with modified standards (89% of Target Bonus of $384)	$341.8	28.5%

Actual plan funding could be determined through an interpolation calculation that determined the payout associated with incremental improvements in performance. If Z Corp achieved an actual EBITDA of $320 million (26.7 percent of beginning gross assets), then the modified performance standards could be applied to the resulting return to calculate actual plan funding. Using an EBITDA of $320 million, the interpolation calculation would result in plan funding equal to 89 percent of the target funding level.[13]

Human resources worked with financial executives to test the new plan before it was implemented. Past performance data were used to compare the new plan with the existing plan. The new plan was also tested with forecasted results to make certain that the payouts it generated would remain competitive and affordable and fit within the company's compensation strategy.

The last task associated with developing the new plan was to educate participants on how it worked. In the weeks before the new plan was introduced, human resources worked with corporate communications to develop materials that explained why a new plan was needed and how it worked. The materials included a brief plan description, examples of plan payouts under different performance scenarios, and a contact list for more information. Next, management and human resources scheduled several meetings to present the new plan and respond to questions. Participants were instructed to contact human resources or their managers if they had further questions regarding the plan.

Checklist for Linking Executive Pay to Performance

Company's Business Strategy

☐ What are the performance objectives?
☐ How are pay programs structured to support the strategy and the performance objectives?

Company Compensation Philosophy

☐ How strong is the link between pay and performance? What is the intended competitive positioning of the pay that is delivered?

Company Compensation Strategy

☐ What pay mix is appropriate in terms of short- and long-term performance objectives?
☐ How do the elements of pay relate to each other?
☐ How much leverage should be structured into the pay packages?
☐ To what extent do competitive pressures affect pay mix, leverage, and pay levels?

Linking the Short-Term Incentive Plan to Performance

☐ Who should be eligible to participate in the plan?
☐ Can lines of sight be drawn between participants and the desired performance objectives?

Measuring Performance

☐ What performance measures make sense in terms of the performance objectives and line-of-sight considerations?

☐ At what level should performance be measured (corporate, business unit, team, individual)?

☐ Can participants manipulate performance measures to achieve desired results?

☐ How much flexibility or discretion should be permitted in assessing performance?

Performance Standards

☐ Is performance measured relative to budgeted performance or last year's performance?

☐ Is performance measured relative to industry peers or the market?

☐ How and how often are performance standards adjusted or renegotiated?

Funding Arrangements

☐ Is there a threshold level of performance that must be met before bonuses are paid?

☐ Is there a maximum funding level or cap in place?

☐ What are the implications of having a threshold or cap?

☐ What are the cost implications of the plan at target and maximum performance levels?

Pay and Performance

☐ Does pay increase linearly with performance, or does the slope of the pay and performance relationship schedule vary with the level of performance?

☐ Is the size of the incentive zone appropriate?

Determining Individual Awards

☐ Are target bonuses used? What, if any, are the minimum and maximum awards in relation to target?

☐ Do individual awards reflect different levels of accountability and responsibility?

☐ How competitive are individual awards from on an internal and external basis?

☐ Does the plan provide for negative bonuses?

Award Delivery

☐ Are awards paid in cash, stock, or a combination of cash and stock?
☐ When are awards paid?
☐ Does a bonus bank or deferral arrangement make sense?

Participant Understanding

☐ How well do participants understand the plan? Do they understand how their actions can help achieve desired results?
☐ Do they understand how their bonus awards are determined?
☐ How frequently are performance results communicated to plan participants?

Notes

■

1. Refer to Internal Revenue Code (IC) 162(m) for more information.
2. Economic performance measures profits or returns in relation to the cost of capital.
3. Total intrinsic value is a company's estimated present value discounted by its prevailing risk-adjusted cost of capital. These concepts are discussed in most corporate finance texts.
4. EVA and Economic Value Added are trademarked by Stern Stewart & Co.
5. Findings from the 1997 Towers Perrin Workplace Index indicate that 91 percent of employees who understand their role and believe they influence success are motivated to help their companies achieve success, while 23 percent of employees who do not understand their roles or believe they have little influence over success are motivated to help their companies achieve success.
6. The Balanced Scorecard is trademarked by Renaissance Solutions, Inc.
7. The Integrated Scorecard is trademarked by Towers Perrin.
8. Incentive plans must specify an approach for measuring peer performance if the composition of the peer group changes prior to the end of the performance period.
9. Size bias issues can be overcome by measuring percentage change rather than specific values (e.g., sales growth, net income growth).
10. Towers Perrin's CompScan Report on the Cost of Management Incentives, August 1997.

11. Performance above the maximum level can provide indirect benefits tied to recognition and long-term incentive plan performance, and enhance the value of stock-based awards through stock price appreciation.

12. According to the 1997 Towers Perrin Annual Incentive Design Study, 59 percent of the respondents expressed maximum individual awards as a percentage of target.

13. First take the difference between the actual EBITDA return and modified threshold EBIDTA return and divide by the difference between modified target EBITDA return and actual EBIDTA return. Multiply the resulting percentage by the difference between the target funding percentage and the threshold funding percentage. Add the resulting fraction to the threshold funding percentage to determine the percentage of target funding that goes into the plan.

4

Aligning Executive Pay and the Creation of Economic Value

· ■ ·

Jude T. Rich
chairman of Sibson & Company

I n a 1982 article in *Chief Executive* magazine, I wrote, "Faced with stiff foreign competition and an ailing domestic economy, leading U.S. companies are trying to look beyond short-term earnings by focusing on the long-term health of their companies. Together with their management teams, CEOs must decide which markets are most attractive and how they can gain and hold an advantage over competitors. But these efforts to think and act strategically are frequently contradicted by outdated executive incentive plans."[1]

In the same article, I advocated using a combination of "stock options, a new form of long-term cash incentive called an economic value incentive, and an annual incentive based on strategic, as well as financial goal attainment." The article went on to define economic value (EV) as the return a company generates on its invested capital above the cost of that capital and to demonstrate that EV correlates closely with shareholder wealth creation (stock price appreciation plus dividends). Exhibit 4-1 provides a brief description of EV.

At the time, very few companies used EV as a business planning tool, and only my client examples, which were referenced in the article, had tied incentives to EV. In the past fifteen years, more companies have adopted EV concepts and incentives. In fact, a 1998 Sibson &

Exhibit 4-1. Definition of Economic Value.

In its simplest form, Economic Value (EV) is the extent to which a company's return on its capital exceeds its cost of that capital. For example, assume the following:

1. A company has equity (net worth) of $80 million and debt of $20 million, which equals $100 million in total invested capital.
2. The company's after-tax cost of debt is 8%, and its cost of equity capital* is 10.5%, the company's weighted average cost of capital is $10 million (or 10% of total capital) calculated as follows: ($20 million debt × 8% = $1.6 million) + ($80 million equity × 10.50% = $8.4 million), which equals $10 million.
3. The company currently generates $15 million after tax earnings or a 15% Return on Investment (ROI), which results in an EV of $5 million ($15 million earnings minus $10 million capital cost). Said another way, the company has a 5% spread between its ROI and capital cost (15% minus 10%).

If this company increases its ROI to 17% and keeps its capital constant at $100 million, EV will increase to a 7% spread (17% minus 10%) or $7 million (7% × $100 million). If the company keeps its ROI constant at 15% and increases its investment by $40 million (80% in equity and 20% in debt), EV will also increase to $7 million ($140 million capital × 5% spread).

As this example shows, a company can increase its EV in two ways:

1. Increase its ROI (by increasing earnings and/or reducing capital).
2. Increase its invested capital (while maintaining a constant ROI or improving its ROI).

There are innumerable adjustments to reported accounting figures that can be made to make EV more precise. Discounted cash flow approaches can also be used. But the above definition gets across the concept.

*Calculating the cost of equity capital is described in many financial management texts, and is omitted here due to lack of space.

Company survey of 200 large U.S. and multinational companies showed that 49 percent of these companies now use EV as a business planning and financial management tool, and 32 percent of the companies used EV as a measure in their annual or long-term incentive plans. Moreover, 29 percent (91 percent of the 32 percent) use EV for business unit (versus corporate) incentive plans.

Despite the greater use of EV today, many companies still do not provide incentives to their executives to create shareholder wealth. This chapter explains how companies can shape executive incentives that truly lead to creation of EV and shareholder wealth.

Guiding Principles

· ■ ·

To design effective executive incentives that focus on the creation of economic value, a company needs to take two major steps. First, decision makers need to establish a set of guiding principles dealing with how incentives will be structured and administered for maximum effectiveness. Second, they need to think beyond traditional approaches in order to design incentives that truly motivate executives to increase EV. These principles provide enduring guidelines for incentive design and cover three key elements:

- Incentive prominence—that is, how influential incentives should be in driving executive actions and decisions
- The risk-reward trade-off

Executive stock ownership expectations

Incentive Prominence

Incentives will have the greatest influence on executive behavior when the following components are in place:

- *Executives in the plan have control over results measured.* Their actions must be able to affect outcomes directly. Of course, the measures should not motivate employees to sacrifice long-term results or the overall interests of the company.

- *The rules are explicit.* Those affected by the plan need to know as specifically as possible what their opportunities are, the results sought, the measures used, and how they can realize the rewards.

- *Pay is truly variable.* If everyone is assured of a safe C, why strive for an A + ? Variable pay means high upside pay potential for achievers and dramatically lower payouts for poor performance.

- *There is adequate latitude by top executives and the board to ensure fairness and credibility.* However, adjustments to goals or payouts should be spelled out in advance whenever possible (e.g., for acquisitions and divestitures), and incentive plans should call for very limited forgiveness. Otherwise, the incentive will become a discretionary reward and will lose most of its motivational value.

To the extent that pay will have real prominence in influencing executive actions and decisions, the four factors above must be present.

Some very successful companies have elected not to use pay as a prominent driver of action and decisions. These companies rely solely on other management tools to ensure that executives focus on the "right stuff." Prominent management tools other than pay include these:

- A strongly held, constantly reinforced mission statement (an example is Johnson and Johnson's Credo) and a set of shared values (for example, those at Hewlett Packard). Such companies typically hire mainly at the entry level and have management teams with long company tenure. By the time a person becomes an executive, the mission and values are so deeply inculcated into the person's psyche that his or her actions and decisions almost always are the right ones for the business. People who do not exhibit the right behaviors are weeded out or sidetracked before they become executives.

- Clear, well-articulated business strategy (as at Enron, for example).

- Regular, in-depth reviews of business performance and future initiatives by senior-level executives (as at GE, for example).

Most U.S. companies nevertheless use pay, as well as some of these tools, to get across key messages. This chapter assumes a company has decided on at least reasonably prominent pay.

Risk-Reward Trade-off

A key guiding principle for rewarding executives for creating shareholder wealth should be a balance of risk and reward. The idea is to spell out just how high the crossbar will be for executives and employees who are working under the plan. To be effective, the plan should provide significant upside rewards, particularly for difficult situations, such as turnarounds and start-ups. But there must also be a real downside potential for nonperformance. The aggregate executive payout available should also constitute a reasonable percentage of shareholder wealth (stock price appreciation plus dividends) created. The schedule of these payouts should be leveraged to ensure that upside pay potential is offset by an equal amount of downside risk. For example, if executives stand to receive a payout of two times base salary for outstanding performance, doing a poor job should result in little or no payout.

There are two key aspects of the risk-reward equation to consider: the extent of pay opportunities that are variable (the fixed-to-variable mix) and the actual range of potential variability.

Fixed-to-Variable Pay Mix

Years ago, fixed pay in the form of base salaries and benefits constituted a significant portion of senior management pay. For example, the CEO of a large U.S. company in the early 1980s would have salary and benefits equal to over 60 percent of total pay opportunity. Now that percentage would be closer to 30 percent. Thus, at the top of the house, there is more than enough variable pay to get people's attention. At lower management levels, however, there are still companies that have over 80 percent of pay opportunity fixed.

All companies should have a principle that calls for a sufficient percentage of variable pay. Moreover, enough of the variable-pay opportunity should be based on long-term results to avoid encouraging executives to "short-term" the business (for example, holding back on needed expenditures to maximize this year's bonus).

Actual Variability

Under too many "incentive" plans, even the variable part of pay delivers handsome rewards with minimal risk or even minimal effort. Short of a major debacle, most annual bonus plans pay off well each year, and goals are often written in ways that virtually guarantee success. Although such plans are presented as performance incentives, boards and CEOs often treat them (accurately) as deferred compensation.

Some companies have also taken the variability out of their stock option plans by "repricing" their below-water options. However, shareholders are stiffening their resistance against repricing. The 1998 annual meeting season, for instance, saw a number of shareholder resolutions target the repricing of executive stock options. The State of Wisconsin Investment Board pressured twenty-two companies to seek shareholder approval before repricing options.

Further pressure to match top executive rewards to shareholder returns is coming through the growth of global competition. Protected markets are crumbling worldwide, and that includes the "protected market" of dependable executive pay for mediocre results. Market integration in Europe and economic turmoil in Asia (which will compel this region to tighten belts and become even more competitive) will accelerate this demand.

Stock Ownership Expectations

One of the best ways to provide executives with incentives to create wealth for shareholders is to make the executives shareholders themselves. Currently, many executives own far too little of their company's stock to have a serious impact on their actions. Executives have less risk of feeling the shareholders' pain if they quickly sell their stock accumulated from options and other stock awards. In fact, executives of the 120 largest New York Stock Exchange companies own a minute 0.04 percent of their companies. Fifty years ago, this figure stood at 3 percent.[2] Recent attempts to put more stock in executives' hands have justified "mega-grants" of stock in options or restricted shares. These still cost the executive nothing, and in such quantity can be viewed as giveaways. Greater stock ownership creates a strong alignment between executive gain and shareholder wealth creation, thereby increasing the pay at risk and the potential rewards. Therefore, many companies use suggested stock ownership guidelines, expressed as a multiple of base pay, which are communicated to all executives. For the CEO, for example, a typical stock holding guideline is five to seven times annual salary, with the multiples becoming smaller further down the executive ranks.

But company leaders should avoid driving aggressive guidelines too deeply into the organization. Although the guidelines are both valuable and reasonable for top executives, they can create a real financial hardship at lower levels. The program should typically concentrate on executives' building their equity over time rather than pushing for immediate purchases. The program guidelines should also spell out the consequences of failure to meet the guidelines (typically, cutting off future stock-based awards), with greater flexibility offered below the ranks of most senior executives.

The CEO and board should take an active role in encouraging executives to obtain and hold company stock. The overall pay plan should be designed to build stock ownership of executives through such devices as stock-for-stock option exercise, highly selective restricted stock grants early in the executive's career, loans to exercise options, and payment of some part of annual incentives in stock. For stock ownership to be an effective incentive, it needs to be a serious percentage of the executive's portfolio.

Expecting top executives to maintain ownership in the company from their own pockets requires the company to consider the options for financing such purchases. One approach is to expect executives to buy stock or exercise stock options with their own money. Executives could also be asked to purchase stock options. To sweeten the deal, each option purchased might then be paired with one or two free ones. Another approach is to sell executives stock financed by bank loans arranged by the company, or to arrange such loans to enable executives to pay the exercise price of options and the tax due, thus enabling them to hold all or most of the shares received upon option exercise.

Incentive Plan Design

· ■ ·

The three guiding principles are a vital first step. Once these principles are in place, we must then bridge the gap between them and the real world of work. This brings us to the second major element of paying executives to create shareholder wealth: incentive designs that reward for shareholder wealth creation. The first step in effective incentive design is to understand economic value (EV) and how to use it.

Economic Value

There is a growing acceptance among business leaders that EV in its various guises (e.g., shareholder value, economic value-added, economic profit) is a highly effective method for measuring company financial performance. Fortune 100 stalwart Coca-Cola, as well as other well-known companies, use EV extensively, often with impressive results, to develop strategies and evaluate acquisitions, divestitures, and specific investments. As these companies have discovered, EV can be an excellent predictor of total return to shareholders—better than traditional accounting measures—because it incorporates critical elements that drive company value: the earnings or cash flow generated by a business, the capital requirements needed to generate the earnings or cash flow, and the costs associated with using that capital.

The trouble is that business leaders' enthusiasm with the concept of EV has been tempered by their growing frustration over the inability to use EV to inspire and mobilize their employees to realize a company's value potential. Even through EV may have been used effectively to make strategic business decisions for the company, it has rarely been successfully incorporated into the management systems that drive and reinforce decisions, behaviors, and performance throughout the company. In the end, despite all the high expectations, EV's full power to energize a company and its people is seldom realized.

There are several reasons for these disappointments, including the following:

■ EV is often presented to executives as a mysterious black box whose key principles are often lost on the vast majority of employees at all levels and in all functions. In fact, many managers, even in professed EV companies, often do not understand the EV methodology and its implications.

 ▪ A company's various incentive plans are often not aligned because they are developed separately and, at best, linked only loosely to EV. This lack of a community of interests often manifests itself in incentive plans that conflict from business unit to business unit. In many sales-driven organizations, for example, it is all too common that variable-pay plans send different signals to sales professionals and general managers within the same business. In such situations, salespeople may be motivated toward volume selling, whereas general managers are rewarded only for increased product profitability. As a result, the two parties often find themselves working at cross-purposes, because there is no mechanism to ensure a value-creating balance between growth and margins.

Perhaps the biggest irony of all is that many companies already— and unknowingly—possess the capabilities to build and utilize EV concepts. In several cases, they have started down the right path by identifying key value drivers and undertaking various initiatives in different parts of the organization, like total quality management or the Balanced Scorecard (examined in Chapter 3), to increase EV. But some companies take a wrong turn when they fail to integrate those initiatives and make them actionable and understandable companywide.

Driving EV creation throughout the company need not be so frustrating or complicated. EV can be a clearly understood, immensely powerful tool for helping to unleash a company's value.

Most public, for-profit companies have a relatively simple and straightforward organizational objective: increase long-term total return to shareholders (TRS). Although TRS represents the ultimate scorecard for company performance, it is not the ultimate measure of performance for all employees. In fact, TRS is best reserved for those top executives who are in a position to influence it. This is why stock options make great sense for top corporate executives. Other employees need to be measured not by TRS but by those key drivers of TRS that they can influence. The first step in incorporating EV into incentive designs is to determine the drivers of EV (see Exhibit 4-2).

Exhibit 4-2. Primary Economic Drivers.

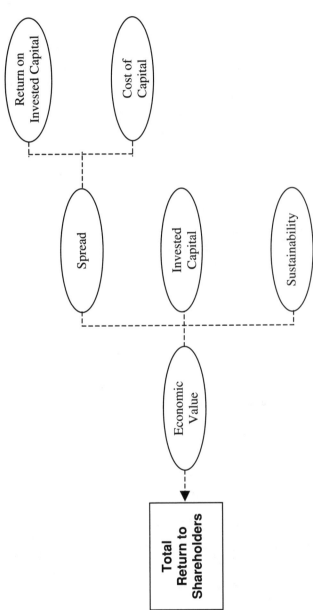

If a company's goal is to influence behaviors and change results, then success is enhanced if employees have a line of sight from their individual efforts to the company's EV. The process of finding clear sight lines begins with unbundling EV's primary economic drivers: (1) the spread between return on invested capital and cost of capital, (2) invested capital, and (3) sustainability.

Using a value creation tree, a company can extend the three "primary branches" through enough successive levels to determine key economic measures for specific functions (see Exhibits 4-3 and 4-4). For example, a value creation tree like that shown in Figure 4-4 can help individuals in a manufacturing organization begin to translate return on invested capital into specific financial measures that they influence directly, such as manufacturing expenses or inventory levels. At the same time, individuals in the sales organization will be able to see how areas over which they have control, such as unit volume, pricing, discounts, and sales and marketing costs, interact to create or deplete value.

To summarize, executives need to understand EV and what drives it.

BUSINESS AS USUAL

A major consumer products company found out what can happen if incentive participants do not understand EV. In its desire to motivate top managers to make decisions that would increase EV, the company adopted EV as the measure for its executive incentive plan. Soon after, a band of financial analysts set about forecasting, modeling, and tracking changes in EV—only to find that there was not much change to measure. The fact is that not much changed—neither behavior nor performance was influenced by EV. Other than the financial experts, no one understood EV, and even senior executives did not know what levers would affect it. In the end, despite a revamped incentive plan, it was business—and poor stock performance—as usual.

Exhibit 4-3. Secondary Economic Drivers.

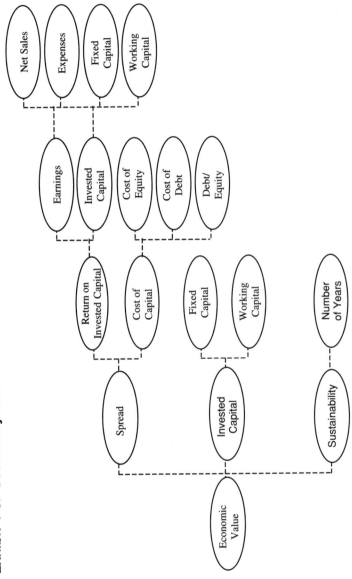

Exhibit 4-4. Extending the Value Tree (a Branch).

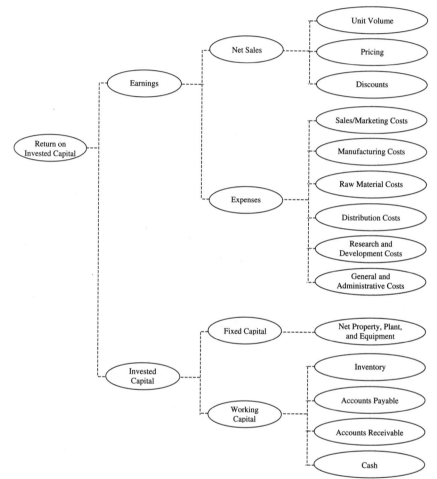

Accountabilities for EV Creation

Once executives understand how EV is created in their company, the next step is to determine which groups and levels of executives control which aspects of EV. Here is how one company assigned accountabilities:

Aspect of EV	Executives Accountable
■ Overall corporate EV, which includes ROI, cost of capital, and level of invested capital	■ CEO, CFO, rest of Management Committee
■ Business unit "Economic Profit" defined as profits minus a corporate-wide capital charge	■ Business unit CEOs and direct reports
■ Drivers of EV, such as:	
— Revenues	■ Sales and product develoment functions
— Distribution costs	■ Distribution functions
— Inventory turns	■ Manufacturing functions
— Product returns	■ Manufacturing and product design functions

Using this approach, accountability for EV can be fixed, and measures for annual and long-term incentive design can be selected for different executive groups. It is important to note that functions should share responsibility for certain EV drivers, as illustrated for product returns in the table. Selecting EV drivers for different executive groups and sharing goals based on these drivers is far superior to classic MBOs. Most MBOs are set within each functional silo, and often are at cross purposes with other silos.

Company-Specific Needs

Armed with an understanding of EV, the next step is to identify the specific company or business unit needs. The case studies at the end of the chapter illustrate how incentive design can be tailored to company needs. The two companies in the case studies had very different needs and therefore developed very different incentives.

Conclusion

=== · ■ · ===

Incentives can be a powerful tool for motivating executives to create shareholder wealth. The keys to success are (1) a set of guiding principles regarding pay prominence, variability, risk-to-reward trade-offs, and stock ownership and (2) incentive designs based on a clear understanding of how the company creates EV and on the specific strategy for improving EV for each business.

Case Study: Providing Incentives for Profitable Growth

Company X, a highly diversified, multibillion dollar industrial company, had long been successful and was well known for its superb management. But a number of its markets were mature going into the early 1990s, so it had been selling off parts of the business that were not generating adequate returns. It had also squeezed out most of the potential profit available through cost control and asset management. Better stock price appreciation would now require growth. Senior management launched a campaign for growth. One of its key initiatives was to redesign its executive pay program.

In the past, division heads negotiated the lowest possible annual goals. Fearing their goals would be ratcheted up the following year from the current year's results, they also carefully managed their results not to exceed annual budgets too much.

The new program encouraged each of the company's more than thirty independent divisions to set "stretch" goals and rewarded executives for growing EV. The new annual incentive is only one-third the size of the previous plan and is based on solely nonfinancial EV drivers, such as customer satisfaction and new product development. Executives below business unit CEOs and those who report directly to them have annual incentives based on the EV drivers they control, or share control of, with other executives.

The most important change was to provide business unit heads with a three-year incentive based solely on their division's EV growth. Previously division heads and staff had received a long-term cash

94

incentive based on corporate return on capital employed and cash flow, plus stock options. The corporate long-term cash incentive was eliminated, and options for division executives were reduced, to help fund the three-year division EV plan.

A look at a division head's compensation, which follows, shows how dramatically the pay program has changed. Division executives now have nearly 75 percent of their combined target annual and long-term incentive based on their own division's performance versus only about 40 percent in the past:

	Old Plan	*New Plan*
Base Salary	$200	$20
Business Unit Annual Incentive	75	25
Corporate Long-Term Cash/Options	10	45 (options only)
Business unit 3-Year EV	0	105

Corporate executives received larger option grants and a small three-year EV incentive, funded by reduced annual incentives and elimination of the prior corporate long-term cash incentive plan.

Divisions now set their own EV goals based on their three-year plan. Corporate management accepted the goals as submitted, but applied a difficulty rating: the greater the difficulty, the higher the potential payout. The payout was capped at 300 percent of the target level, compared with an average of 160 percent for other U.S. companies. Division executives could now set stretch three-year goals rather than setting readily attainable annual goals and holding back to avoid having next year's goals raised.

Another important requirement of the EV incentive was to encourage the sound acquisitions and other major capital outlays that this company's growth strategy called for. Since such investments often take more than three years to pay off, executives could be penalized under the EV incentive without some adjustment. On the other hand, removing the costs and capital required from incentive calculations would fail to hold executives accountable for poorly performing investments.

The solution was to normalize the effects of investments above a *certain size, as follows: assume a division has a goal of $100 million over three years and senior management approves a capital appropriation request for an acquisition that would reduce EV by $10 million over three years. Normalization means the actual EV results will be increased by the $10 million projected EV decline. If the division achieves $90 million in EV, it will just meet its $100 million goal when the $10 million is added on. This approach has the added benefit of encouraging realistic projections, versus overly optimistic appropriation requests.*

Company X's new pay plan sent a loud message deep into the organization: "Go for long-term growth that creates value." The results: in the plan's first two years, sales increased nearly 25 percent and stock price increased 40 percent , compared with three previous years of flat sales and virtually no stock price appreciation.

In company X's case, the CEO and other top corporate executives now have reduced annual incentives, but much smaller three-year EV incentives than business unit heads. Instead, these top officers have much larger option grants. This makes sense, since these top officers have the most control over stock price appreciation and dividends. Therefore, they can be measured more directly on shareholder wealth creation. Business unit executives, on the other hand, are now paid more on the elements of the business unit EV they control, and less on overall corporate shareholder wealth creation directly via options.

Case Study: Rewarding Economic Value Creation

Company Y, one of the largest companies in South America, has six geographic divisions in six different countries, each of which produces, markets, and sells food ingredients and products. The divisions had operated autonomously until a strong new CEO arrived. The new CEO and his CFO initiated an analysis of each division's strategy and incentive plan. They came to the following conclusions:

*   ▪ *Two divisions had ROIs below their capital costs and would need to dispose of low-performing assets and product lines. Their opportunities for growth were limited, since they operated in mature markets with dominant competitors. These divisions were destroying*

EV, but their incentive plans were paying out each year based on attainment of operating goals. The CEO dubbed these divisions "Streamliners."

- *Two divisions had ROIs well above their capital costs and had been growing at a reasonable pace, with the potential to continue to do so. Incentive plans paid out based on operating earnings (50 percent) and margins (50 percent). These were the "Steady-Staters."*

- *The last two divisions had very high ROIs (well above their capital costs) but virtually no growth. To grow, they would have to invest more capital in new facilities, product development, and acquisitions. They were the "Investors."*

The CEO and division presidents wanted to have a common incentive architecture but with the incentives that would drive and reward execution of the different division strategies. Management wanted to use EV, but was cautioned that most executives were marketing oriented, so going to an elaborate EV system would take years of education.

The conclusion was to measure all the divisions on the two measures that accounted for nearly 90 percent of EV creation based on correlation analyses: return on capital employed (ROCE) and total capital employed ("Capital"). These were measures already incorporated into management reports and were understood and accepted as controllable by division executives. The factors accounting for the other 10 percent of EV (e.g., different capital costs, cash flow) would be carefully managed and tracked by division and corporate executives. While the same two measures were used for all divisions, there were three different payout matrices for the three different division types. The matrices are illustrated in Exhibit 4-5 using simplifying assumptions (e.g., the same three Capital and ROCE points on all three matrices, and 12 percent capital cost of all divisions; only three points versus ten points on each matrix).

The calculation of incentive payouts would be based on the interpolation between the performance levels shown.

These matrices were used for 50 percent of the annual incentive (the other 50 percent was based on controllable value drivers and

Exhibit 4-5. Incentive Payout as Percentage of Guideline Incentive Levels.

Streamliners

		250%	300%	400%
	20%	200	250	300
ROCE	15%	150	100	**50**
	8% *Current*			
		$0.5	$1.0	$2.0 *Current*

Capital ($ billions)

Steady-Staters

	125%	300%	400%
	20	**100**	150
Current	0	0	0
	$0.5	$1.0 *Current*	$2.0

Capital ($ billions)

Investors

	100%	300%	400%
Current	50	75	150
	0	0	0
	$0.5 *Current*	$1.0	$2.0

Capital ($ billions)

98

talent management) and 100 percent of the three-year incentive, which was the company's long-term incentive since it is privately held, so stock is not available.

Streamliners will receive higher payouts for reducing their capital and increasing their ROCE, because they will destroy less EV and ultimately create more EV by sending capital back to the corporation to be given to the investors. Note from Exhibit 4-5 that they must increase their ROCE or reduce their capital from current levels or they will receive less than 100 percent of guideline incentive payout. In the past, these divisions were receiving 100 percent or more for meeting operating earnings goals, while destroying EV because of their low ROCE.

Steady-Staters will receive higher payouts by maintaining or increasing ROCE while growing their businesses.

Investors will be handsomely rewarded for growth at current ROCE levels and will receive 150 percent of guideline incentive if they increase their capital dramatically while maintaining an ROCE of 15 percent (3 percent above their cost of capital).

In addition to motivating what each division will need to create EV (grow, increase returns, etc.), the matrix takes into account the absolute level of EV created and the amount of improvement. For example, the Streamliners will increase EV by $60 million if they cut their capital to $0.5 billion but do not improve their ROCE. (Currently they get an 8 percent ROCE, which is 4 percent below their capital cost of 12 percent ; thus, they destroy 4 percent of $2.0 capital, or $80 million. At 8 percent ROCE and $0.5 billion in capital, they destroy only $20 million of EV, which increases corporate EV by $60 million.) They will receive 150 percent payout for this achievement. The Steady-Staters and Investors will also earn 150 percent when they increase EV by $60 million.

The matrix approach is very different from designing a payout schedule around a goal. The matrix gives the division executives the flexibility to decide whether to increase capital at current or better ROCE, reduce capital, or increase ROCE at constant capital levels. A goal-based approach commits the divisions to a single course of action unless the goal is changed in mid-cycle, when the strategy changes. Thus, the matrix is superior when new and untested strategies are used as the basis for incentives, as was the case at Company Y.

Notes

· ■ ·

1. Chief Executive, "Pay Executives to Create Wealth," Number Twenty One, Autumn 1982.
2. Based on an analysis of proxy statements.
3. Excerpted from CEO Magazine, "Get the Growth You Pay For," May 1988, by the author.

5

Aligning Compensation and Stock Ownership

· ∎ ·

Eric P. Marquardt
senior vice president of Compensation Resource Group (CRG)

The joining of two common company goals—raising the bar of performance and identifying ways to cut costs—has triggered a high level of interest in programs that treat employees like entrepreneurs, giving them a stake in the success of their company in return for sharing the risks. Facing challenges from both domestic and foreign competitors with lower labor costs, companies everywhere continue to seek ways to reduce fixed labor costs. With the tight labor market, however, the downsizing and cutbacks so common a few years ago are no longer a feasible strategy to reduce costs except in financial crises. As an alternative, companies have turned increasingly to owner-ship incentives, ranging from profit-sharing schemes to stock awards that hold out the promise of additional income if the company succeeds. Stock-based compensation arrangements continue to have tax and accounting advantages and at the same time offer significant upside potential for gains that can be far greater than typical payouts from cash programs.

One of the earliest employee ownership programs was the Western Partnership, created in the mid-1980s. After four straight years of significant losses, Western Airlines gave employees a 32 percent ownership stake, a profit-sharing plan, and two seats on the board in return for wage cuts of up to 18 percent. The next year, the company paid out over $10 million in profit sharing to its workforce. In the next subsequent year, when Western was acquired by Delta, each employee got approximately $8,000 in cash and Delta stock for shares worth about $1,500 two years earlier at the start of the program.

Today an increasing number of companies are seeking a competitive edge from a new source, the commitment and innovation of their employees, prompted in part by the creation of an ownership culture. In order to be successful in meeting today's business challenges, companies are using stock-based reward systems to facilitate a level of employee engagement not present in traditional work environments. Simply stated, people do not feel obligated to wash rental cars, and companies need more than a workforce that is rented by the hour.

In a 1996 survey conducted by Compensation Resource Group, 80 percent of 125 CEOs of Fortune 1000 companies indicated their belief that executive ownership programs have a significant positive impact on executive behavior. However, fewer than 50 percent indicated a belief that broad-based ownership programs also positively affect employee behavior. In this area of broad-based programs, executive views still differ widely on the value to the company of employee ownership.

Establishing Ownership

Few ideas in U.S. business have attained the status of mom and apple pie as rapidly as the idea that executives should own substantial stakes in their companies. Over half of the top 100 U.S. companies adopted executive ownership guidelines in the five years ending in 1997. Moreover, according to ShareData, 45 percent of companies with option plans and 5,000 or more employees now grant options to all of their workers.[1] Ownership at all levels is a growing trend.

Executive ownership programs emanate in part from traditional corporate governance where there has long been a separation of ownership—typically in the hands of shareholders—and control—typically in the hands of management. Traditional pay programs that focused on recognizing the worth of an executive and until recently on cash compensation have done little to bridge this separation.

In the 1970s and 1980s, corporate boards addressed this separation of management and control by granting stock options to executives, saying that they wanted these individuals to be motivated to *think* like owners. In the business environment of the 1990s, these same boards are modifying their executive pay practices. Most now say that they want their executives to *be* owners. The issue has not changed from one decade to the other. However, the sharp rise in the stock market in the 1990s coupled with higher levels of executive pay (average salary plus bonus for CEO's in the Fortune 500 exceeded $2 million in fiscal 1997) and generous severance arrangements have reduced the risks of stock ownership and made it more attractive.

Can a company get its executives to think and act like owners if they are not actual owners? The answer is yes, but. . . . Bonus or option schemes will get executives caught up in the action of finding ways to make money for their company and for themselves. However, unless they are actual owners, the process is not complete. Equity ownership maintained throughout an executive career with a company is a foundation for longer-term thinking. It is the best tool for prompting executives to pay attention to the details, and for the right reasons.

Broad-based employee ownership programs, on the other hand, are a new phenomenon and not everyone views them as contributors to success. Why, in the face of aggressive employee ownership programs in successful companies like Wal-Mart, Compaq Computer, and Eli Lilly, do other companies continue to have limited ownership programs? A simple answer may be ignorance or greed. However, there are three more common reasons:

1. *If the stock price does not go up, you will rue the day you gave them the opportunity.* This reason reflects a perception that employees do not know how they affect the value of stock and that they become very cynical if the stock does not yield the expected pot of gold. This concern has been valid in some cases. However, where the employer has invested in educating its workforce about the business and the realities of the stock market, workers have demonstrated that they are interested in becoming owners in the same way that their management counterparts do.

2. *Employees should not put all their eggs in one basket.* An employer that permits employees to take out cash and invest in different kinds of financial instruments provides those employees greater security, independence, and control. Employees who are owners do not necessarily feel in control and may not want more company stock. Viewed only as an issue of financial security, this too is a solid concern. However, I take the contrary view that employees who invest in their own company invest in themselves. They are making a commitment to creating returns through the employer.

3. *Managers don't make good owners, and owners don't make good managers.* Ownership is perceived to create conflicts of interest, especially between someone's responsibility as an owner and as an employee. For example, first-line supervisors may assume an inappropriate, almost controlling authority in employee relations if they are also owners. In this case, equity is not the concern but rather is the excuse. The problem is simply the differences among individuals. In many cases, equity encourages individuals to see the bigger picture and merge the interests of owners and employees.

Defining Ownership

· ■ ·

Companies define ownership in different ways. With the variety of compensation and benefits plans in place, a simple definition of ownership is elusive. Exhibit 5-1 shows that anything from stock ownership in a 401(k) plan to phantom stock may be considered ownership.

The most straightforward type of ownership is holding company stock. Employer awards of restricted stock or employee investments in company stock in a 401(k) plan, for example, create legal owners.

Some companies also include a phantom or deferred interest in their definition of ownership. As Exhibit 5-1 shows, the distinction in whether a phantom interest is considered ownership lies in the means by which the phantom interest was acquired. Almost 40 percent of com-

104

Exhibit 5-1. Stock Ownership Arrangements

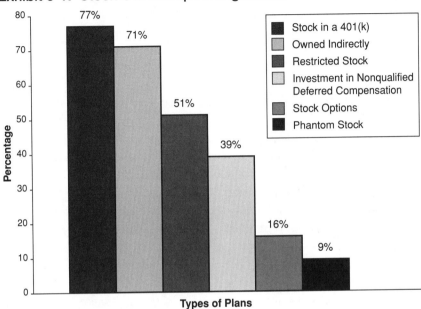

Source: Compensation Research Group.

panies consider that an executive who defers current pay (in a nonquali-fied deferred compensation account) in return for a phantom ownership interest is an owner. Many of these same companies disclose this "own-ership" in the beneficial ownership section of the company proxy. On the other hand, an outright grant of a deferred or phantom interest through such things as stock options or phantom stock is rarely consid-ered ownership.

An important dimension of ownership is the number and value of shares owned. The definition of executive ownership should also con-sider how ownership is measured: in terms of shares owned, the value of the shares, or both.

When a company discloses executive ownership to its shareholders in the annual proxy statement, the measure of ownership is the number of shares (and percentage of total outstanding shares) the executive owns. This measure focuses on the voting power of the executive share-holder.

In the majority of corporate stock ownership guideline programs, the ownership sought from executives is measured in the value of shares, expressed as a multiple of the executive's base salary. A CEO, for example, may be expected to own shares having a fair market value of between four and six times that same CEO's annual salary. Here the measure of ownership is the amount at risk, the dollar value of the executive's stake in his company.

This decision on how to measure ownership will significantly affect the design of an executive stock compensation program. For example, a company focused on the number of shares owned will have guidelines for stock option awards expressed in numbers of shares. Generally the value of these stock option awards will fluctuate from year to year, but the numbers of shares covered by the stock option will not. A company focused on fair market value of ownership will have guidelines for stock option awards expressed in terms of the value of the option grant. From year to year, the value of shares covered by a stock option will be held constant, though the numbers of shares will adjust in line with changes in value.

The debate over how to measure executive ownership does not extend to the broader employee population. Generally the main purpose of spreading ownership beyond executives is to spread both the financial benefits and a sense of ownership as widely as possible throughout the company.

A common question in defining ownership for employees is whether that ownership is a liquid or illiquid position. In other words, are the financial benefits of ownership intended to be short term or long term, or both?

Many of the common vehicles for creating broad-based ownership are longer term in nature. Two examples are the employee stock ownership program (ESOP), with long-term (typically seven-year) vesting required for the employee to take the shares with him or her when leaving the organization, and the 401(k) plan, where any distribution occurs at termination. These longer-term plans must be well communicated if they are to create the sense of ownership needed to motivate employees in the short term.

The longer-term nature of broad-based ownership plans is also designed to protect the company. For example, the author of a recent *Forbes* article,[2] in a discussion of earnings dilution from option programs, indicated a concern that an all-employee stock option with a common vesting date can get out of hand and hurt the company if a majority of the option holders choose to exercise and sell on or around the common vesting date. Some pro rata vesting, on the other hand, can give employees a chance to buy in, realize some gains, and promote a general understanding of the power of ownership, all without risking an artificial downward pressure on stock price.

Programs for Creating Executive Ownership

Executive stock ownership programs typically require an executive to acquire a specified amount of company stock, expressed as a multiple of the executive's base salary, over a period of years. Shares are acquired on an ongoing basis through the executive compensation program, often through performance incentives paid in stock, exercise of stock options, awards of restricted stock, or stock given in lieu of salary increases. Executives do not typically have to dig deeply into their own pockets to comply.

The table shows an example of a typical executive stock ownership guideline program:[3]

Provision	Typical Practice	
Eligibility	All appointed and elected officers	
Targeted Ownership Levels	■ CEO	5 times Salary
	■ President	3 times Salary
	■ Divisional President	2 times Salary
	■ Senior Vice President	1 times Salary
Timing (for Compliance)	5 Years	
Company Assistance	Incentive awards paid in whole or in part in company stock	
Rewards (for Compliance)	Additional grants of stock options	
Penalties (for Noncompliance)	Reduced participation in various incentive programs	

Note: Data are from stock ownership plans disclosed in the 1995 proxies of Fortune 500 companies.

107

At first glance, these programs appear to put executives in the same boat as shareholders, with not only significant upside potential for price appreciation, but also downside risk should the stock price fall. Certainly Albert J. Dunlap took a risk when he invested $3 million in Sunbeam in 1996 when he took over as CEO of the company. C. Michael Armstrong also took a risk shortly after he joined AT&T as CEO in 1997, telling Wall Street analysts that he and his top officers would each buy stock worth five times their salaries.

The definition of risk is elusive, however. Institutional investor groups, such as Institutional Shareholder Services of Bethesda, Maryland, often argue that the various rewards for compliance reduce risk and make these programs a bribe. Still others, such as Baxter International, which loaned its top officers the money to buy an aggregate of $122 million in company stock, take away downside risk directly. Baxter's loan had a downside protection feature that said if the executive held the shares at least three years, the company would reimburse up to 50 percent of the loss if the stock fell in value.

A more detailed examination of the key design elements follows:

Eligibility

In the initial program, the eligibility includes the CEO and elected officers in the vast majority of cases. Few programs initially have broader participation. However, at the completion of the first compliance period or as the original group achieves its guidelines, it is also typical to add a layer of management to the program.

Target Ownership Levels

In the earliest executive ownership programs, top executives were typically expected to own three times their base salary in their company's stock. In many of these same programs, executives achieved their targeted level of ownership in large part from the run-up in their company's stock price and converting the after-tax paper profits in their stock options into stock ownership. The significant increase in the price of most stocks in the period 1995 through 1997 has led to a call for guidelines to prescribe higher ownership levels and a shift from guidelines expressed solely as a value to guidelines expressed in shares. New programs and second-generation programs typically convert the salary multiple to fixed shares when the guidelines are established and then hold the executive accountable to acquire that number of shares, regardless of price appreciation or declines.

Higher guideline levels are (and will continue to be) countered by those who believe too much ownership will make executives risk averse. Executives, it is argued, will avoid taking otherwise prudent business risks and stay the course, fearing that any failed risks will significantly damage their personal financial health. At the end of 1997, according to Pearl Meyer & Partners in the 1997 study *The Equity Stake*, the CEOs of the 200 largest U.S. companies had average stock ownership in their companies valued at $29 million. Interviews with these executives conducted by the United States Trust Corporation found that the majority were concerned that their portfolios were not diversified enough.

Timing for Compliance

Most of the executive ownership plans established time for compliance over which the officers could use company-sponsored compensation plans to achieve their objectives. Few expected substantial individual investments from an executive's existing savings or investments. Over five years, for example, a CEO with a combined annual target for a cash bonus and a long-term incentive of 100 percent of base salary could use the combined after-tax proceeds (60 percent after tax times five years) to buy three times salary in stock.

Rewards for Compliance

Rewards for compliance have taken many forms, from grants of restricted stock that vest upon attainment of the guideline ownership level, to an additional year's stock option grant, to forgiveness of loans used to purchase the shares. All of these programs not only reduce some of the downside risk of ownership but also replace some of the liquidity lost by the executive in the effort to comply with the ownership guidelines.

Penalties for Noncompliance

Direct penalties for noncompliance are only rarely part of the executive compensation program. Compliance or noncompliance is more commonly judged as part of the executive's overall job performance. Mechanically administering penalties for noncompliance can also have negative consequences beyond those intended from the executive stock ownership program. For example, a large southeastern equipment leasing company established an ownership program for its executives just prior to a downturn in results and a sustained decline in company stock price. (See the case study at the end of the chapter for details.)

Programs for Creating Broad-Based Employee Ownership

If a company decides to share equity with all of its employees, there are only so many ways to go about it (ESOPs, stock options and internal trading programs), each with its own unique complexities.

Employee Stock Ownership Plans

A technical discussion of the design of an ESOP is well beyond the scope of a chapter on ownership; there are too many types of plans and regulations. A simple example of one type, a leveraged ESOP, is as follows. A company borrows a sum sufficient to purchase a block of shares equal to 10 percent of the company. The shares are pledged as collateral for the loan. Each year, the company pays back a specified portion of the loan. When this is done, the corresponding portion of the shares is released to the trust and credited to the accounts of the employee participants. The employees vest in the shares credited to their account over a period of seven years. The individual accounts grow in value based on the growth in the value of the company stock credited to each account.

In many cases, the ESOP will become the largest single shareholder of the company, often managed by a committee of employees. It also is a means for a company to raise capital at below-market rates. Banks are given financial incentives from the Internal Revenue Service to loan money at below-market rates for ESOPs, and some of this savings is passed on to the companies. ESOPs can also be a retirement plan or severance plan. As a retirement plan, it often replaces a formal pension or profit-sharing program. In change-of-control situations, the ESOP may be a primary source of income continuance for employees terminated as a result of the acquisition. The plan will specify a minimum value for the shares that the acquiring company must pay and will call for a cessation of the plan and a distribution to employee participants.

It is this range of diverse purposes, from tax-advantaged capital generation to retirement savings, and the variety of rules required by the Internal Revenue Service and the Department of Labor for compliance that can dilute the impact of ESOPs as ownership programs. Also, many of the companies that use ESOPs today also use more traditional management practices. The stakeholders in an ESOP may be more likely to consider themselves career stakeholders in these traditional companies rather than financial stakeholders. Traditional management practices support a quid pro quo between employers and employees in which the long-term commitment to the company is rewarded with financial security at retirement.

Stock Option Plans

Broad-based stock option plans have been on the rise since the beginning of the 1990s. The data in Exhibit 5-2 show that during a period of rising stock prices (and therefore rising stock option value), the number of shares granted annually in stock options (as a percentage of outstanding shares) by the Fortune 200 companies rose sharply. This growth is not caused by bigger share grants to the same participants but by growth in the number of people receiving options.

In some companies *broad based* means all employees. Companies such as PepsiCo, Merck, and Bristol-Meyers Squibb have granted stock options on more than one occasion to all of their employees. In the case of Pepsi, all employees receive an annual grant of a number of shares whose purchase price equals 10 percent of the employee's salary. In the

Exhibit 5-2. Average Annual Equity Grants as a Percentage of Shares Outstanding, Fortune 200 Companies.

A bar chart with y-axis labeled "Average Annual Equity Grant as a % of Shares Outstanding" ranging from 0.00% to 2.00%, and x-axis showing years 1989 through 1997:

Year	Value
1989	1.05%
1990	1.15%
1991	1.08%
1992	1.23%
1993	1.15%
1994	1.24%
1995	1.64%
1996	1.49%
1997	1.80%

Source: Pearl Meyer & Partners, *The Equity Stake—1997.*

case of Merck and Bristol-Meyers Squibb, all employees twice received a grant of a fixed number of shares, 300 and 200 each, respectively. In all three of these companies, the options vested and became exercisable over five years.

A number of factors limit the growth of stock option grants to all employees. The most important is the number of shares required. Many employers cannot absorb the potential earnings per share dilution caused by such a broad share grant. In Merck, the very high ratio of market capitalization (total outstanding shares times the fair market value per share) to employee keeps the dilution low and makes a broad-based grant financially feasible. High market capitalization combined with high employee turnover has made a broad-based stock option plan feasible at PepsiCo.

The biggest challenge to granting stock options to all employees is maintaining the motivational aspect. Both Merck and Bristol-Meyers

Squibb stopped these programs after two awards for fear the programs would be perceived as entitlement. However, little changed in the management of these businesses or in the sharing of information with employees following the grants to avoid this concern.

Among a larger group of companies, *broad based* means a significant percentage of the employee population, typically 15 percent to 25 percent. Although this is far short of 100 percent or even a majority, it is also much more broad based than participation in traditional stock options used solely as a management incentive. In these plans, participation of 1 percent to 3 percent of total employees would be typical.

Two approaches for selecting participants are used in a broad-based stock option plan where participation is less than 100 percent. In the *line in the sand approach*, all employees above a threshold are declared eligible. Thresholds may be salary levels, organization levels, individual performance levels, or job level. The *management discretion approach* is designed to get an ownership interest to key contributors, regardless of job or salary level. A budgeted number of shares are set aside for stock options sufficient to fund stock option awards to a specified percentage of the population. Senior managers then decide the actual participants and numbers of shares for each, subject only to the budget share limits.

This second type of broad-based plan acknowledges the financial limitations of 100 percent participation and directs ownership instead to the key contributors or those with key responsibilities. It is far from a perfect solution. However, it is a step in the right direction in the sense that more ownership is better than less.

Internal Equity Markets

One other type of broad-based ownership program bears mentioning. This program appears primarily in private companies, particularly professional services organizations. Employees at all levels are encouraged to own shares. Shares available for purchase generally come from existing shareholders wishing to sell. Buyers are employees as well. This type of program gives new employees a chance to buy into their company and longer-service employees a chance to realize some gains; it generally creates an awareness of the company's stock and stock price growth.

In addition to the internal trading, some common characteristics of these programs include the right of the company to buy back shares from any employee owner who quits, dies, or otherwise leaves the company. The buyback occurs over a number of years. Also, windows of opportunity every two or three years allow current owners a chance to sell shares back to the company, subject to sufficient financial resources.

One other unique feature of these plans is the use of nonvoting stock. When used, these shares let the participant share in the financial risks and rewards of ownership. The ultimate legal authority on most major issues rests with the owners of the voting stock, often the founder or the senior management team. Sharing ownership does not mean giving up control of a business, as some owners of private companies fear. However sharing ownership and information creates a larger pool of people to whom an owner can turn to for help.

Factors Contributing to Successful Ownership Programs

The success of ownership programs can be measured by their ability to affect executive and employee behavior positively. The Compensation Resource Group survey mentioned at the start of this chapter found the changed behaviors observed most often to be commitment, integrity, and flexibility. Although two large corporation and benefits consulting firms, William Mercer and WatsonWyatt, have attempted to show a statistically significant connection between the presence of ownership programs and improved company results, neither has succeeded. There are far too many intervening factors for this to occur.

What can be seen are numerous examples of ownership programs and improved company performance. Companies with ownership programs often are managed differently and are more successful than those that do not have these programs. Companies such as Wal-Mart, South-west Airlines, and Intel are examples of high-performing companies that emphasize broad-based employee ownership.

In the Compensation Resource Group survey, a clearly communicated and understood philosophy on executive stock ownership was perceived by executives to be the key to achieving the desired affect of a program mandating stock ownership. Where executives felt their company had a clearly communicated stock ownership philosophy, they were far more likely to perceive the program as positively affecting executive behavior than executives who did not perceive their company to have a clearly communicated philosophy.

Jack Stack, the proponent of open book management,[4] indicates that successful companies with employee owners work to communicate and ensure that all employees know how the company makes money, what the keys to long-term success are, and how shareholder value is created. With employees, you get what you give. If you have informed employee owners, he says, people will set their own goals, and if employees set their own targets, generally the goals will be accomplished.

Communication is not the only key to a successful ownership program. The following additional factors contribute to successful ownership programs:

- *Employees have a voice in how a business is run.* By giving people a voice, a company can tap into the universal desire of people to win and make that desire a competitive advantage.

- *All employees are encouraged to think beyond their job and accept broader accountability.* When employees focus only on their jobs, they do not function as part of one company, and they are not flexible or even likely to enjoy work. Teaching them the bigger picture can alter behavior toward flexibility and motivation, and toward being a team player.

- *Numbers are used as building blocks.* Too many companies use numbers as controls. Numbers used as standards can educate and empower employees to take control of results.

- *All employees can win (through rewards) and win often.* Incentives give employees a focus. They have a challenge and a reason to work as smart and hard as they can. Well-designed incentives guarantee that if the organization meets its performance targets, the stock price will rise. In this way, employees pay attention to both the short and long term.

Conclusion

=== · ■ · ===

Sharing equity with executives and employees will not make the existing owners poor. Greed, however, will. Companies must start by giving something to get something back. Encouraging and creating executive and employee owners is a starting point.

Next, executives and employees must *want* to succeed before they *will* succeed. There are many obstacles to success in the marketplace, but an even bigger obstacle exists inside all employees: their will to win. Ownership helps motivate employees by giving them a meaningful stake in the company's success.

Finally, executives and employees must share a common definition of success. The value of ownership can be that common scorecard that gets all executives and employees working to achieve common goals.

Case Study: Using Stock Ownership to Align Rewards and Results

In 1992, a large southeastern transportation company established executive stock ownership guidelines for the first time. The company felt that the guidelines would give a positive message to the investment community and support stock price growth.

Executives were given five years to comply with guidelines requiring them to acquire between two and four times their base salary in company stock. Those who failed to comply with the new ownership guidelines would find their annual stock option grant reduced by 20 percent in each subsequent year beyond the scheduled time for compliance.

Many longer-service executives had current ownership close to the guideline amount at the start of the ownership program. Many shorter-service executives elected at the start of the program to have the after-tax portion of their annual bonus paid in stock. Still others indicated their intent to hold after-tax gains from option exercise in company stock. The program appeared initially as if it would have the desired effect.

Trouble began three years into the program, when the stock price went into an extended decline. By the end of the third year of the program, it had lost almost 50 percent of its initial value. The decline in value was due in part to poor financial results, which meant that annual bonuses were below targeted levels. Executives lacked cash to purchase stock, and those who thought they were in compliance now faced a serious shortfall. The impending penalties for noncompliance appeared as a reason for executive turnover at a time when continuity of management was critical.

The company CEO and the board decided it would be poor shareholder relations and a poor leadership decision to back off from the desired ownership levels in the face of the stock price decline. However, they did decide to reconfigure the guidelines and add an incentive for compliance.

First, the guidelines were converted from value to numbers of shares. The targeted share ownership was set using the dollars derived from the desired salary multiple and dividing by the price of the stock at the start of the program. In this way, the guidelines were no longer subject to price fluctuation.

The change lessened the ownership burden in the short term. However, management added a second five-year ownership program, generally raising the ownership levels by one times salary. For example, an executive required to own two times his or her salary by year 5 now had to own three times his or her salary by year eight.

Further, management did not drop the penalty for noncompliance, but it instituted a 20 percent stock option premium for any executive attaining and remaining in compliance with the initial five-year ownership program. This premium remained in effect until the second targeted ownership levels applied in year eight.

At the time of this writing, the company's stock price has returned to a small premium above those at the start of the ownership program. In addition, nearly all of the executives were in compliance with the ownership guidelines

Notes

· ■ ·

1. "Stock Options Are Not a Free Lunch," *Forbes,* May 18, 1998, p. 213
2. Ibid., p. 212.
3. Data are from stock ownership plans disclosed in the 1995 proxies of Fortune 500 companies.
4. Jack Stack, *The Great Game of Business* (New York: Doubleday, 1992), pp. 5–21.

6

Aligning Directors' Compensation With Company Performance

Pearl Meyer
president of Pearl Mayer & Partners

T hese are challenging times in corporate America. We live in an era of mega-mergers, restructuring, intense global competition, and rapidly evolving technologies that cause companies to come and go in the blink of an eye. As a result, the responsibilities, risks, and performance expectations associated with independent directorship are rising exponentially. Driven by aggressive corporate governance initiatives, new strategies for compensating directors are keeping pace.

With new compensation vehicles, regulatory changes, ever-increasing institutional ownership, and heightened accountability for directors, the pay-for-performance story at the board level can be told in one word: ownership.

Directors as Owners: Resurrection of an Old Role

Equity has skyrocketed to a position of indisputable prominence in compensating the outside director for board service, restoring an ownership stake to directors that hearkens back to the earliest days of corporate America, when many directors were founders or direct investors in the companies on whose boards they served. Today this ownership stake serves a different though equally critical purpose: to link irrevocably the financial interests of board members, through their compensation, with those of the shareholders whose fiduciary interests they represent.

Stock ownership for directors is a breakthrough advancement in board governance. Most movers and shakers in the business and investor communities believe that all stakeholders—management, employees, and the community, as well as individual and institutional shareholders—benefit when board members are placed on an equal at-risk footing with stockholders. As John L. Vogelstein of the Warburg Pincus investment firm put it simply: "I have observed that directors who own meaningful amounts of stock pay more attention. . . . If we want directors to represent the best interests of the owners and the long-run interests of the company, they must think like owners, and there is only one way to see they do."

Still, there is a contrary movement afoot to pay incentives to directors for achievement of annual quantitative corporate results.[1] This competing type of pay-for-performance strategy, which has been adopted by a handful of companies, has significant downside, unlike the direct use of equity.

Linking board pay to annual corporate results is fraught with incendiary potential. Short-term incentives for board members can ignite a blaze of turmoil and dissension within the boardroom and with management, as well as a firestorm of deserved criticism. Simply put, this type of pay scheme contrasts starkly with the independence outside directors need to chart courses of action that are in the best long-term interests of shareholders. Examples of this incentive pay approach are found in companies that base annual option or stock awards on minimum annual increases in return on equity (ROE) or earnings, generally 10 percent.

Achieving board independence from management and fostering its long-term strategic perspective has been one of the corporate governance movement's greatest success stories thus far, but the key to preserving director independence is recognition of the fundamental divergence between the duties of a public corporation's board and its management and the need to reflect their different roles in the design of their compensation. A program that subjects outside directors to management's annual pay-for-performance standards is a threat to board members' capacity to act in a truly disinterested manner.

The far wiser and almost universally lauded practice adopted by an ever-growing number of companies puts meaningful amounts of company equity in the hands of directors. Stock-based compensation applies the pay-for-performance concept to directors' remuneration in a positive and productive manner for all constituents by tying the long-term results of directors' corporate oversight to the long-term value of their shareholdings and those of all stockholders.

Directors' pay has always been one of the best buys in American business. Until now, it has been the "how" of board compensation, not the "how much" that has been in question. Considering the expertise, judgment, breadth of knowledge, and experience that directors bring to the table, their pay levels have not been out of line in most cases. However, the value of the "buy" has grown dramatically for shareholders and will continue to do so, now that directors, through their pay, have become owners of meaningful stakes in the companies on whose boards they serve.

The Cash-to-Equity Shift in Directors' Pay

Corporate governance initiatives sparked the cash-to-equity shift more than a decade ago at the senior executive level, causing corporations to move an increasing portion of management, and even employee, remuneration into company stock to motivate and reward the creation of shareholder value. With equity firmly entrenched inside the corporation, governance activists turned their attention to directors. Thus began the initial stages of a similar movement at the board level to align pay with stock performance and, most important, with shareholder interests. Equity accounted for a trifling 2 percent of a director's total compensation among the 200 largest U.S. corporations in 1985. By 1997, in a dramatic about-face, equity had skyrocketed to previously unheard of levels, constituting an average 45 percent of total director compensation (see Exhibit 6-1).

Companies are rapidly approaching the groundbreaking recommendations of corporate governance activists that were made in 1995 to

Exhibit 6-1. Cash versus Equity as a Percentage of Total Director Compensation, Excluding Pension.

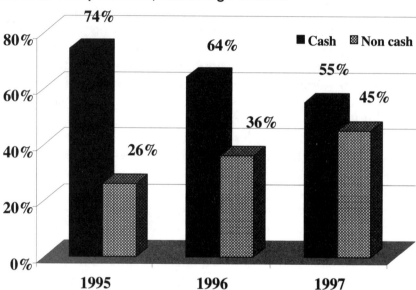

increase this stake to no less than 50 percent. In fact, if trailblazers such as the National Association of Corporate Directors (NACD) and its Blue Ribbon Commission, CalPERS, TIAA-CREF, and the Business Round-table have their way, this 50 percent goal will be reached and surely surpassed in the near future. With heavy use of outright stock grants and stock options, widespread eradication of board pension plans and replacement in many cases with equity, and with all or a portion of cash retainers increasingly being paid in equity, it is quickly becoming clear that equity is king.

Pensions Out, Equity In

Director ownership is receiving a boost from what once would have been deemed an unlikely source: a dramatic move to abandon director pension plans, prompted by conclusions drawn in the NACD Blue Rib-bon Commission Report on Director Compensation in 1995, and sec-onded by other powerhouse activists and investors. The emphasis now is on ensuring that directors maintain a meaningful equity stake in their companies during board service rather than upholding the promise of cash pension payments once directorship has ended.

In the early 1990s, approximately three-fourths of the 200 largest U.S. corporations had pension plans on their books for outside directors. In the 1994–1995 proxy season, a handful of companies anticipated the Blue Ribbon Commission's findings and downsized their pension benefits. Since the issuance of the NACD report, companies have done away with board pensions in droves. In fact, 90 companies bought out their pension plans in the last two years, leaving only 41 of the top 200 companies with pension plans remaining at year-end 1997. All indications are that this trend is continuing in full force. Proxies from 1998 provide evidence that more companies are eliminating their nonemployee director pension plans. By the time we reach the millennium, it is quite likely that pensions among major corporations will be obsolete.

With respect to terminated pension plans, in almost all cases, companies have set aside the funds representing the benefits accrued to date in deferred compensation arrangements. While these funds may be paid out currently, such accrued benefits are most frequently converted into director stockholdings using a number of vehicles.

The Prevalence of Stock Vehicles

· ■ ·

By the late 1990s, almost all of the 200 largest U.S. companies had included stock in the compensation of their outside directors versus a mere handful ten years ago. Equity vehicles vary widely—from outright full-value current grants to deferred shares, restricted stock, and stock options—and are often used in combination. While the vast majority of companies pay their directors in stock of some kind, a small percentage offer only elective deferral programs that permit tax-sheltered investment of current cash retainers and/or meeting fees into company stock.

Among the top 200 companies using some form of stock compensation for outside directors, outright grants continue to outweigh stock options by far, although use of both types of vehicles is on the rise (see Exhibit 6-2).

123

Exhibit 6-2. Full-Value Grants Versus Stock Options.

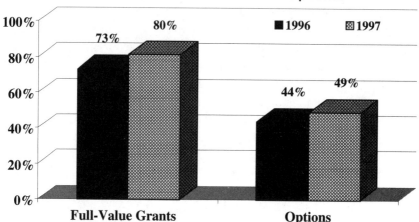

Note: The options are nonadditive since sixty-eight companies use at least two forms of stock-based pay, including stock options, stock retainers, current stock, restricted stock, and deferred stock. "Full-Value Grants" include stock retainers, current stock, restricted stock, and deferred stock.

From a governance perspective, full-value grants are deemed the preferred choice for board remuneration. Unlike options, grants provide directors with an ownership interest that offers both upside opportunity and downside risk, as well as full voting and dividend rights, on par with stockholders. Stock awards also provide a boon to the growing challenge of board recruitment by providing one-time only "welcome-aboard" grants to new board members, along with ownership at entry, both of which encourage immediate motivation and commitment.

While there are those who fear that stock options may focus directors too heavily on short-term stock price performance rather than strategic progress and long-term value creation, stock option grants can play an important role in certain situations. In our ongoing executive and board compensation practice, we find that stock options are the vehicle of choice in turnarounds, before initial public offerings (IPO)s, start-ups and high-growth companies—clearly cases in which maximum leverage is needed to attract and compensate valuable board talent and, in some instances, where cash may be in scant supply.

A good example is a high-technology company that split off from its parent company through an IPO to form a new public entity. A sizable one-time stock option was granted to outside directors at the time of the IPO and continues as the sole form of payment when new directors join the board. The option vests in equal installments on the first, second, and third anniversaries of the date of grant. Outside directors receive no other compensation for their services. Interestingly, the new chairman and CEO, who was brought on board at the IPO, negotiated for a mega-stock option grant on about 2.5 percent of the outstanding shares as his only form of pay for the year of the IPO and ensuing years thereafter in exchange for salary, bonus, and all other compensation.

Shifting From Cash Retainer to Stock Retainer

One of the most striking manifestations of the cash-to-equity shift in director compensation can be found in the growing number of companies now paying part, and in selective cases all, of the traditionally cash retainer in stock. Among major U.S. corporations, prevalence of stock retainers has almost doubled in the past several years. Stock as an integral part of the retainer represents a clear step toward institutionalizing equity as a vital component of board pay rather than the enticing "add-on" of past years.

Major corporations that pay 100 percent of their retainer in some form of stock include Campbell Soup, Colgate-Palmolive, and Chrysler. A closer look at one of the companies using a stock retainer provides insight into the reasons that boards make this commitment, placing heavy reliance on equity for their own compensation.

RELYING ON STOCK TO COMPENSATE DIRECTORS

This company, now a financial services giant, began in 1986 at the time of a major acquisition to pay its outside directors solely in stock. Previously the company used traditional executive and board compensation programs heavily reliant on cash. Therefore, one of the top priorities of the CEO and board at the time of the acquisition was to redesign and implement executive and board compensation programs geared to shareholder value creation.

A true forerunner, compensation for this company's board has consisted since 1986 solely of an annual retainer payable in common stock. Today the value of the annual stock retainer is $100,000, receipt of which may be deferred at the election of the director. Directors who do not make such an election are paid partly in cash to cover the current tax liability incurred on receipt of stock.

The board of this giant enterprise made its position unequivocally clear from the beginning. As stated in the proxy, since 1986, directors have been paid solely in shares to ensure that they have an ownership interest in common with the stockholders. And in the most recent proxy, the report of the Compensation Committee on Executive Compensation explicitly described board policy with respect to director stock ownership: all director fees are paid in company stock, and all members of the board have made a commitment (along with the executive group) not to dispose of any company stock they hold as long as they remain directors.

This is an unusually complete proxy disclosure, but this company is not alone in its commitment to board stock ownership and concomitant linkage with shareholder interests.

Director Share Ownership Guidelines

Boards are in the singular position of setting and approving their own compensation. While many boards should be applauded for their responsiveness in dealing with corporate governance and investor pressures to make equity a vital component of board pay, a growing number are doing even more. Many boards are now taking the critically important step of ensuring share retention and significant levels of continuing ownership by adopting stock ownership guidelines for directors similar to those previously instituted for their corporate executives.

Several companies fully disclose their requirement that directors own from three to five times their annual retainer in stock, with a minimum number of shares of stock to be acquired within a few years of joining their board. In some companies, rewards are offered to directors who meet or exceed guidelines. For example, one company grants a supplementary option if the number of shares owned exceeds its five-times guideline. Another grants a special option when 1,500 shares are held by a director, and ownership of 2,000 shares is required for eligibility for the next grant in five years.

Although only a small, albeit growing, number of companies voluntarily disclose formal director ownership guidelines, the fact is that many companies, large and small, are using stock to pay their directors, and more will follow. It is clear that board members are quickly accruing real ownership stakes on a direct, meaningful basis, with or without guidelines.

A Different Slant on Director Incentives

In the spirit of making directors owners in concert with shareholders through equity-based compensation, a new, and for the first time, positive, trend in incentive pay for directors is emerging. A small group of major corporations have begun to offer their directors a premium if they elect some form of stock payment in lieu of payment of some or all of the annual retainer in cash—for example:

- Offering a stock option priced at a discount from fair market value
- Electing to exchange the cash retainer for options based on a Black-Scholes valuation (which is a widely used econometric approach to estimating a stock's future value)
- Crediting directors' deferred stock accounts with a premium ranging from 10 percent to 25 percent above the value of the forgone cash retainer

Such incentives strictly reward directors for electing stock over cash; annual corporate performance plays no role whatsoever.

Discretionary Stock Plans

A significant change in Rule 16b-3 of the Securities and Exchange Commission in 1996 has brought us to the threshold of a new era in board

127

compensation as traditional formula-driven stock plans are being re-placed by discretionary plans for the first time. Public companies now have far greater flexibility in granting options and stock-related awards to directors.

Since the 1950s, Rule 16b-3 had strictly limited the way in which a company could implement exempt stock-based compensation pro-grams for directors. Among other things, the rule required shareholder approval of the plan and any material amendments to the plan, and awards could be granted at the discretion of "disinterested directors" (a director was "disinterested" in this respect under Rule 16b-3 only if his or her awards were nondiscretionary) or on a nondiscretionary basis by means of fixed grants or formula grants specified in the plan. Since employee directors are most often executive officers paid at least par-tially on a discretionary basis, boards generally lack "disinterested" di-rectors qualified to make discretionary grants to other board members.

Companies therefore complied with old Rule 16b-3 by adopting shareholder-approved plans that made fixed awards to nonemployee di-rectors. A typical plan provision might authorize the grant of an option or stock award on 5,000 shares to each nonemployee director at the date of each annual meeting of shareholders. Directors who received only this type of award would qualify as "disinterested," and therefore they could sit on compensation committees that made discretionary grants to executive officers under shareholder-approved plans covering those officers. In this way, both nondiscretionary grants to directors and discretionary grants to executive officers would be exempt under old Rule 16b-3, meaning that they would not incur short-swing profits lia-bility.

As completely revised in 1996, Rule 16b-3 eliminated shareholder approval as a strict requirement for exemptions and dropped the re-quirement that directors be "disinterested." Although the new rule in-cludes an exemption for grants made by a committee of nonemployee directors (an especially good way to exempt grants to executive officers), the definition of "nonemployee director" turns on whether the director receives payments from the company for anything other than services as a director. It no longer matters under the rule whether the director receives discretionary grants rather than fixed grants. An award may be granted in any manner, so long as it is compensation for services as a director, without jeopardizing a director's status as a nonemployee director. Moreover, grants to directors are exempt under new Rule 16b-3 if they are simply approved by the board (which is the general practice for corporate law purposes, in any event).

As a result, Rule 16b-3 is no longer the primary regulation shaping stock-based compensation for directors. Other concerns, such as shareholder approval requirements imposed by stock exchanges and NASDAQ rules and the view of institutional shareholders that they should be permitted to vote on stock plans for directors, have assumed greater prominence as Rule 16b-3 has receded. Nevertheless, companies now have greater freedom to adopt plans for directors (or even to amend existing plans that were designed to meet the rigid requirements of old Rule 16b-3) that permit boards to determine the type of award, size and timing of grant, vesting, forfeiture, and other award terms.

Since the rule change in 1996, companies clearly have been taking advantage of their new flexibility. In fact, an informal review of new director plans starting in 1997 indicates the emergence of a new trend: whether director plans are incorporated into executive or all-employee stock vehicles or remain stand-alone plans, the flexibility of omnibus plans is replacing rigid formulas. This means that for the first time, directors are eligible to receive everything from stock appreciation rights to performance shares, dividend equivalents, and stock unit bonus awards. Some companies favor the benefits of joint executive-director omnibus stock plans. Typically, more shares are reserved under joint plans, and combining the plans simplifies the shareholder approval process.

Proponents of discretionary stock plans for directors believe that it is now more likely that board pay will be closely linked to corporate performance. However, there are those dissenters who fear that permitting directors the sole discretion to determine their own stock awards will encourage grants that are too generous. Further, there is a concern that the trend toward performance evaluations for individual directors, coupled with greater flexibility and discretion in making stock awards, might lead to stark differentiation in pay levels within a corporate board for the first time. Until now, the only individual differences in pay on a board have been determined by services rendered: the number of meetings attended, committee chair service, the number of board committees on which individual directors serve, special or consulting services rendered, and so on. It is clear that in realizing the positive benefits of these flexible, discretionary plans, it will be necessary at the same time for directors to avoid short-term, "island unto oneself" orientation.

One company's journey through the as-yet roughly charted waters of the new flexibility illustrates the manner in which a discretionary plan can be used in a positive way to reel in surging pay levels for directors.

"Increased Flexibility Enhances Stock Ownership Plans"

In its most recent proxy, the board of a major financial services institution disclosed that it had taken advantage of changes in Rule 16b-3 by recommending alterations in its existing directors' stock plan. The changes reflected in the revised plan were intended to give the board greater sway in setting the terms of stock-based compensation for nonemployee directors. The revised plan no longer specifies the number of shares subject to options or restricted stock grants, but instead permits the board to determine the size of future grants.

Such flexibility permits the type and size of options grants, restricted stock, or deferred stock to be more readily adjusted to maintain reasonable and appropriate levels of board compensation overall and at the same time take into account changes in the market value of the company's shares. In fact, the stock of this company has performed so well for so long that under its rigid, formula-driven plan, directors' pay packages have been overly enriched. Management and the board have wanted to rein in director pay, and they viewed changes in Rule 16b-3 as a golden opportunity to adjust board compensation downward now, knowing that with this new flexibility, they can adjust the number of shares granted up or down in the future, depending on market conditions. More specifically, the board has announced plans to:

- Decrease annual option grants by a specified percentage
- Replace its annual grant of restricted stock with a new annual grant of restricted stock having a value equal to a certain specified percentage of the annual retainer

- Take advantage of its increased flexibility to provide a more substantial equity-based component to new nonemployee directors
- Provide nonemployee directors with a means to invest their cash in company stock on a tax-deferred basis

The Future of Board Pay

In an amazingly brief period, equity has become the new cornerstone of board pay. Stock in all its forms will continue to provide a firm foundation as directors solidify their independence, build stronger relationships with the stockholders, demonstrate commitment through immediate responsiveness to good corporate governance practices, and establish parity with shareholder interests.

In this scenario, linking directors' pay to company performance works. When ownership is the link, everyone benefits.

Case Study: The Odyssey of Two Corporations

A close look at the 1996 merger of two Fortune 100 companies dramatically illustrates the flight from pensions to stock and brings to the light other critically important director remuneration considerations. We will call the acquiring firm Company A, the acquiree Company B, and the newly created entity (our client) Newco, now a megacorporation in its industry.

Company A had sixteen directors, of whom only two were employees: the chief executive officer and the chief operating officer. Company B had a larger board, with twenty-one directors, of whom three were insiders: the chairman, the chief executive officer, and the chief operating officer.

The service of individual directors varied widely on both boards, ranging from less than one year up to twenty-six years. Average service was lengthy but different for the two boards: ten years on average for Company A and fourteen years on average for Company B. Ages of the board members also ranged widely, from the fifties and sixties to age seventy, the oldest on both boards. Average ages were sixty-two and sixty-five in Company A and B, respectively.

Our firm's mission was to develop an appropriate compensation program for Newco's board, which was slated to have seventeen directors: seven from Company A and six from Company B, plus the chief executive officer (who was the former head of Company A) and the chief operating officer (the previous chief executive of Company B). In addition, there were two vice chairmen, one from each predecessor company. The new board is typically diverse: it includes females and African Americans, educators and CEOs at ages ranging from fifty-four to sixty-seven years.

Three Key Issues

Among the immediate issues to be addressed, we identified three areas of critical concern:

1. *Convergence of two different pay patterns, including the use of stock*
2. *Fairness to both continuing and retiring directors*
3. *Developing a competitive package appropriate for the new entity*

In beginning this project, we were told that the two companies' programs were comparable in design and value. Company A had a much smaller retainer ($25,000) than Company B, but unlike Company B, it also made separate deferred stock grants. When valued and added to the cash retainer, these deferred shares brought board pay at Company A exactly up to Company B's retainer of $54,000. The Company B retainer was, in fact, a composite of $30,000 in cash and annual grants of 400 shares worth $24,000. Amazingly, the annual meeting fees and chair fees were so similar that they came within $1,000 of each (see Exhibit 6-3).

In addition to these almost equal direct compensation amounts, each company also had a retirement plan. Unlike the direct pay elements, we found two very different pension programs. Company A's lifetime benefit was limited to the $25,000 retainer. Here, retirement

Exhibit 6-3. Directors' Pay Packages at Company A and Company B.

	Company A	Company B
Retainer, including stock	$25,000	$54,000
Other stock	29,000	0
Meeting fees	41,000	40,000
Direct compensation	$95,000	$94,000

at age sixty-five required at least six years of service for a lifetime benefit.

Company B's lifetime benefit was also based on its retainer. However, included in the annual retainer was the annual share grant, which raised the amount of the total retainer to $54,000, contrasting sharply with Company A at $25,000. Lifetime benefits for directors of Company B were earned based on retirement after age seventy (rather than sixty-five) and ten years of service (rather than six).

In order to receive a lifetime benefit, Company A had a vesting cliff of six years' service and age sixty-five. If those two conditions were not met, then the full benefit was limited to the years of actual service. Company B had a more generous plan. For a limited benefit, the company simply prorated the lifetime benefit amount by 10 percent per annum for less than ten years of board service.

The spousal benefit was another point of differentiation. In the event that a director died, Company A provided a partial benefit to his or her spouse, whereas Company B offered no such benefit.

Overall, the imbalance between the two packages became apparent when we took pension values and provisions into account. In fact, annualizing the pension of each company demonstrated that Company A directors had a benefit that was about half the value of Company B. The resulting total remuneration was quite different: $110,000 for Company A and $125,000 for Company B (see Exhibit 6-4).

The first two issues—merging two different pay packages and developing an appropriate program for both ongoing directors and retiring directors—became much easier because our client wanted to

Exhibit 6-4. Total Directors' Remuneration at Company A and Company B.

	Company A	Company B
Retainer, incl. stock	$25,000	$54,000
Other stock	$29,000	0
Meeting fees	$41,000	$40,000
Direct Compensation	*$95,000*	*$94,000*
Pension present value	$15,000	$31,000
Total Remuneration	*$110,000*	*$125,000*

do the right thing. As a newly created corporation, Newco wished to follow good corporate governance guidelines by eliminating its pensions and emphasizing stock.

First, let us look at Newco's new program, since it took far less time to develop than ensuring parity for retiring directors.

To address the third issue of developing a competitive program for the new entity, we studied the marketplace from several angles. We first compared our predecessor companies with typical Fortune 100 companies. In this analysis, we also reviewed industry comparators and other major director-affiliated companies whose pay patterns and levels were found to be similar to the Fortune 100 survey results.

Our client wanted a pay program that would fall in the average to above-average range. After reviewing all the market data and the two existing programs, we developed a new plan for the thirteen outside directors who were continuing with Newco. The proposed plan offered the smaller cash retainer of $25,000 with the same committee and chair fee structure yielding $40,000, plus a larger annual stock award. In addition, we instituted a deferred compensation plan under which all or any portion of board compensation could be electively deferred. The deferred accounts were initially funded with shares from the pension buyout.

An interesting side issue was whether to grant stock awards as a fixed number of shares or a fixed dollar amount. We chose the "number of shares" approach so that annual board remuneration would be directly affected by shareholder value rather than increasing grant size in years of declining value and cutting grants when the stock price appreciates. This design feature in any company clearly helps focus directors on the rise and fall of shareholder value.

At the time we designed this new plan, 500 shares of stock equaled about $50,000. A range of reasonableness was set at $30,000 to $70,000. The total package was targeted at $115,000 and was designed to range from $95,000 to $135,000, with review planned for every two or three years to ensure competitiveness and adjust the number of shares, as necessary (see Exhibit 6-5).

Exhibit 6-5. Newco's Directors' Compensation Package.

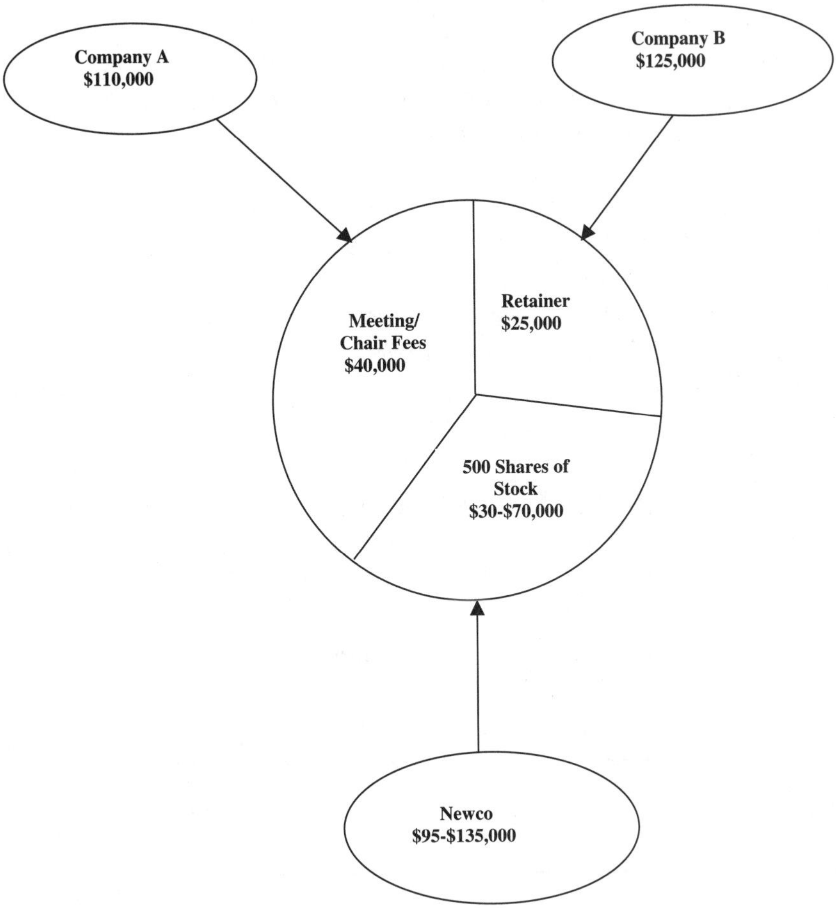

Although the NACD guidelines call for at least 50 percent of directors' compensation in stock, our client opted for 43 percent in stock and 57 percent in cash (see Exhibit 6-6).

However, directors were given the opportunity to defer all elements of their compensation into stock on a tax-sheltered basis. Remember that this was a diverse board. While several directors took immediate advantage of this deferral feature, the program's flexibility permitted those with current cash needs to be paid currently while others could choose deferral to retirement.

Retirement Buyout

Buying out the two pension plans developed into the thorniest issue. In buying out the retirement benefits of the directors of Companies A and B, Newco joined the other ninety companies in the Fortune 200 that terminated board pensions in 1996 and 1997. The design that we structured for other clients in prior years, and is now standard, was also used at Newco, although some companies offer less flexibility in terms of payout timing.

For Newco, we calculated the lump-sum present value of each director's projected retirement benefit, which became a complex and tedious process due to the following issues that required consideration:

- Should the terminal value be based on each director's age and service now or, because the promised benefits were prematurely terminated, should credit be given until normal retirement?

Exhibit 6-6. Compensation Breakdown.

	Newco Balance	NACD Recommended Balance
Cash	57%	50% to 0%
Stock	43%	50% to 100%
Pension	—	—

136

■ *What discount rate should be used?*

■ *Should actual service and age and gender norms be used?*

■ *Should the nearest birthday or the last birthday be used in calculating years of service?*

■ *Under which plan should each director retire: his or her own company's plan, the better of the two plans, or a composite plan that was better yet?*

Since most directors would have continued service had it not been for the merger—and thirteen did—our client decided to buy out all directors using Company B's more generous normal retirement benefit with accelerated vesting.

Finally, after completion of preliminary calculations and with the approval of all parties gained, the number of deferred shares to be delivered to each director was determined in the window period for insiders. Depending on age, this resulted in lump-sum present values ranging from $150,000 to $500,000 paid in deferred stock units to both retiring and continuing directors. While the new (and ongoing) board remuneration program was valued toward the lower side of its two predecessor companies, Newco retained its competitive compensation edge on a direct, rather than indirect compensation basis—that is, with cash and stock compensation rather than pension. This multifaceted project resulted in a program that merged two major corporate boards into one, provided a fair package for both retiring and continuing directors, and established a framework for paying the new board competitively, all the while adhering to today's mandate for good corporate governance. This shift from pension to stock ownership has resulted in director compensation that more closely mirrors the fortunes of the board's principal constituent, the Newco stockholder.

Checklist for Linking Directors' Pay to Company Performance

☐ Does the company provide equity participation to board members?

☐ Which equity vehicles are used?

- [ ] Full value grants versus stock options?
- [ ] If full value, are grants outright stock awards or awards with vesting requirements?
- [ ] Stock retainer?
  - [ ] If yes, all stock or partial cash and partial stock?
- [ ] What percentage of board compensation is in stock?
- [ ] Are share ownership guidelines for directors in place?
- [ ] Can directors electively defer cash retainer and/or board and committee fees into company stock?
  - [ ] Does the company provide an incentive to encourage deferral?
- [ ] What is the status of director stock plans with regard to new Rule 16b-3?
  - [ ] New, flexible, omnibus stock plan or standard, formula-driven plan?
  - [ ] Stand-alone director plan or all-inclusive plan (executives, directors, and employees)?
  - [ ] How many shares remain available for grant under existing plan(s)?
- [ ] Is any element of director pay contingent on achievement of quantitative performance goals?
- [ ] Is there a director pension plan?
- [ ] Are some or all of the equity awards mandatorily deferred until retirement or termination?
- [ ] Do directors receive other benefits?
- [ ] Does the director pay program include a charitable contribution benefit?
- [ ] Do directors attend at least 75 percent of board and board committee meetings?
- [ ] Are board members paid attendance fees for board and board committee meetings?
- [ ] Do committee chairs receive additional fees or retainers?
- [ ] Is there a lead director?
- [ ] Is there a separate chairman and CEO?
- [ ] Does the board have a structured performance evaluation process in place?
  - [ ] Of the board as a whole?
  - [ ] Of individual directors?

☐ Is the CEO's performance evaluated by the board or a board committee on a structured basis?

☐ How is the level of board total remuneration determined?

    ☐ Marketplace positioning relative to an appropriate peer group?

☐ How is the peer group determined?

☐ How does it differ from that used to assess the competitiveness of executive compensation?

☐ Is board remuneration reviewed on a regular basis?

☐ Is independent compensation counsel consulted, or does management or the compensation committee make its own recommendations without outside counsel?

☐ How and how much do directors benefit financially in the event of a change in control or other corporate transaction?

☐ Does the company uphold sound corporate governance practices in compensating its directors?

Note

1. Our firm's annual analysis of proxy statements shows a small but growing number of corporations that tie directors' compensation to financial results.

SECTION II

===== · ■ · =====

ALIGNING BASE PAY AND EMPLOYEE CAPABILITIES

The traditional model for managing wages and salaries evolved in an era when control was the primary objective. It was developed by industrial engineers in the 1930s and 1940s and reflects the labor-management climate of this period. The process started with highly detailed job descriptions that documented each duty and task that an employee was expected to perform. That document was effectively a contract that defined each worker's job. Then pseudoscientific job evaluation systems were applied to determine each job's relative value or, more accurately, its rank in the hierarchy of jobs. The analyses and related decisions were handled by a centralized staff of specialists who controlled every aspect of the program.

The initial programs were developed for a blue-collar environment. White-collar workers were small in number through the first half of this century. Wage increases in the early factories were across the board or based on longevity, although in smaller companies, supervisors had a great deal of discretion to handle all pay decisions. When the first formal pay systems for white-collar employees were developed after World War II, the framework used in manufacturing was extended to them with little conceptual change. The new concepts introduced over the next couple of decades reinforced the centralized control orientation.

The only significant difference between the typical base pay programs for white-collar and blue-collar employees is the announced emphasis on linking pay increases to performance. For managers and professionals, merit pay is essentially universal in the corporate world. It is less prevalent for clerical support personnel but still the predominant practice. For blue-collar and service employees, especially in larger companies, it is rare to find merit pay.

The more-or-less standard model used to manage base pay until the beginning of the 1990s fits the traditional, command-and-control organization. Internal job evaluation systems have been the basis for determining a job's relative value. The announced premise of these decisions is the need to maintain internal equity, but in reality job evaluation systems serve to reinforce and perpetuate the existing job hierarchy. Annual salary increases have become virtually automatic, which has created a widely shared sense of entitlement among employees in every sector. Merit pay predominates, but there is commonly little difference in the increases granted to the best and worst employees.

This traditional model was accepted and served its purpose until the era of downsizing and restructuring started a decade or so ago. As companies have initiated the changes to respond to competitive pressures, they have come to realize that they need more flexibility. That has triggered an explosion of interest in new program ideas. One of the most prominent of the new concepts is broad banding, which effectively throws out the controls that were so important in a traditional program and makes managers and supervisors much more responsible for managing the base pay of their people.

In a broad-banding environment, the traditional emphasis on determining each job's value and on micro-managing annual increases no longer makes sense. Organizations now may have as few as five or six salary bands instead of what were often twenty or thirty salary ranges. The difference in percentage terms from the lowest salary to the highest is 100 percent and those bands are typically 100 percent from the bottom to the top. In the traditional model, the decision to evaluate each job and determine an appropriate range required an investment of hours on the part of everyone involved. When an organization shifts to banding, it reduces the need for the human resources specialists customarily involved in "policing" the pay program.

Banding facilitates a shift from the value of the job to a new emphasis on the value of the individual. The new program concept for accomplishing this is referred to as *competency-based pay*. Competencies are best understood as the personal capabilities an employee needs to perform at high levels. The focus on individual capabilities represents a radical change that introduces an incentive for employees to enhance their competence. That is the subject of Chapter 7 by Jim Kochanski and Howard Risher.

The related alternative, skill-based pay, is the subject of Chapter 8 by Marc Wallace and Fred Crandall. Skill-based pay has been in limited use for over twenty years but has had renewed interest in settings where multi-skilled workers provide increased flexibility. It has been limited in application in the past to manual jobs, but that is also changing. With skill-based pay, workers can increase their base pay by demonstrating that they have acquired new skills or enhanced existing skills. It represents a shift to the value of the individual.

To this point, the work to develop and refine these concepts has been carried on independently and by different groups. Both concepts focus on worker capabilities and provide incentives to develop the capabilities to perform at a high level. Wallace and Crandall use the words *competency* and *skill* interchangeably, and contend that the differences are largely semantic. They also point out that *skills* are used with hourly employees, while *competencies* are typically reserved for professionals. They argue that distinction has become counterproductive.

These concepts reflect a subtle but important distinction from the traditional merit pay policy. Merit increases were understood to be a reward for last year's performance. In theory, each employee's supervisor looks back at the individuals' successes and failures over the year and determines an appropriate increase. In contrast, both skill- and competency-based pay look into the future and use the anticipated future contribution as the basis for granting increases.

There has been a rush to adopt new ideas in wage and salary management. These concepts have been around for a long time, but only in the past two or three years have they had widespread adoption by major corporations. A few companies have experienced problems, but the concepts are still being refined. As with any other innovation, there are skeptics, and since any change in a pay system can make people upset, it is not surprising to find vocal critics in organizations with new programs. Still, the high level of interest in the new concepts is clear evidence of the dissatisfaction with traditional programs. For that reason the number of skill- or competency-based pay programs will undoubtedly continue to grow.

7

Paying for Competencies
Rewarding Knowledge, Skills, and Behaviors

· ■ ·

James T. Kochanski
a principal in Sibson & Company
Howard Risher
a senior fellow in the Center for Human Resources, Wharton
School, University of Pennsylvania

There has been a dramatic increase in the use of systems that reward factors that contribute to results, in addition to rewarding results themselves. The growing importance of knowledge, the changes in the way work is organized and managed—the new work—and the pressure to be more responsive and flexible have made many jobs more dynamic, complex, and autonomous. These changes have also made it difficult in many situations to attribute results to individuals. In this new environment, organizations are backing away from a number of the traditional management tools and searching for new alternatives.

The foundation of people management in the new work is the systematic understanding of what it takes for employees to perform at high levels—the job competencies. Competencies are the knowledge, skills, and behaviors that lead to high performance. Just as the job description and listings of assigned duties and tasks were the foundation for the previous era of work, now competencies will be the basis for managing people as they move up and across organizations.

Why Competency-Based Management?

· ■ ·

Competency-based management (CBM) can bring a source of focus and order to the complex web of tasks, responsibilities, goals, skills, knowledge, and abilities in today's knowledge-based roles by clarifying the critical few competencies that differentiate high performance. Most managers recognize that the factor that differentiates an organization's performance comes from its people. The organizational capabilities that are essential for success are based in the competencies that employees demonstrate.

But the traditional suite of people-management tools—objective setting, job descriptions, performance appraisals, and merit pay, to name just a few—seem to have lost their impact on performance. There is a sense that these tools belong to an earlier era. Consequently, many managers have allowed the traditional tools to fall into disuse. For example, when an audience of managers is asked if their management system is based on annual objectives, almost everyone will raise their hands affirmatively. But if they are then asked if their objectives are still relevant at the end of the year, less than a third will usually respond affirmatively. While many human resources practitioners chalk this up to bad management, it is in some cases because the available methods are inappropriate or ineffective in the new work paradigm.

Why are two-thirds of managers not updating their employees' objectives if that is the basis for the management system? In some cases, it is bad management, but in others it is because the environment is too dynamic for traditional objective setting, or the work is so independent and knowledge based that the manager cannot set objectives for an employee. In other cases, the work is so team based that individual objectives are not relevant.

If the traditional people management processes are failing managers, imagine what little benefit or value these practices are to the majority of employees. From the employees' perspective, programs for recruitment, training, promotion, job and organizational design, and base pay management are just entries in a mind-boggling array of poorly understood policies and processes that should relate to their work but do not, really. Like total quality management, self-directed work teams, and reengineering processes, these programs are changed so frequently that the skeptical workers and managers at many large companies sarcastically refer to them as "the flavor of the month."

To make matters worse, often the only threads that link the traditional processes and systems to employees' work are an individual manager's opinion of what makes an employee successful and that particular manager's perception of the employee. If you start with the different biases of each manager and then add in the biases and beliefs of every other employee in the company, it is no wonder that employees learn what it takes to be successful through legend, hearsay, and trial and error. This mix of advice means that each employee has a somewhat different, and only partially accurate, view of how to be effective in his or her work.

CBM approaches create a focus on the critical few factors that differentiate high performance, and because these factors tend to be more enduring than the immediate priorities, they can clarify and simplify the management of people. This is not to suggest that competency-based management is a panacea. It requires a significant investment of time to get it off the ground. When it succeeds, it introduces a wholly new basis for people decisions and for managers to help employees understand how to be successful. When it fails, it is often because a company attempts to define competencies as everything that employees do in a job and thus creates a system even more complex than what it replaced.

The competency focus has been around for over twenty years but only recently has become a mainstream tool. It flows from the emphasis on performing at high levels. It complements the growth in knowledge- and team-based work. The increased use of competencies is due to the development of practical methods for identifying and defining competencies and in improvements in assessment methods.

Putting Your Money Where Your Competencies Are

=== · ■ · ===

If competencies are the "wheels" for managing knowledge work, pay remains the engine. In most organizations it is not enough just to reveal the most critical competencies or to provide training and development in competencies. The problem is that employees keep paying attention to whatever gets reinforced by pay even if that is just the individual biases of their managers. Company after company has come to the same conclusion about managing with competencies: nobody really cares until they are linked to pay.

In the new work environment, the development and demonstration of competencies is one of the most effective measures on which to anchor the pay system. It focuses employees' attention on what they need to do to be successful and at the same time gives managers the flexibility to deploy people as demanded by the business.

The term, *competency-based pay* (CBP), has been adopted to refer to a base pay system that links wage and salary increases to demonstrated competence. Most successful applications of CBP are combined with an incentive system, with elements of the reward system tied to different performance factors: base pay tied to competencies and individual results or group results tied to bonus opportunities. The term *competency-based pay* has been adopted because base pay is the foundation for a reward system.

It sounds simple enough and intuitively correct: people should be paid for their competence. CBP, however, is a different paradigm that is new to managers and employees. It is a shift away from job based pay where wage and salary rates are based on the value of the job. With CBP, the focus is on the relative value of the person. The old credo, "Pay the job, not the person," is being used less and less as organizations find the traditional model for managing salaries out of sync with the work paradigm. CBP requires a different mind-set—people have to think about pay in a new way—and is most effective when it is a component in an integrated people management system that is used for staffing, career management, development, and rewards. For salary management, it involves new measures, new assessment methods, and new pay delivery mechanisms.

One of the most frequent mistakes is confusing CBP with other pay approaches, thus diluting its effect. CBP is not another subtle variation on MBO (management by objectives) and its companion, the merit increase. In fact, one of the most common reasons for adopting CBP is that merit pay has lost its effectiveness and is beyond repair in the particular organization. In most companies, MBO involves setting annual objectives; merit increases cluster around a narrow range and are delivered annually to virtually every employee. Substituting competency objectives for results objectives is one way to link competencies to a traditional pay system, but this short-cut will not have as much impact as creating a complete CBP system.

Competency-based pay also differs from its cousin, skill-based pay (SBP), in that its primary use is not to reinforce operational flexibility. With the typical skill-based pay model, people are paid progressively higher pay levels for developing new skills that give them the ability to perform additional tasks. Rather than measuring the breadth of operational skills, CBP usually assumes that basic technical job skills are the minimum job requirements. Wage or salary increases then ride on demonstrated technical depth and other competencies that differentiate high performance from average performance.

Skill-based pay is used primarily in operational settings where manual skills are important. There the employee is paid for his or her skill. That concept does not fit work settings where people are paid for their cognitive abilities and the work requires the application of knowledge for problem solving. The connotation of the word *competence* is broader than *skill* and is commonly understood to refer to an ability to perform at high levels. That fits any job or occupation.

When to Use Competency-Based Pay

· ■ ·

Paying for competencies is not for every category of employee. For example, salespeople may need to be trained in competencies, but to the extent their work is individual and measurable, their pay should continue to be based on results. Similarly, executives who are responsible for the results of a business unit or a company should be rewarded primarily for the results of that unit. But for many categories of employee, including some managers in functional roles, most knowledge workers, and many people who work in teams, it is difficult to attribute results to individuals. Their value rides on what they can do, and CBP is still important and needs to be aligned with something enduring.

149

In a traditional work setting, the base-pay program focuses on jobs and job incumbents. The work is routine and more or less static, and performance is measured individual by individual. That traditional model is disappearing rapidly. Exhibit 7-1 captures the basic changes. Organizations that have moved into quadrant four have found that the traditional program model no longer fits the environment.

In a dynamic environment, where priorities and goals are constantly changing, or where the work is knowledge or team based, it is the individual component of the pay system. For example, in a team- or knowledge-based work setting, one might conclude that the easy solution is to pay everyone on the team the same base pay and to deliver pay increases or bonuses based on team results. In that context, the message is that everyone is equal. That might work in some cultures, but most companies (at least in North America) want an individual element in the reward system. The focus on individual competence fits that environment and rewards employees for being as good and competent as they can be at performing their jobs.

Identifying and defining competencies requires leadership, time, and resources. Some companies focus the use of competencies, including pay, on a few particularly strategic groups of employees, where the investment in developing and implementing a CBP system has a clear payback, rather than using competencies with all employees.

For several reasons, then, CBP may not always be the best answer

Exhibit 7-1. Changing Nature of Work.

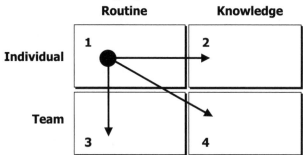

Quadrant 1: Predictable with measurable individual results
Quadrants2–4: More dynamic and complex result attribution

for all employee groups. On the other hand, where the need exists and the other readiness factors are present, CBP is a powerful approach for focusing employees on factors that lead to high performance.

Defining Competencies: Focusing on What Matters Most

· ■ ·

The first step in developing CBP is to understand the patterns that are repeated by the most effective employees in their knowledge, skills, and behaviors—the competencies that enable them to be high performers. By highlighting these competencies, companies can provide managers and employees with guidance on how to increase employee effectiveness, while enabling individuals to control or manage their own development and performance.

Companies can then use their understanding of requisite competencies as a foundation for staffing, learning and development, rewards, and other capability-building programs. In addition to improving employee performance and overall capability, CBP can be used to reinforce other imperatives, such as time to market, customer satisfaction, and responsiveness. It also supports employees' need to have greater personal control over their career success.

A telecommunications company needed new ways to measure and manage its product line managers (PLMs). The PLMs were key to business success but operated in a team environment without direct control over sales, R&D, or manufacturing. A competency model was developed that identified twelve competencies along with five or six behavioral descriptors for each competency that differentiated high-performing PLMs from others.

The company used these competencies and behaviors to develop tools for employee self-assessment, assessment by others, development planning, a developmental activities guide, career planning ideas, and selection tools. The model and the tools were rolled out through a training program led

151

by a senior PLM executive and a human resources professional. Groups of PLMs worked in teams, using an action learning approach, to develop specific competencies while they did their jobs. The competencies were used in performance appraisal and tied to base pay increases and succession decisions.

Setting the Foundation

An essential building block needed to develop CBP is the "architecture," or format and structure, of the competencies. Too many organizations have charged off and started to define competencies without knowing how many distinct models they would need and how they should be formatted. Rather than creating full-blown competency models for every job, it is better to start by reviewing some examples from other companies or by mocking up some competencies. This exercise will help to develop an architecture for the competencies that work with the intended pay (and other) applications.

Competency Models and System Architecture

A *competency model* is the list of differentiating competencies for a role or job family, the definition of each competency, and the descriptors or behavioral indicators describing how the competency is displayed by high performers. The maximum number of models equals the number of distinct jobs in the organization, but most CBP systems use a fewer number of models. Options include developing models for entire families of jobs (e.g., all programmers) or even whole departments, such as all information technology employees. The maximum number of models creates a complex system that is difficult to maintain, while the departmental approach may overly generalize, so there is a tendency toward the job family architecture.

Competencies can be tiered or prioritized from high to low based on their relative importance or simply listed and treated as equal. For example, one petrochemical company determined that it would use a simple architecture for the competencies within each job family because the organization leaders decided to include the critical few competencies that differentiate high performance from average performance. But to make the competencies useful in the performance management and pay system, they decided to tier the descriptors within each competency into two levels: basic and mastery.

There are two types of competency models. *Descriptive competency models* define the knowledge, skills, and behaviors known to differentiate high performance from average performance in the current environment or recent past. Descriptive models can have high validity because they are built from actual data about the difference between average and star performers. *Prescriptive models* lean toward describing competencies that will be important in the future. They are helpful in dynamic environments or to help drive a major change in culture or capabilities.

Sometimes descriptive and prescriptive models are blended. In one office systems company, descriptive models were built for each job family by interviewing panels of high performers. In addition, several competencies were added to support the strategic direction set out by a new leadership team.

An example of a competency shows several of the architectural options. In the example in Exhibit 7-2, the competency label is Project Management, which is part of a category of several competencies called Change Management. The competency has a definition, and in this case the situation in which the competency is used also is described. Descriptors of the competency in action are listed and are tiered, low to high, among three levels. For most knowledge-based roles or job families, there will be eight to twelve competencies, such as the one shown in the competency model in the exhibit.

There are several acceptable methods for defining competencies, all based on a process of discovering the differentiating factors. Competencies are not simply made up.

Competency Discovery Methods

Approach	Strength	Limitation
Analysis of a single "star"	Reveals "secrets" of pros	Job specific
Analysis of multiple "exemplars"	Validity, multiple jobs	Long process
Statistical survey of "experts"	Fast, statistical validity	Low touch
Compilation of external models	Best of the best	Low buy-in
Interviews with leaders	Future oriented	Personal bias

Exhibit 7-2. Competency Example.

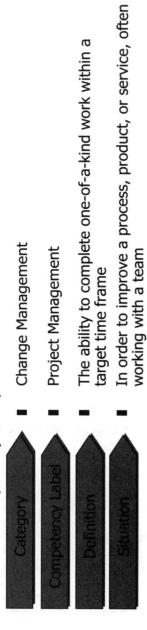

Category	■ Change Management
Competency Label	■ Project Management
Definition	■ The ability to complete one-of-a-kind work within a target time frame
Situation	■ In order to improve a process, product, or service, often working with a team

Descriptors

1.11	Follows project plan to complete tasks as expected
1.12	Makes extraordinary effort to complete tasks on schedule with quality
1.2.1	Engages others to take responsibility for portions of a project (including vendors)
1.2.2	Evaluates the capability of others to contribute to project objectives
1.2.3	Enables team coordination by creating and communicating project plans
1.3.1	Identifies needs and establishes challenging project objectives
1.3.2	Encourages others to stay on track with project commitments
1.3.3	Manages linkages to other projects or systems inside and outside human resources

In addition to being valid, competencies need to have the buy-in of those employees and managers who will use them. Broad involvement in defining competencies, through focus groups or interviews, helps gain buy-in and reduces any sense of elitism or exclusion among employees. Exhibit 7-3 summarizes the relative validity and prospects for buy-in across the basic approaches for defining competencies.

Competency models that define the unique factors that differentiate high performance as they are displayed in the organization's context are generally preferable to off-the-shelf versions from an external source, such as a trade association. Although an organization should not simply adopt someone else's competency model, there is no need to start from scratch. The process of defining competencies can be made more efficient by beginning with a language of possible competencies, called a *library* or *dictionary* (see the example in Exhibit 7-4). The library can be provided from an external source or, in companies that already have some competency models in use, it can be developed by merging existing models. The library is used to "code" or analyze interview or focus group output and to narrow the competencies to the critical few. The few differentiating competencies then are defined as they apply to the particular job family.

Organizations that already have competencies defined and in use for applications other than pay may be able to skip the step of defining competencies, but they may face more constraints in pay system design than the organization that starts fresh. When competencies are already in use, there is sometimes a reluctance to tinker with them so they are appropriate for use with the pay system. For example, in one company, several functional groups had defined their own competencies using different standards and formats. One function had defined competencies as minimum standards, while another had defined them as differentiating high performance. Those differences made it impractical to use the models in the same competency-based pay system. The solution was to revise the competency models to a minimum standard and for all new models to be based on that standard. Although it was somewhat onerous for the group that had to modify its competencies, the change was an improvement.

This example also illustrates the need for competencies to be dynamic. Although the competencies that distinguish high performance in

Exhibit 7-3. Process, Validity, and User Buy-In.

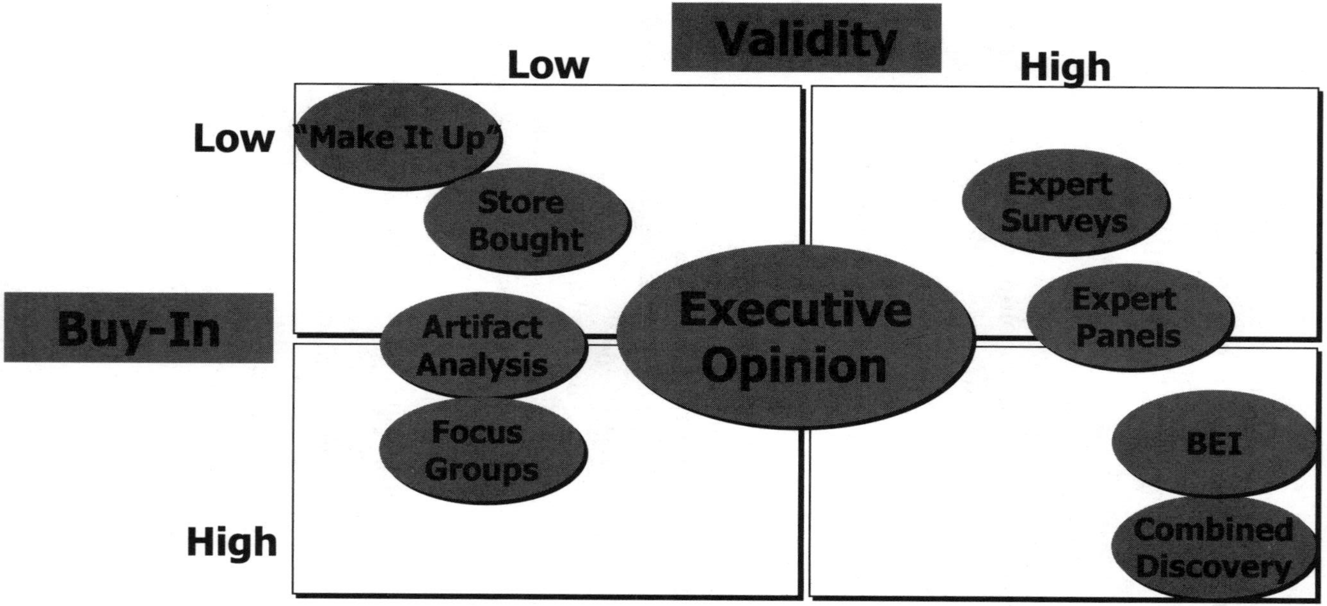

Validity: Low — High

Buy-In: Low — High

- "Make It Up"
- Store Bought
- Expert Surveys
- Expert Panels
- BEI
- Combined Discovery
- Executive Opinion
- Artifact Analysis
- Focus Groups

Exhibit 7-4. A Competency Library Example.

- Analytical Thinking
- Assertiveness
- Broad Business Knowledge
- Business Orientation
- Coaching and Development
- Collaboration/Teamwork
- Commitment/Accountability
- Communication
- Conflict Resolution
- Creativity/Innovation
- Customer Focus
- Efficiency Orientation
- Flexibility/Adaptability
- Influence Advocacy
- Initiative/Proactivity
- Interpersonal Sensitivity/Empathy
- Leadership

- Learning
- Negotiating
- Networking/Relationship Building
- Organizational Agility
- Planning/Organizing
- Problem Solving/Decision Making
- Project Management
- Relationship Building
- Results Orientation
- Self-Assurance (Self-Confidence)
- Service Orientation
- Social Objectivity
- Stakeholder Focus
- Strategic Vision
- Systemic Thinking
- Teamwork
- Technical Depth

a role will not change as often as the objectives or the priority tasks, competencies do and should change and be updated.

Conventional wisdom suggests that competencies be used for safe (low risk of failure or rejection) applications first, like employee development and training, until the competencies are well accepted and understood. This strategy is easier to accept because there are no immediate consequences and the competency development process is less threatening.

The problem with the safe route is that often the competencies do not take root or become important to managers and employees. Then the time is never right for attaching rewards to the competencies. An approach that blends the conservative and aggressive approaches is to determine how the competencies will link to pay as early as possible, let employees know when and how the pay system will connect to competencies, and then cut over to the new pay system at the designated future point.

Nuts and Bolts: Elements of the CBP System

Dissecting a CBP system reveals how each of the elements is designed to reward competencies and results and enable administration of the system.

Pay Structure

CBP is enabled by a flat, broad-banded structure. Imagine trying to define competencies for twenty-five salary grades and fifteen different job families. It would be difficult to define more than four or five levels of competencies for most professional roles, such as engineers, scientists, marketing, operations, or staff roles, in a way that would be valid and usable by managers and employees. Consider further that if there are three to five distinguishable levels of competencies for professionals, and two or three for administrative and direct labor roles, and another two or three for leadership roles, then the whole competency architecture would have a maximum of seven to eleven levels.

The optimal pay structure for CBP mirrors the competency architecture and is much flatter than traditional job-based grades. For example, in one rather egalitarian company, the pay structure and competency architecture has the same five levels from the bottom to the top of the organization.

Although most CBP systems rely on broad-banded pay structures, not all broad-banded systems are based on competencies. On the average, broad-banded systems have salary ranges with a spread of 100 percent, for example, $25,000 minimum to $50,000 maximum for one band. This broad range enables another aspect of CBP: the flexibility to adjust pay levels according to the competencies of the person, rather than targeting pay to the job, as with narrow grades. To realize this flexibility, companies need to adopt alternative pay delivery methods that allow employees in the same band with different competency levels to achieve different pay potential.

In most CBP systems, the bands are defined by job responsibilities, stage in a career ladder, or organizational tier. In other words, employees need to get a distinctly different job with higher-level responsibilities in order to move to a higher-level band. In some organizations, especially scientific or technical groups, there are clusters of two or three bands in which employees may move on the basis of their competencies without changing jobs.

The level of accuracy between the market and internal pay levels is harder to pinpoint for any broad-banded structure versus narrow grades. CBP trades off some level of accuracy versus the market for the ability to be flexible and to reward the individual rather than the job. In most roles, it is difficult to rely on published surveys to pinpoint market rates for competencies since the data are job based. Companies using CBP continue to price the structure by comparing benchmark jobs at the top and bottom of the band to the market. Market positioning considerations are the same as with traditional job-based pay, for example, the cost versus the benefits of being at the seventy-fifth percentile. Actually banding provides considerably more flexibility than a traditional salary structure to pay critical jobs or job families at specific market levels.

Three main ways are used to control salary costs and maintain market positioning with CBP systems. The first method is to give managers budget responsibility for salaries so that they are accountable for any escalation. They have a salary increase budget and are accountable for making sound decisions. The second is providing access to market data, so they can take market positioning into account while exercising their responsibility for making individual pay decisions. The second method, combined with the first, provides a basis to control the escalation of pay levels through pay delivery guidelines requiring extraordinary approval for any out-of-guideline increases.

Pay Delivery

Pay delivery in CBP is generally designed around the logic of setting the ongoing base pay level according to the ongoing value of the person and rewarding the past results with one-time bonuses. This is an important distinction from traditional merit increase policies. Competency-based pay is future oriented. Increases are based on the assumption that greater competence will increase an individual's future value.

Following this logic, base pay increases are primarily competency based and may or may not be on an annual basis, since significant increases in competence do not occur on an annual basis. Bonus awards in such a system are clearly targeted to reflect results delivered in the prior performance period. In several companies, this logic has yielded a matrix such as the one shown in Exhibit 7-5.

With broad pay bands, upward promotions are less frequent than in narrow-graded systems; therefore, provisions need to be made for in-

Exhibit 7-5. Pay Delivery Example.

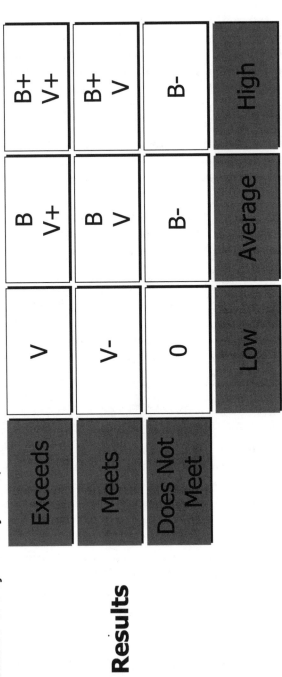

Results			
Exceeds	V	B V+	B+ V+
Meets	V-	B V	B+ V
Does Not Meet	0	B-	B-
	Low	Average	High

Competencies

B = Base pay increase target.

V = Variable-pay target.

band competency pay progression beyond the level of market movement or with additional vehicles. For example, if the matrix in Exhibit 7-5 targets base pay increases to market movement of 4 percent, then an additional vehicle can be used to recognize extraordinary competency progression. This additional base pay delivery vehicle, sometimes called *in-band promotion, career development pay,* or *competency increase,* is sometimes designed to be separate from the regular base pay increase, such as those in the pay delivery matrix in Exhibit 7-5. This is to ensure that the additional competency increase, usually budgeted around 1 percent of payroll, is not seen as an entitlement as was the old merit increase.

The additional pay increase vehicle can be targeted to reward increases in competency depth, breadth, or both. Competency depth within a role is often important for scientific and technical employees who may work in essentially the same research or design role for many years, have results that are difficult to measure, and whose value increases as they get increasingly deep in their discipline. Competency breadth may be more important for people on a management track whose value increases by understanding more and more of the business.

Several companies have created decision matrixes to help managers determine who should be eligible for in-band competency increases. The range for these increases is usually set about the same as for regular base pay increases, at 0 percent to 8 percent, but eligibility assumptions are set to control the budget and to prevent frivolous use of the pay vehicle. In companies that make the change to a broad-banded CBP from narrow grades, the savings from fewer grade-to-grade promotions is used to fund the in-band competency increases. Depending on the historical turnover and growth, this usually enables a target of 15 percent to 30 percent of employees to get in-band competency increases.

A few companies have tied bonuses in part to competencies. They do so to get employees to pay attention to competencies, especially when they are newly introduced or when they are seeking to reinforce a behavioral change. For example, one company based 25 percent of its executives' annual bonus on the results of a multirater feedback survey that measured demonstration of a new set of leadership competencies.

Promotions to another band in CBP, as in almost every other reward system, are highly valued because they not only involve significant base pay increases and eligibility for higher-level bonuses and other rewards, but promotions also provide significant recognition. In CBP companies, people get a job in a higher band only if they have the competencies required to do, or at least learn, the job. Pay treatment associated with band-to-band promotions usually includes bringing the individual up to the minimum of the new band, or a significant percentage increase, say, from 15 percent to 20 percent.

Competency Assessment

Assessment of results, or in the case of CBP, competencies is often where otherwise well-designed systems break down. Having well-defined competencies helps improve assessment but does not make the process less manager intensive. In fact, CBP usually increases rather than decreases manager discretion and the time required to conduct assessment. Competencies enable multiple inputs, which improves assessment quality. For example, you can get four-way or 360-degree feedback from customers or subordinates, peers, self, and manager. Competency evaluation does not require written four-way feedback, although it has grown in use.

Assessment still comes down to managers' making decisions about who gets what pay. Best practices include group reviews where managers review assessment decisions and approval of manager's recommendations by the level above. Assessment must tie in with pay delivery so that if the pay delivery is based on absolute level of competencies demonstrated rather than competency development, then the assessment must also measure competency demonstration.

Some companies have used CBP to increase the responsibility of employees for their own assessment. For example, one company asks employees to initiate their own competency evaluation whenever they seek an in-band competency increase. The argument in favor of such an approach is that competency models make the success criteria public and less based on individual managers' biases, so employees should be better able to take responsibility for their own assessment and development. The argument against such an approach is that it favors the bold employee who is not reluctant to ask for an increase, for feedback, and for development.

Many people use the failure to differentiate among employees as the evidence that an assessment approach is not working. CBP is not foolproof in this regard, but it can improve differentiation. In one company, the tendency to rate most employees near the top of the assessment scale was reduced significantly when the organization went to CBP with three-way feedback from self, manager, and customers. CBP cannot give managers the ability to deliver differentiated messages to employees, but it can give them the language to do it. Another company handles the assessment by having groups of managers develop a relative ranking of all employees to minimize bias.

No particular trend has emerged with regard to assessment scales in CBP. Either absolute level of competency demonstration (proficiency) or the level of competency development (improvement) is used as an assessment factor in CBP systems. Despite the predictions that CBP would herald the true beginning of the ratingless system, it is not so. In fact, CBP systems are often driven by the rating scale used in multirater feedback instruments. And because employees really do have different levels of competence and do develop competencies at different rates, a pay system based on competencies should reflect these differences.

In most CBP systems, the method of reflecting the difference in competence or competency development is in differentiated pay increases or in the timing of increases. The method for determining those differences is most often where the individual employee falls on a scale relative to the competency model. A few companies have sought to avoid using a scale, and thus labeling employees, by force-ranking employees relative to other employees, using a competency model as the criterion. Although this method does improve differentiation, it does not really avoid labeling.

Summary

·■·

Competencies can be used to bring order to the otherwise chaotic system of increasing employee effectiveness and capacity and rewarding them appropriately. The people management system can be grounded in a rather simple framework of the factors that distinguish high performance, organized into competency models for major job families. The focus on individual competence is an important new message in many companies.

Remember these five success factors about competency-based pay:

- *Require supervisors to use the system.* Because CBP in a broadband environment is less cumbersome than the combination of job evaluation, performance evaluation, and related practices that go into a traditional salary program—and because it helps shift career responsibility to the employee—CBP is likely to be embraced by most managers. However, expect a few holdouts. Some managers will want to retain power and control by using their own success factors or biases to evaluate employees rather than using CBP. Others will not use CBP because they practice favoritism or discrimination. Still others are just comfortable using a more traditional management approach. If this type of environment is prevalent, then CBP will not work because, as one savvy employee put it, "what interests my boss fascinates me."

- *But don't overuse it.* Even the best competency models still are generalizations of a very complex phenomenon, so competencies can be overused to the point of becoming tyrannical or counter to diversity. Even the best models of a general management competency, for example, represent only about 50 percent of what makes an organization effective. The point here is that competencies are not all encompassing and should be used accordingly. In a worst-case scenario, an employee feels punished for displaying behaviors that are different from, but not in conflict with, the competencies.

- *Rely on a valid process to develop competency model(s).* A frequent response to the suggested process for discovering and validating competencies is that it can be simplified by "just getting some people in a room and making a list." While on the surface this may be just an attempt to speed things up, more often it is an effort to incorporate personal biases into the model. However, that approach is inconsistent with the shift away from managerial personal bias, renders the model useful only as long as the current leadership who creates the list remains intact, and assumes that the list makers' personal views are accurate and superior to the views of others in the organization. Skeptics of CBP almost always are mollified knowing that someone did not just make up this list and that a valid process was used to develop the model.

- *Don't create fear of the competencies.* Beginning CBP by using the competencies to fire, demote, reprimand, or transfer is good way to keep employees from adopting and using the competencies. Although there is a natural desire to do something concrete with the model at the outset, it is best to use the competencies for a balanced set of uses that are seen as positive, including selection, development, and salary management.

- *Keep the number of models reasonable.* One competency model probably is not enough for the entire company, but a model for each job in the company would be an overwhelming level of complexity and unnecessarily bog down the human resources system. The interest in many models is in part driven by the true differentiation between job families that should be revealed through a competency discovery process. It also can be driven by a desire on the part of some stakeholders to see a competency model with very little stretch or one that will confirm, rather than challenge, their current—that is, limited—abilities. The former reason for multiple models should be honored and the latter rejected.

Case Study: Competency-Based Pay in a Technical Organization

An R&D organization faced high turnover in the increasingly competitive market for high-tech talent as its world-class hardware, software, and network engineers were being raided by other companies.

With rapidly changing technology fueling new business revenue—and even entire new businesses—the loss of even one key technologist on a project could be devastating to the business. In addition, the nature of the technology projects had changed to be more team based, integrating a number of different disciplines and de-emphasizing hierarchical management and vertical career paths. It also was critical to keep top technologists working directly on development projects rather than moving them into administrative management roles.

The company's traditional approach to career and pay progression was inconsistent with the business needs and the business environment. It was in a catch-22 situation with technology employees. If employees remained on projects over the long term, they perceived their career as stagnant and were susceptible to overtures from competitors. But if the company moved the person to another project or to a management role, then the success of the technology project was jeopardized.

In addition, the engineers were unhappy with vague and inconsistent success criteria. Their individual performance was difficult to measure because their work was knowledge and team based, the projects did not start and stop according to a calendar or fiscal year, and the best possible outcome for some projects was to end them without a product's going to market.

The leadership of the organization realized that something had to change and set out to develop a more person-based rather than job-based approach. A team was convened, with the help of a consulting firm, to design a career track separate from the traditional management track, pay grades, and pay-delivery methods. The challenge was to create a system more consistent with the business environment.

The team began by examining the number of discernible differences in competency and contribution levels among the population. A hypothesis was developed that there should be four career steps and a parallel structure of pay ranges. The team considered a structure of many mini-career steps but concluded that more than four levels would be too hierarchical and advancement could become based on time rather than on talent.

The four-level model was tested using two methods. First, management teams did a pro-forma slotting of technical staff into four levels, without any criteria other than the differences they themselves noticed among the people. Each of the management teams was able to slot all of the staff into four levels with few borderline cases and without any levels being empty. This result gave initial confirmation that the hypothesis of four competency levels was not only valid but also usable by managers.

Second, exemplar employees were nominated from the pro-

forma slotting of each of the four levels. Behavioral event interviews were conducted with the exemplars from the four levels. The interviews were coded, and the analysis revealed common competencies at all four levels of the job family. Development of the descriptors for each competency revealed that most indicators (but not all) were different by level. One of the competencies and its descriptors is shown below.

Competency Model (partial)

Competency	Descriptor	MSS	SMSS	DMSS	PSS
Business Perspective *Project Demonstration*	• Demonstrates awareness of how current design decisions can impact a project's success.	✓			
	• Incorporates awareness of long-term project implications into the development of specific design recommendations	✓			
	• Balances cost implications and technical features when selecting vendors and products.	✓			
	• Balances customer needs and business objectives in determining project direction.		✓		
Business Demonstration	• Optimizes quality and cost considerations when making project decisions.		✓		
	• Identifies product development opportunities based on technical expertise and understanding strategic direction.			✓	
	• Assesses vendor viability as part of making vendor selection decisions.			✓	
	• Stays abreast of competitor activities and incorporates knowledge into the development of project and business strategies.			✓	
	• Demonstrates cultural sensitivity when representing the business with customers.			✓	
Industry Demonstration	• Influences strategies which result in development of marketable technologies.				✓
	• Develops and implements strategies which result in marketable technologies.				✓
	• Identifies potential new business opportunities which shape global strategy.				✓

The initial slotting of the staff also was used to identify jobs for the purpose of market pricing the four levels, or bands. In addition to using existing survey data, a special survey was developed and faxed to a target set of companies. The market data were used to define the salary bands. A conversion chart was created to compare the new bands to the old grades because employees would figure it out even if the comparison were not provided.

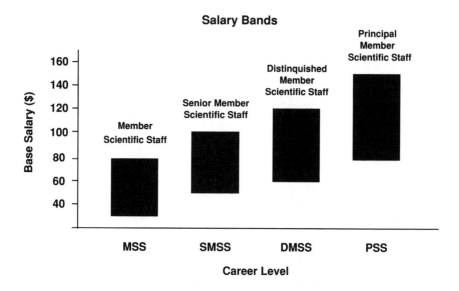

Salary Bands

To retain employees in technical roles and to encourage depth in competencies within levels, an additional pay delivery vehicle was created to allow in-band progression beyond what was available with merit increases. The additional pay delivery vehicle, growth pay, was funded in part by the reduction in grade-to-grade increases due to the conversion to broad bands. It was estimated that approximately 25 percent of employees would receive growth pay annually. Most employees continued to earn a performance-based increase each year, so the new program would not be considered a take-away. The matrix below shows the guidelines that managers use to determine the eligibility for and amount of growth pay.

Several common features of technical ladders and CBP were not adopted because the design team understood that they would be inconsistent with the culture and the design objectives. Manager and self-evaluation of the competencies and performance was maintained, rather than using multirater surveys, to avoid administrative burden and to encourage manager and employee dialogue. Also,

Growth Pay Matrix

Expected growth in competencies 0% Approximate distribution 75%	Significant increase in competencies, high in salary range 0%–3% Approximate distribution 15%
Significant increase in competencies, low in range 0%–6% Approximate distribution 5%	Extraordinary growth and demonstration of competencies 0%–10% Approximate distribution 5%

while some technical ladder programs require employees to self-nominate for promotions and use a panel of peers to evaluate candidates, the design team chose to administer advancement through the regular management decision-making process.

Checklist Status of Current Salary Program

☐ Is the existing program meeting the needs of the organization?
☐ Does the program reinforce the "right" culture? The desired behaviors?
☐ Is it sufficiently flexible to respond to organizational change initiatives?

Related Work Management and HR Initiatives

☐ Is the new work paradigm a front-burner issue?
☐ Are teams important? Permanent? Temporary?
☐ Is quality management still important? Is continuous improvement?
☐ Is organizational learning important? Is individual development and learning a priority?
☐ Are employees responsible for their personal development?
☐ Is individual development recognized?

☐ Is employee development an important priority?

☐ Is the company investing more in employee development than three years ago? Less? About the same?

☐ Is knowledge management an issue? Who has the lead?

Competency Management

☐ Does the organization have any experience with competency management? If yes, has that initiative been successful?

☐ Can existing competencies be used as the basis for salary management? Are they current?

☐ Is the goal to drive cultural change? To sustain and enhance performance?

☐ What process will be used to identify and define competencies?

☐ Who will be involved in the process?

☐ Who will conduct the assessment of individual competencies? Does the organization have experience with multirater assessment?

☐ How important is validity? How important is management support? Employee buy-in?

☐ How many competency models are needed? Will they be defined in job tiers or job ladder stages?

☐ Will competencies have other applications?

New Pay Policies

☐ Are any aspects of the base pay program leading edge? Is the organization open to leading-edge practices?

☐ Has there been any benchmarking of pay practices in other organizations?

☐ Has the linkage between pay and performance been reconsidered recently?

☐ Is individual growth and development rewarded? Is it reflected in salary management?

☐ Does the shared understanding of internal equity reflect individual competence?

☐ What role do managers play in salary management? Will they accept a new program? Will they require extensive training?

☐ Is risk taking encouraged and rewarded independent of the salary program?

☐ Does the reward system enable employees to share in the company's success?

☐ Do managers currently look to human resources for help with pay problems?

8

Paying Employees to Develop New Skills

· ■ ·

N. Fredric Crandall
Marc J. Wallace, Jr.
founding partners of the Center for Workforce Effectiveness

A client of ours faced a crisis. The company, a manufacturer of decorative wall-covering products, had 80 percent of its sales concentrated in four large customers—and they were angry. They issued the following ultimatum: drastically reduce costs, certify perfect quality, and service just-in-time inventory systems by delivering the products in a twenty-four-hour window rather than on a two-week delivery cycle.

Clearly radical reinvention of the company's processes was called for. The alternative was to go out of business. The senior leadership group of eight executives recognized the gravity of the situation. The problem was that eight hundred other people working for the company had no clue. And the state of blissful ignorance was reinforced by the way they were paid:

■ *The base pay system was modest and predictable.* Everyone in the same pay grade made just about the same amount of money, there were many pay grades, and base pay movement from year to year was very predictable. Every employee had become accustomed over the

Portions of this chapter were adapted from N. Fredric Crandall and Marc J. Wallace, Jr., *Work and Rewards in the Virtual Workplace* (New York: AMACOM, 1998).

past twenty years to receiving an increase that pretty much kept pace with inflation.

- *Production employees (engaged in making the product) were paid on a piece-rate incentive system.* Under the program, an industrial engineer analyzed the job and judged how many piece parts (units of product) a worker under normal circumstances and at a normal pace should be able to produce each hour. A piece-rate incentive of twenty-five cents per piece was established for any additional piece parts produced in the hour. The standard had not changed in the past twenty years, and the average production employee was earning nine dollars per hour in base wages and an additional six dollars per hour under the piece rate system.

Under the circumstances, the reward or compensation system was sending the wrong message. Rather than signaling that a wolf was at the door, posing a dire threat to the business and jobs, the pay system was reinforcing a false sense of security best summarized by the Bobby McFerrin hit, "Don't Worry—Be Happy!"

This example underscores three key principles about the role of rewards today:

1. How we reward employees sends clear messages about the company's circumstances, direction, values, and goals.

2. The message people receive by those rewards will have a long-term impact on what they do and do not do. Simply put, people will act and perform in ways that get rewarded. They will not act and perform in ways that do not get rewarded. Thus, the rewards encouraged workers at our client's company to produce quantity even at the cost of quality. In addition, focusing on quantity at each step of production created huge amounts of work-in-process inventory, making the overall operation of the plant inefficient and driving up project cost.

3. How we reward represents a powerful opportunity (missed in our client's case) to teach the business and continuously improve performance on key business metrics.

In this chapter we explore how the changing workplace is prompting companies to reconsider the use of their base pay program to provide the incentive to develop the skills needed for success.

Base Pay and Base Pay Progression

=== · ■ · ===

A consideration of base pay requires a stern look at the role of jobs and how they will change.

The Central Role of the Job in a Traditional Organization

The idea of a job has been so central to our thinking about work that it is difficult, even counterintuitive, to consider what the workplace would be without it. The job has been almost synonymous with work and important for these reasons:

- We talk of work in terms of "jobs."
- We organize work activities into jobs and call them job classifications.
- We recruit and select people with a job in mind.
- People "own" jobs. One's identity is defined by the job one holds.
- Power and authority in organization stem from the job. Senior managers are more powerful than junior managers, and that is related to their jobs.
- People's careers are defined by job changes. True advancement comes only when by leaving a job behind and stepping into a new job.
- Jobs are turf. You can't do my work if it's in my job description, nor can I do your work if it's in your job description. I can't take your job until you vacate it.
- Jobs are neatly bunched into functional silos in a traditional workplace. All engineering jobs, for example, are arranged hierarchically in an engineering department. All claims jobs in an insurance company are sorted into a claims department.

The Job and Base Pay

The job paradigm lies at the heart of traditional human resources practices and has since the 1930s. Traditional practice with regard to setting base pay levels and managing base pay progression is based on the use of the job as the unit of analysis:

- Market pricing practices force us to benchmark internal jobs with external jobs surveyed in external labor markets.
- Job evaluation methods have evolved since their inception in the 1930s as a tool to evaluate the relative worth of a job.
- In a traditional base pay program, jobs are slotted into hierarchically arranged pay grades, each with a minimum and maximum, within which the employee's base pay must remain so long as he or she holds the job.

The first rule in evaluating a job is to think of the job, not the person who occupies it. In a traditional workplace, then, one's base pay level is determined by the job one holds.. Base pay progression is limited to the range of rates defining one's job pay grade. Modest increases in pay may be based on annual merit reviews, but the empirical data show that most people in a given pay grade rise with the same tide of annual structural or market-driven adjustments. Significant pay movement requires promotion to a higher job in a functional hierarchy.

The job concept served traditional organizations well. Work has been organized in a command-and-control bureaucracy characterized by functional specifications and hierarchy. It is a paradigm shaped by early twentieth-century thinking of Max Weber and Frederick W. Taylor, implemented by Henry Ford, and cast in the legislation of Franklin D. Roosevelt's New Deal of the 1930s.

Unfortunately the paradigm no longer serves us because the job has died.

Death of the Job

The globalization of production and the technological revolution have forced employers into a postindustrial model for producing goods and service. To become more responsive to customers and to deliver higher levels of performance, companies have begun to tear down their hierarchy, do away with functional specialization, and organize all activities according to entire business processes that cut across traditional departments and occupations.

A traditional insurance company, for example, would have over four hundred job classifications, distributed across ten or more separate departments, organized into as many as thirty pay grades. When that company shifts to a new work paradigm, it may, in contrast, have ten to fifteen work matrices. The traditional hierarchy is steep (perhaps eight management levels), while in the new company, the hierarchy is flat (perhaps three to four levels). In the process, the job has died, and its death raises difficult questions about traditional base pay practices.

The experience of an insurance company illustrates the challenge.

Does the Salary Program Fit the Work Paradigm?

Prior to the transition to a new work organization, the company's operations were segmented by functional silos. Sales represented accepted applications, underwriting evaluated the risk, and policy service issued the accepted policy. The scorecard, which records the experience with previous practices, for issuing a new policy: two weeks' cycle time, high cost, and many hand-offs. When the work was reorganized, the company created a full-service team (consisting of fifteen people) that cut across sales, underwriting, and policy issue, as illustrated in Exhibit 8-1.

Rose was a member of the new team. In the former organization she had been assigned to the policy issue department at an annual salary of $30,000. Now that job had disappeared and she instead occupied a role (represented by the shaded blocks in Exhibit 8-1) that required much more breadth and depth. In fact, she was now dealing with customers and participating in the sales and underwriting process (within specified limits). The adjustment was not easy for Rose. She had a lot more to learn and had to take risks and make decisions that people superior to her used to make.

One day she had a question for her team leader: "Tom, I made $30,000, and I was okay with that. But now the company is asking me to take on a broader role. I know the other

Exhibit 8-1. Policyholder Service Team.

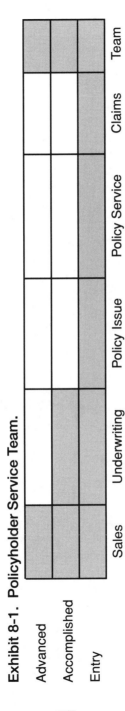

jobs are evaluated at higher pay grades and are paying more than $40,000. Are you going to pay me that?" Clearly the answer is no. But what is the right answer?

ANOTHER EXAMPLE OF A POOR FIT

The research and development unit for a large high-technology firm faced a dilemma. The director wanted research engineers to broaden their value by gaining practical experience in the operations of the company. It seemed like a relatively straightforward choice to ask the engineers to take on assignments in the field. The problem, however, was that the only job open in the field was evaluated in a lower pay grade than the engineers' current job. Of course, the engineers took the assignment, and, of course, they held on to their current pay. But the point is that the traditional job definition, job evaluation, and base pay practice constituted a barrier—something around which exceptions had to be made in order to do the right thing.

New Base Pay Model

Both cases illustrate the need for a new base pay model—one that supports new work designs, sends appropriate messages, and eliminates barriers.

In effect, the job has been replaced by a role, often on a team that has much vaguer boundaries and requires greater depth and breadth of skills and abilities. Rose, for example, raised a valid point. Her newly acquired skills added to her personal worth to herself, her team, and her company. She did not change jobs, but she changed her capacity to perform work. Consider the following: if Rose's capacity to perform customer service, underwriting, and expediting policies lowers unit cost by 30 percent, speeds cycle time from two weeks to one day, and results in loyal customers, has her personal asset value to the company increased? The answer, of course, is yes.

Paying the Person

Let us say that Rose's company, a small, family-run operation of a preindustrial age, never had a formal job evaluation system, never even had formally defined jobs. The boss would have put Rose to work on some basic tasks. He would want to run as lean as possible, so if Rose was capable of taking on more, he would try her out. He would also watch her progress. And he might even match her increased value (because of an increased ability to handle different parts of the operations) with increases in pay.

The simple picture from the past that has become a reality is that a traditional company pays the job rather than the person (see Exhibit 8-2).

In the new workplace people are paid not for the job they hold but for the role they are expected to play. The role is less formal and more flexible, and it overlaps much more with other roles than did jobs.

When work is structured as flexible roles rather than static jobs, we cannot determine a person's worth by looking at the job he is assigned

Exhibit 8-2. Base Pay Model in the Traditional and New Paradigm Workplace.

	Traditional	*New Paradigm*
Unit of analysis	Job	Person
Basis for determining value	Job evaluation	Personal evaluation
Pay determinant	Work performed	Capacity to perform
Base pay progression	Modest movement within grades to midpoint. Pay is controlled to midpoint	Significant movement from entry rate to target based on individual capacity.
	Required promotion for significant advancement.	
Base pay structure	Many, narrow pay grades, hierarchically arranged	Few, broad bands

to now. Rather, we must ask, "What can he personally do for us?" The more of a business process he can perform effectively, the greater his value is. The more valuable a person is, the more we are willing to pay. This base pay model is not constrained by job assignments and narrow pay grades. Rather, a person's growth in capacity to perform is matched by base pay increases until he reaches the full capacity his team or organization needs and his base pay reaches a target rate representing the fair market value for the skills he or she possesses.

Such a system is called *skill-based pay* or *competency-based pay*. The system is neither time based nor annual. Fast trackers will move more quickly than others. The premise is that demonstrated skills are reliable measures of an individual's capacity. The intent is to recognize and reward employees for adding or expanding their skills. Questions shift from how well Joe has done his job this year to whether is Joe making expected progress in developing and renewing the capacities needed in his role.

The more skills a person exhibits, the more valuable he or she is to the organization, and the more he or she can expect to be paid. A person's growth in capacity to perform is matched by base pay increases. An employee who is new to a job starts at an entry level of pay, and her pay is increased as she develops new or broader skills. Her base pay reaches a target level once she is fully qualified, that is, when she is able to demonstrate that she has acquired all of the requisite skills.

The following specific elements distinguish skill-based pay from a traditional base pay program:

- *Skill units as the basis of pay.* Employees are paid for the number of skill units they can demonstrate. Pay is incrementally granted for learning new skills.

- *Focus on repertoire of skills.* An important assumption is that it is organizationally valuable for employees to be multiskilled, that is, to be able to perform several functions.

- *Skill certification.* In a traditional salary program, it is assumed employees have the required skills or are willing to develop them. By contrast, most skill-based pay plans incorporate formal processes to assess and certify skill attainment.

▪ *Job changes without pay changes.* In the new compensation model, changing jobs or roles does not necessarily involve a promotion. Employees are expected to apply their skills as required. They do not move to a higher pay rate when they move to another job requiring the same skills.

▪ *Advancement opportunities.* The acquisition of new skills is the basis for advancement.

Skill-based pay is not for every company. It can be expensive and requires a substantial investment in training and development. Our research shows that an average company experiences a 15 to 20 percent increase in wage rates, a 20 to 25 percent increase in costs of training and development, and initial increases in head count and slack built into work schedules to allow people to cross-train and move around, which at some point should balanced by decreases in head count due to the new versatility of the team members.

Defining Skills and Competencies

Skills are understood best in the broader context of competencies required for effective performance. There are three distinct types of competencies:

▪ *Strategic competencies*, required to achieve competitive advantage (e.g., world-class service)
▪ *Individual competencies*, the characteristics that underlie an individual's capability to be effective and are used in selection (e.g., written and oral comprehension, manual dexterity)
▪ *Process competencies*, which reflect the requisite knowledge and skills defined by a customer-driven work process

The process competencies are the basis for skill-based pay. At the process level, competencies and skills are interchangeable. Process competencies or skills provide the foundation for defining work and worker requirements. Process competencies are the underpinnings for work design and provide the framework through which jobs or roles are defined and performance expectations defined. At this level, the competencies or skills tell a worker what he or she has to be able to do. We have found that it is useful to focus on three components of process competencies:

- *Knowledge*—the information or ability that is necessary to perform work. Knowledge may be gained through structured training or experience. General knowledge is often acquired externally through schools, whereas knowledge specific to core processes is typically developed in-house. Knowledge requirements can be defined through subject matter experts involved in the process or from equipment or training manuals (provided by vendors).

- *Activities*—the work steps that form the basis for delivering (or enabling) value through core or support business processes. Regardless of how work is performed (e.g., a manufacturing process, an engineering design process, or a customer service process), there are steps that can be analyzed along the way. It is important to concentrate on the activities in processes rather than functions (where similar work occurs) so employees can see how the activity delivers value to customers.

- *Results*—the outputs from a given process. They provide the confirmation of effective performance and should be based on quantifiable, or at least verifiable, standards, such as quality, cost, service, and efficiency. It typically takes time to define performance standards, but as baseline measurement data become available, the standards are integral to determining if an employee has developed the competency or skill.

Exhibit 8-3 displays an example of process competencies or skills (expressed in terms of knowledge, activities and results) at an aircraft manufacturing facility.

Combining Competencies and Skills to Define Roles

With the transition from jobs to processes and roles, it is still fundamental that people know what they are expected to do on a daily basis. As the basis for defining roles, many organizations are grouping or bundling process competencies and skills together. This approach

Exhibit 8-3. Process Competency Example: Assembler for an Aircraft Manufacturing Facility.

Knowledge	Activities	Results
Understands FAA quality/safety specifications and standards	Selects appropriate materials for assembly	99.8 percent first time quality standards maintained
Ability to review appropriate equipment and design manuals	Operates hand tools	96 percent adherence
Knowledge of just-in-time inventory process	Programs machinery	FAA safety standards upheld
Ability to operate hand tools	Applies rivets and welds to sheet metal	The aircraft is sound
Understanding of jig assembly procedures	Inspects for quality adherence	The customer is satisfied

allows them to balance the degree of process breadth versus specialized depth of skill in planning the composition of a work team responsible for a process. Exhibit 8-4 displays an example of processes bundled together into a matrix for a team-based sales and service organization. [Note for Exhibit 8-4 that "lead generation" refers to the generation or identification of leads and "lead qualification" is the assessment of the quality or potential of leads to become sales.]

In order to move from bundling groups of competencies to defining specific expectations for individuals, we often develop a matrix to examine holistic performance along work processes. The matrix collapses process requirements into specific levels of work based on complexity and arranges competencies according to blocks of similar skills. Exhibit 8-5 shows the sales and service processes from Exhibit 8-4 broken into competency and skill blocks. The blocks at Level I show the knowledge, activities, and results required to perform the process effectively under normal conditions. Level II shows the requirements to troubleshoot the process and handle nonroutine problems. Level III is for more advanced levels of performance (improving, redesigning, and developing better ways to handle the process).

183

Exhibit 8-4. Process Bundling Example for a Sales and Service Organization.

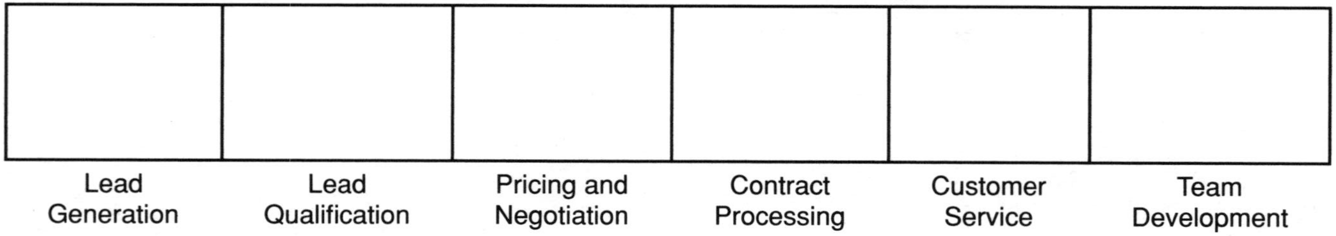

Lead Generation	Lead Qualification	Pricing and Negotiation	Contract Processing	Customer Service	Team Development

Exhibit 8-5. Process Bundling Competency and Skill Blocks for a Sales and Service Organization.

	Lead Generation	Lead Qualification	Pricing and Negotiation	Contract Processing	Customer Service	Team Development
Level III						
Level II						
Level I						

Each block of the matrix sets forth the knowledge, activities, and results required at different levels of employees involved in the process. Exhibit 8-6 illustrates this information for entry-level people in lead generation.

Exhibit 8-7 illustrates a role and requisite levels of competency for a senior person, Alice, who specializes in the generation of sales leads. She is expected to function at Level III in lead generation, which is to say that she is one of the best at this role. To complement this proficiency, Alice is also expected to perform at Level II in lead qualification and at Level I in price negotiation, contract processing, and customer service. Other employees on the sales and service team, who concentrate in these areas, will work with Alice and expect her to pass along leads that she generates. Each individual has an area where he or she is proficient at Level III and has sufficient mastery of other skill blocks to work effectively as team members.

Each individual's role is defined using skill blocks that represent the breadth and depth of competencies that the team requires. The team members necessarily have to complement each other, and that is addressed in staffing and training. In this example, it makes sense for the team members to specialize, although that may not be the best answer in another situation.

Exhibit 8-6. Process Competency Block Example for Lead Qualification, Entry Level.

Knowledge	Activities	Results
Understands qualification criteria	Identifies potential leads	Number of qualified leads generated
Recognizes potential leads	Communicates effectively with potential leads by listening, questioning, and building trust	Ratio of qualified leads who actually become clients
Understands costs and benefits associated with pursuing various leads	Effectively qualifies leads	Average transaction cost

Exhibit 8-7. Example Role for a Lead Generator.

	Lead Generation	Lead Qualification	Pricing and Negotiation	Contract Processing	Customer Service	Team Development
Level I	■	■	■	■	■	■
Level II	■	■				■
Level III	■					■

Establishing Pay Levels

A skill-based pay system has the same basic objectives as a traditional wage and salary program: to attract and retain adequately qualified employees. That means that entry-level wages have to be aligned with prevailing market levels, and as employees progress up the career ladder, pay levels have to be competitive with market levels for people with comparable skills.

As employees demonstrate proficiency with new skill blocks, they at some point will possess broader or deeper skill sets common in other organizations, and that justifies pay levels above those paid in a traditional job environment. Performance levels should also be higher, and in fact it is generally true that comparable results can be achieved with fewer people. The difference in staffing should more than offset the higher pay levels. Organizations that have incurred increased payroll costs are typically those that fail to utilize the new skill sets fully.

With a skill-based pay system, the most common basis for increases above the entry level is a defined dollar or cents increment for mastering each skill block. Each pay increment has to be planned so that it reflects the difficulty of the skill block and the perceived value to the employer. When the employee masters the final skill block, the new wage has to be competitive and attractive relative to other similar job opportunities available in the labor market. The mechanics of this approach to skill-based pay are illustrated in the case study at the end of this chapter.

That logic can be used with both competency- and skill-based systems. The focus is on the employee's ability to demonstrate the new set of skills or competencies. The pay increments or steps can be equal and tied to a single skill block, or if some skills are more difficult to develop than others, it may justify increases of two or more steps for selected skill blocks. Alternatively, pay increase ranges can be defined and discretion provided to supervisors to determine the amount of the increase.

It is sometimes argued that skill-based pay systems cannot be aligned with market-dictated pay levels. Salary surveys, of course, focus on benchmark jobs that are seen as comparable across organizations. Organizations with competency- or skill-based pay systems are, however, competing for talent with other employers and competing directly for entry-level people. At the higher levels, organizations that define roles in terms of competencies or skills offer superior career opportunities, rich learning environments, and more diverse work experience, but those benefits are not a substitute for higher pay levels. It is unlikely that skill-based pay will be successful if pay rates are below the prevailing levels available to qualified people in the labor market.

A strategy for market pricing that meets this need is referred to as the *market basket approach*. This approach is based on the calculation of a composite market pay level using data for a series of more common survey jobs. The approach is otherwise similar to traditional market pricing in that it requires the same attention to the definition of the labor market, the selection of quality data sources, and the same analytical rigor.

The primary difference between traditional market pricing and the market basket approach is the way that positions are matched to industry benchmarks. Traditional market pricing is based on the identification of generic jobs (e.g., secretary, chemist) and comparing their pay levels with the amounts paid by other organizations employing people in similar jobs. The market basket approach is used when multiskilled jobs require broader capacities and roles that are effectively a composite of the jobs in other organizations. For example, a skill-based role that involves machine operation, equipment control, equipment maintenance, and team leadership would be compared to a market basket of more traditional jobs requiring some portion of these skills. The survey data are weighted to reflect the relative importance of the different jobs and sets of skills and a weighted average calculated. Some analysts then add a factor to the calculated market rate to reflect the complexity and unique value of the multiskilled job. The adjustment factor is typically 10 to 20 percent. Exhibit 8-8 illustrates a typical calculation process based on the logic of the market basket approach.

Creating a Certification Process

The most important administrative protocol associated with skill-based pay is the system for confirming the acquisition or demonstration of current or new skills in a given performance period. This process, called

Exhibit 8-8. Process for Developing Market Basket Survey Data.

1. Develop comparative understanding of labor market
   - Industry
   - Geography
   - Scope
2. Bucket competencies to create model "job descriptions"
3. Identify market survey sources
4. Collect competitive rates on all jobs representative of the multi-skilled jobs

Survey jobs	Median Market rates
Machine operator	$18,000
Equipment technician	$22,000
Engineering technician	$24,000
Lead/working supervisor	$28,000
Maintenance technician	$23,000

5. Weigh each job by the skill allocation and derive an estimated market rate by taking a weighted average of the Median Market Rates:

Survey jobs	Weight	Median Market rates
Machine operator	30%	$18,000
Equipment technician	10%	$22,000
Engineering technician	20%	$24,000
Lead/working supervisor	20%	$28,000
Maintenance technician	20%	$23,000

Weighted average
$(.30 \times \$18,000) + (.10 \times \$22,000) + (.20 \times \$24,000) + (.20 \times \$28,000) + (.20 \times \$22,600) = \$22,600$
Note that this job does not have a market rate similar to the pay levels for benchmark jobs because the "job" does not exist in the market place (or in the available surveys). The weights represent an assumption about the relative mix of skills. We also assume that the benchmark jobs are "pure" measures of comparable skills.

6. Adjust the derived market median rate (step 5) by a factor recognizing the uniqueness of the role and the additional market value associated with the specific combination of competencies and skills. This step is optional and based on the judgment of the analyst.
   $\$22,600 \times 110\% = \$24,860$
7. Establish pay range, band and/or steps.

certification, is closely aligned with the performance management system and makes a powerful statement regarding expected proficiency levels, the credibility of the pay system, and the fairness of the system to its employees.

Creating the certification process requires the following decisions:

- *Certification oversight team.* This group is responsible for designing and administering the certification process. The team also plans how the system will be set up and how to resolve disputes, and it decides when the system needs to be improved. Successful organizations usually involve someone from each of the following groups: line management, employees, human resources, and union representatives (if relevant).

- *Certification evaluators.* These are the people who are responsible for certifying new skills. In more traditional organizations, the certification is handled by human resources specialists or managers. In some cases, team leaders serve as evaluators with employee input. In a 360-degree feedback environment, all employees in the organization could be asked to play a role.

- *Frequency of certification.* Some organizations allow employees to certify for newly acquired skills whenever they feel they are ready. Generally these companies have skill modules that require a relatively long period (e.g., nine to twenty-four months) to complete. When the skill acquisition period is relatively short, companies typically limit the certification to quarterly or semiannually. If employees can have skills tested monthly, the time spent in testing can detract from their concentration on work. Annual processes tend to be too infrequent to be credible in high-performance, fast-paced organizations.

- *Recertification schedule.* Organizations need to decide if and how frequently employees will be required to have their skills revalidated. Recertification can be done on a set schedule or on a random schedule throughout the performance period. Other employers rely on a rotation work schedule to give employees a chance to use their skills regularly, which makes recertification unnecessary.

- *Automated or manual certification.* It is generally preferable to develop automated certification processes whenever possible. Manual certification can work effectively, but it can be cumbersome, inflexible, and time-consuming. Automated systems, which are computer-based, are advantageous whenever there are large numbers of employees to be certified, multiple locations, lean administrative staff, complex skill sets, or elaborate record-keeping systems.

Topping Out

One of the common complaints from employees is that they top out when they acquire the full complement of skills. Most skill-based pay systems are planned so that employees can complete the acquisition of skill blocks within three to seven years. The common policy is to review the pay structure annually and make annual adjustments to keep it competitive. That means small increases to everyone, but when an employee has reached the top, the larger increases linked to skill blocks are over. Realistically that is also true in a traditional base wage system when an employee reaches the top of his or her career ladder.

Skill-based pay is often accompanied by a variable-pay plan that can continue to provide employees with an incentive. Other alternatives for base pay include periodic lump-sum awards to recognize special accomplishments and special assignments with additional pay.

Camping Out

Not all employees will be interested in gaining additional skills, some will "camp out," wishing to remain at the same level.. Employees who have done well in a traditional environment, especially long-term employees who are seen as the functional experts, may resist the idea of cross-training. By tradition, the individual with the highest skill levels in a functional career ladder has the highest pay level. Now, these functional experts will be expected to learn additional skills to increase their base wage.

Furthermore, traditional ladder organizations have allowed employees to identify a job level where they feel comfortable and to stay there. In fact, organizations often require that employees seek a level because they do not want to pay everyone at the top of the pay scale and there is no justification to have everyone at the highest skill level. Hence, long-term employees become comfortable and have formal or informal seniority rights that enable them to "own" a particular machine, process, or customer base. We have worked in plants where workers have literally scratched their names on machines to confirm their ownership. We have had hotel clerks refuse to leave the front desk because after years of service that is where people expect to see them.

In a traditional hierarchical organization, that behavior is often rewarded. Competency- or skill-based systems, in contrast, give all employees the opportunity to increase their pay based on individual growth. Organizations moving to a skill-based system must decide if they are willing to allow employees to camp out in a narrow role or specific work area.

The benefit to the organization of having employees who do not aspire to broader roles is that veteran employees with deep skills can serve as mentors and role models for employees who need to acquire the skills. This, however, can have a cost to the organization if the campers create bottlenecks in a system geared otherwise to flexibility and operational effectiveness. Their pay may also have been "red circled" or frozen when the skill-based system was adopted. Finally, other employees may begin to resent them if they are allowed to forgo the struggle of learning new tasks. We strongly recommend taking a decisive position on the issue of camping out (versus the continued effort by employees to add additional skills) before implementing a skill-based pay system.

Ten Hard-Won Lessons of Skill-Based Pay

Following are ten hard-won lessons from companies that have succeeded with skill-based pay:

1. *Build the economic model first.* Develop an understanding of the fundamental economics underlying the work design. Be able to show how the work design will lead to additional economic value (for example, through higher labor productivity, faster cycle times, lower unit cost, or lower inventory) so that it will more than offset the higher pay levels of the skill-based system.

2. *Be careful about what you call a skill or competency.* Competency has become an overused term that applies to a wide range of uses. Let us be clear by what we mean by a skill or competency in the context of the new workplace. First, we are focusing on process skills that relate to economic value. Second, with our definition, a skill or a competency must have the three components of knowledge, activity, and results. Our definition of a skill covers all levels of work, from that of the CEO and senior executives to the operator on the floor.

3. *Be careful when drawing distinctions between a skill and a competency.* There is a temptation to draw a hard distinction between a skill and a competency. Skills are often perceived as narrow, tangible, and lower-level tasks. A competency, in contrast, is often considered broader and related to higher-level, more strategic work.

Although this distinction has some face validity, it is dangerous and raises more confusion than it is worth. It has led some companies into the trap of maintaining the job evaluation system and hierarchies they have been trying to get away from. For example, skills would be the basis for valuing low-level, blue-collar, nonexempt work, while competencies would be reserved for higher-level, exempt, salaried, managerial work. Thus, skill-based compensation would become the province of blue-collar work. Salaried work would remain within the confines of traditional compensation programs, serving only to reinforce the system we need to move away from.

Our counsel is that a skill is a skill is a skill. The discipline of specifying knowledge, activities, and results applies at all levels of work.

4. *Do not pay for (that is, reward) broadly defined traits.* The current market is awash with competency models that variously define competencies as personality characteristics, behavioral potential, or general behavior patterns. Certainly such characteristics are important in many work roles, but we are struck by the logic of the distinctions Nobel laureate Gary S. Becker draws between general and specific learning.[1] The broad traits we have just cited are what Becker describes as general learning. Such skills or competencies are general in nature and create value in many different settings. They are not unique to any organization. Becker's key insight is that the value created by the application of general learning accrues directly to the employee. There-

fore, the cost of acquiring and maintaining them should be borne by the employee rather than the employer.

Our counsel is to treat broad traits as foundation competencies: those things you expect people to have as a condition of employment. Screen for them in selecting and expect, people to obtain them if they do not have them. Do not, however, pay incremental base pay for them.

5. *Watch out for "camping out."* The changes in the way work is organized in the new workplace are not for everyone. Almost every time one of our customers has reorganized work around processes, someone does not like it. The person often is a specialist and perhaps has been doing the same job for fifteen to twenty years. He or she says, "I don't need more money; I'm happy to continue doing just what I'm doing, so leave me alone!" The temptation is to do just that: "Let Mary camp out, and we will work around her." The problem with this decision is that it creates dysfunction that detracts from process effectiveness. Working around Mary creates bottlenecks. Other team members do not get trained on Mary's work. The result is high unit cost, slow cycle time, and lower quality.

We suggest adopting stern career and pay management policies. Employees are given ample time to adjust and achieve full capacity. If they do not make the change in the allotted time frame, they are then counseled into more appropriate roles or out of the organization.

6. *Make sure skill certification systems are user friendly and valid.* One of the most frequent complaints we hear about skill-based pay systems is that they are cumbersome. Team leaders complain about the volume of paperwork and the constant barrage of people seeking the next pay steps.

Keep things simple. Institute windows (perhaps every three months) during which skill certifications occur. Involve people other than the team leader in each assessment; for example, use 360-degree feedback procedures. Focus the assessment and certifications on the demonstration of observable results.

Finally, use timesaving software applications to ease the paper burden.[2] User-friendly software exists that allows the team leader to track members of the team, maintain progress in skill paths, and update certification and pay decisions.

7. *Plan ahead for training and development resource requirements.* When we ask clients who have introduced skill-based pay, "What would you have done differently?" near the top of everyone's list is, "We underestimated the training resources required." In planning make sufficient provision for the training and development resources (instructors, materials) you will need, sufficient time for the employee to get to off-the-job and on-the-job training, and sufficient slack in head count and schedules to allow people the flexibility to cross-train and learn.

8. *Make sure that team leaders understand that performance management (not just appraisal) is one of their most important accountabilities.* Performance management is a continuing cycle that begins and ends with goal setting around performance and competency. The cycle includes ongoing coaching, performance assessment, performance development, teaching, and evaluation. The process of performance management should be job number one, where a team leader spends up to 80 percent of his or her time.

9. *Be ready when employees top out.* At some point, all of us reach full capacity in our role. On some teams it might take three or four years, in other cases longer. We are often asked by customers, "What do we say to the employee who reaches the target goals and asks; 'Is that all there is?' " We counsel that the best answer is, "Yes, that's all there is! Your pay represents fair market value for the skills you possess and are using in your role." There may also be additional rewards: periodic adjustments to base pay reflecting external market movement, promotion to a new role reflecting a substantial change in responsibility and competency (putting the employee in a new pay band), and variable-pay opportunities based on team or individual achievement against goals (see the discussions of variable pay in Chapters 9 and 10).

10. *Watch out for bottlenecks in the skill-based system.* Often organizations build unintended bottlenecks into their work designs. For example, assignments that everyone must experience create bottlenecks. The best way to avoid bottlenecks is to build enough time diversity and flexibility into skill paths. Allow for a variety of paths and opportunities to develop skills and put them to work.

Case Study: Aligning Skills and Rewards to Improve Results

A client company, the Orthopaedic Division of Smith and Nephew, concluded that it had to find ways to develop price-competitive, high-technology products, without sacrificing quality, and focus anew on customers' changing requirements. The company leaders undertook a transformation that involved an integrated approach to simultaneous process redesign, work redesign, and rewards redesign. They determined on a full-scale redesign as opposed to taking a piecemeal approach to the elements of the redesign process.

Three lessons emerged from their experience that relate to the value of an integrated, radical approach to organizational transformation:

- *Combining process and work redesign provides a foundation for significantly and radically transforming an organization.*
- *Integrating work and rewards design aligns skills development, base pay, and performance-based incentives with strategic goals.*
- *Providing employee ownership of the redesign process increases the knowledge of the employees involved and boosts companywide investment in the change process.*

The process redesign phase was led by a design team of fifteen members, representing all hourly and salaried departments in the unit, chosen by senior management. The team set ambitious goals for cutting manufacturing costs while improving quality and productivity. The goals called for specific, drastic reductions in inventory levels, processing and order time, paperwork, and hand-offs during processing.

The design team collapsed what had been ten process steps into just four steps. Each step in the old process represented a de-

A longer version of this case study appeared in *Team Pay Case Studies: A Special Report from Compensation and Benefits Review.* Copyright © 1997 American Management Association. Reprinted by permission. All rights reserved. http://www.amanet.org.

partmental distinction and, thus, a hand-off. At each of these transfer points, material typically would sit on carts awaiting pickup.

The same team pursued the work and rewards redesign phase as rigorously and comprehensively as it had the process design. The design team began by defining the individual skills and structures the organization would need to maximize the potential of the new process. This led to a decision to rely on self-managed teams, compensated through a combination of skill-based pay and a goal-sharing variable-pay plan. The work and rewards designs were integrated from the start with the goal of creating a multiskilled, self-managed workforce that is paid on performance.

Exhibit 8-9 outlines the basis for the new multiskilled work teams. As shown, every manufacturing associate was expected to possess seven core skills:

- Applied mathematics
- Reading
- Applied technology
- Listening
- Teamwork
- Writing
- Locating information

Associates were also expected to possess entry-level proficiency in every one of the seven skill block areas:

- Material deployment
- Machining
- Finishing
- Packaging
- Maintenance
- Quality
- Team skills

Depending on the skill block, associates could increase their skills to the accomplished or advanced level. For example, packaging and maintenance were considered entry-level proficiency, which

Exhibit 8-9. Core Skills and Skill Development Steps.

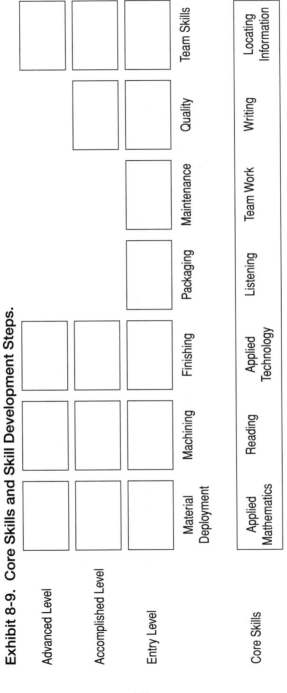

means there are no higher skill blocks. With material deployment, machining, finishing, and quality, associates could acquire higher-level skills and earn a pay increase.

Since every manufacturing associate must have the core skills and an entry-level proficiency for each skill block, career paths become combinations of accomplished and advanced skill proficiencies. Exhibit 8-10 and 8-11 illustrate two career paths for material deployment and machining. These career paths give front-line employees a chance to direct their careers and master many skills. They also support the self-managed teams that provide associates with autonomy and responsibility on the shop floor.

The skill-based pay system was designed around the career path plans. Each career path contained a mastery of core skills and thirteen blocks, each with a specific pay rate assigned, based on a common entry rate. Exhibit 8-12 illustrates this model (with hypothetical pay rates).

Pay steps 1 through 7 correspond to the entry-level blocks required of all associates, while Level 2 and Level 2/3 skills (depending on the career path) are voluntary. The progression through the first seven blocks is fifty cents per block; through Level 2 skills, eighty cents per block; and through Level 2/3 skills, one dollar per block.

The unit assessed all associates for their current skill attainment and placed them accordingly in the new structure. There is now a schedule for attainment of each skill block in anywhere from six to twenty-four months, depending on the level.

In addition, there is a goal-sharing plan with payouts based on four goals: customer focus (customer quality), operations focus (manufacturing costs), financial focus (cycle time expectations driven by the sot of capital), and innovation and learning focus (skill development). Payouts can vary between 2.5 percent and 10 percent of the base pay budget.

The company made dramatic changes with a dramatic method—and all at once, with no concern about traditional parameters. The experience shows that piecemeal implementation of redesign efforts not only is not essential, it is not even desirable. A radical transformation allows an organization to integrate all aspects of its

Exhibit 8-10. Material Deployment Career Path.

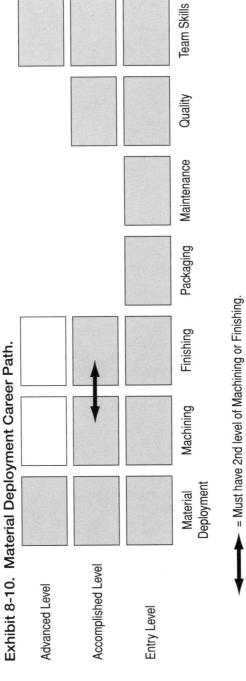

Advanced Level

Accomplished Level

Entry Level

Material Deployment   Machining   Finishing   Packaging   Maintenance   Quality   Team Skills

= Must have 2nd level of Machining or Finishing.

Exhibit 8-11. Machining Career Path.

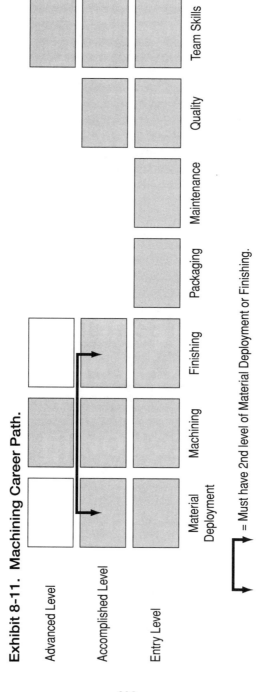

Advanced Level

Accomplished Level

Entry Level

Material Deployment | Machining | Finishing | Packaging | Maintenance | Quality | Team Skills

= Must have 2nd level of Material Deployment or Finishing.

Exhibit 8-12. Skill-Based Pay Structure.

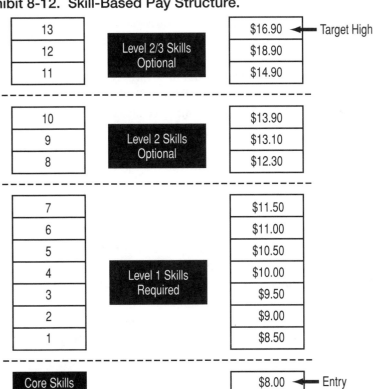

process, work, and compensation design in one mutually supportive and effective operation.

Checklist for Skill-Based Pay

Organization Readiness for Considering Skill-Based Pay

☐ Is there a potential to improve performance? What is a reasonable performance expectation?

☐ Have we defined the core and support processes that will be the basis for a skill matrix?

☐ Are we currently taking advantage of available technology? If not, how would that affect job performance and work design?

☐ Have we identified the framework for work teams?

☐ Is the philosophy of skill-based pay compatible with the way our workers have been managed? If not, what further steps should we take to ensure that workers accept the changes?

☐ How should we define management's role? Is a credible senior executive ready to be a champion of the changes? What managers will be instrumental in making the initiative successful?

☐ What are the goals in evaluating the effectiveness of skill-based pay? What problems do we hope to solve with the new pay system?

☐ Will the existing culture support the planned changes?

The Employees

☐ Do employees rotate among the various steps in the work process? Do they now play different roles at any time during the workday, workweek, or a longer period?

☐ Would it be advantageous for all employees in the group to develop interchangeable or redundant skill sets?

☐ Will added skills enhance group performance? Reduce costs?

☐ Will employees have adequate opportunities to apply new skills that they develop?

Determining Pay

☐ Are our pay levels currently competitive? What is our long-term total compensation objective?

☐ If pay levels are low, how much would it cost to reach competitive levels? Can we afford the additional cost? How much would productivity have to increase to offset the additional cost?

☐ Can we "price" entry-level roles and the target high role?

☐ How much should we pay someone with the full complement of skills? What is the schedule for incremental increases? Should the increments be equal or planned to reflect the value, difficulty, or criticality of each skill set?

☐ Do we plan to introduce a group incentive system (e.g., gain sharing or goal sharing) covering these jobs? Will the incentive focus exclusively or in part on these jobs? How would incentives affect the alignment with market pay levels?

Certification Process Issues

☐ Who will be accountable for this process?
☐ Do we need new training programs? Who will be responsible for training?

Necessary Changes to Related Systems

☐ Are changes needed to the payroll system?
☐ Are changes needed to the information system?
☐ Are changes needed to the accounting system?

The Transition Period

☐ How long should we allow for the transition to the new pay model?
☐ What turnover do we expect?
☐ Can we afford any fall-off in results during the transition?

Notes

1. Gary S. Becker, *Human Capital* (3rd ed.) (Chicago: University of Chicago Press, 1993).
2. The Center for Workforce Effectiveness has developed TeamTrack software available for review at www.cwelink.com.

SECTION III

==== ■ ====

ALIGNING PAY AND GROUP RESULTS

There is a long history of incentives for employees below the executive level. Profit sharing, with roots in the nineteenth century, is still used in thousands of companies. Gain sharing was adopted in the 1930s. Piece-rate incentive plans go back to the same period and are still in use. Sales commission plans are used extensively in some industries. Despite the history, the number of employers with incentives for nonexecutives has been small; surveys have showed less than 10 percent until the last half of the 1990s.

Incentive compensation has been criticized from a number of angles. There are those who argue that incentives serve only to raise costs. These critics discount any possible value of incentives to improve performance. Others argue that it should not be necessary to pay anything more than an adequate wage. That is a deeply held belief in some quarters. Still others contend that incentives serve as a justification to hold down base pay levels. From this vantage point, a "good" employer would simply increase wage levels. Finally some would argue that employers should rely on intrinsic satisfaction—that is, satisfaction from performing the job at a high level—and that incentives cause more harm than good.

Profit sharing has been shown over and over to be a very effective incentive. There are, in fact, employers who advocate the concept vociferously. In the right situation, it can be a powerful incentive, but it is clearly not a panacea. In larger organizations, employees often have no ability to influence profits; there are too many other intervening factors, like the world economy. When employees do not feel they can influence the results, the linkage between performance and payouts is too tenuous, and that vitiates the incentive power of the plan. Private or closely held companies are often reluctant to disclose profits, and that minimizes the impact of profit sharing as an effective incentive.

Gain sharing was conceived to overcome some of the problems inherent in profit sharing. By focusing on the financial measure that employees can control or influence—payroll costs as a percentage of total costs—it is possible to create an effective incentive plan linked to controllable factors. The earliest plans were the idea of Joe Scanlon, a union leader in the 1930s. His concept compared payroll costs, as a percentage of total production costs, with the same costs in a prior base period. If the percentage falls, it means the workforce has become more productive. The "gain" is then shared with employees. Over the years a couple of variations on this theme were developed, with various names coined to refer to these ideas. But there are also problems with pure gain-sharing plans. Not the least is that the business world has become too dynamic to compare one year with a prior year. The idea was to assume that any gain was attributable in part to worker initiatives. Now, with everything in an ongoing state of flux, the comparison with a base period has lost some of its meaning. From a different perspective, reducing costs may not be the highest performance priority, but it will be when its tied to incentive payouts.

Perhaps the most important consideration, however, is that the focus in a classic gain-sharing plan is cost reduction. The clear message is that the workforce is seen as a cost and that workers are best managed as a cost that should be reduced.

That is changing in the new work paradigm. The current generation of group incentives, still often referred to as gain-sharing plans, recognizes that employees have a lot to contribute. The performance measures are now broader and include such things as on-time delivery and customer satisfaction. New phrases are being used to refer to the plans—*success sharing, goal sharing,* and *achievement sharing* to name a few—and the underlying philosophy reflects a belief that plan participants are more than a cost.

That shift in thinking has also opened another important door. With a traditional profit-sharing or gain-sharing plan, every employee participated on a more-or-less equal basis. Payouts were typically in equal dollars or an equal percentage of base pay. That is consistent with the belief that internal equity is an overarching goal.

Now, as organizations begin to focus on the use of incentives as a management tool, it prompts the thought that incentives can be used to accomplish or support specific programs or goals. That leads to the use of separate incentive plans for specific groups. Sales personnel, of course, have always had separate incentives, but it would be extremely rare in most companies to have separate plans in other functions. The possible adoption of specific work group plans is a big philosophical hurdle for a company, but a growing number have gotten over that barrier.

Chapter 9, by Tom Wilson, provides an overview of the planning that goes into group incentive plans. He has learned that there are as many as one hundred decisions that must be made in the development of a group incentive plan. A decision to introduce profit sharing is by comparison straightforward. His chapter is planned to enable program planners to be reasonably certain they have addressed all of the issues.

This shift coincides with another change in the paradigm: the use of self-managed teams. Teams are understood to function best when they are rewarded as a team, and that translates into specific incentives and possibly changes in the base salary system to enhance team effectiveness. Team-based pay systems are probably best viewed as a subset of the trend to introduce group incentives, but they represent an important change in philosophy. Steve Gross discusses these problems in Chapter 10, where he sets forth an approach to develop effective team-based pay systems.

These changes then need to be considered in the context of global management problems. The beliefs about compensation and reward systems reflect the heritage and culture of the United States. When the goal is to motivate desired employee behavior, it is essential that the employees react positively and as expected to the way they are compensated. Incentive plans have not been widely used outside the United States because it is widely believed that the concept is incompatible with the local culture in many countries. The possible problems in introducing incentives in a global business environment are the subject of Chapter 11, by Neil Coleman.

The importance of how a new program is perceived and the reactions it generates makes communications at least as important as plan design. If employees do not understand a plan, misinterpret the intent, or develop a negative perception, it could easily fail. From a different perceptive, employees are accustomed to aggressive advertising. Company communications are competing for attention with the media blitz, and that affects the way employees react to any type of communications. That is the subject of Chapter 12, by Rick Anthony.

Chapter 13, by the editor Howard Risher, presents the argument for using incentives. People like to be paid from incentive plans and there is solid evidence that incentives can trigger improved performance.

9

Aligning Pay to Group Results

· ■ ·

Thomas B. Wilson
president of the Wilson Group

Although the United States celebrates individual achievement and views the individual as a symbol of our capitalist economy, most meaningful work is accomplished not by individuals but by groups. Today it is rare for any one person, no matter how proficient at his or her job, to create a new product or service single-handedly. In fact, groups commonly play a role at each stage, from research through distribution. Some group members may contribute more than others, but it takes a cohesive group to bring new products and services to market.

Organizations are formed because as the work activity grows beyond the capabilities of a single person, additional people are needed, and at some point specialized expertise is needed to function at the highest levels. If individuals could accomplish more than groups or if specific functional expertise were not needed, we would all be self-employed. In a group, workers can generally be more productive than when they work alone.

In a true work group, all group members depend on each other, regardless of reporting relationships or organizational affiliations. Recognizing this interdependence, group reward systems were created to provide a shared fate. If the reward system works, all group members work to achieve the same performance objectives. Recognition of the importance of group effectiveness is forming the basis for new models of management and new management tools, including group incentive plans.

Role of Group Incentives

· ■ ·

Group incentive plans provide a mechanism to identify and allocate rewards based on achievement of goals or exceeding a predetermined performance standard. The success of each participating employee becomes tied to the success of the group, because the more the group succeeds, the greater the reward is for each employee. Often a key question is: Who should be included in the group? Is it a team within an organization, a department, a division, or the entire company?

That question is central to the design of effective incentive plans. At one extreme, the answer can be as broad as an entire company. At the other extreme, it can be as focused as a work team incentive, and in this case, it may make sense to develop multiple plans, with payouts dependent on the performance of a separate team.

A variety of incentive plans have been used with varying success since the 1930s. Sales commissions and piece work are two examples of incentive pay that reward individuals based on individual productivity. Group incentive plans are closer in design to profit-sharing plans. But as the marketplace has become more complex and the definition of success goes beyond just profits, employers have come to appreciate that simplistic profit-sharing plans have become ineffective in motivating desired behaviors.

How can group incentive plans be developed that best suit the needs of today's organization and its employees? How can group incentives work if different group members are motivated by different incentives? And what happens when a group member fails to conform to group standards? Anticipating the issues that will have an impact on the organization's group incentive plan before the plan is designed can strengthen the probability that the plan will succeed.

Getting Comfortable With the Design Process

—— · ■ · ——

There are no standard issues to address when designing group incentive plans. Each organization must identify its own issues, determine why they are important, consider alternatives, and chart the best course of action.

For some organizations, determining performance measures is the most difficult and important issue. Some will find that establishing eligibility criteria is the most critical concern. For others, identifying the sources of funding will be the most complex and troublesome part of the process. During the design process, some organizations will find that a group incentive plan is not the best solution. For those organizations, other reward strategies are available.

Although different issues arise for each organization, one constant they may all face is frustration with the complexity of designing a group incentive plan. From developing hundreds of incentive compensation programs for all types of organizations, we have learned that more than one hundred decisions must be made during the plan development. At times, the task may seem so overwhelming and so complicated that success will be unattainable. Eventually, though, the right model emerges if commitment is sustained, the expertise is present, and the process is healthy. Trust the process.

The design process can be complicated, but the resulting plan must be simple (though not simplistic) so that the participants can easily understand it. Unless it is easy to understand, it will not be effective at motivating the desired behaviors. This double-edged requirement of a comprehensive process and a simple plan can be achieved with a full understanding of the critical issues.

Critical Issues for Group Incentive Plan Success

—— · ■ · ——

The factors that are often commonly important to a plan's success are listed in Exhibit 9-1. You may wish to supplement this review of critical

Exhibit 9-1. Key Issues in Designing Group Incentive Plans.

1. Understand the real reasons that the plan is being developed.

2. Balance team focus and individual focus.

3. Identify the right performance measures.

4. Determine how much money is enough.

5. Define participation requirements.

6. Determine sources of funding and return on investment.

7. Involve the participants in plan design.

8. Introduce incentives into a culture of entitlement carefully.

9. Know what managers need to do differently.

10. Recognize when it is time to modify or terminate the plan.

issues by reviewing a step-by-step process.[1] This list of issues should contribute to the organization's ability to develop a highly effective incentive plan.

Understand the Real Reasons That the Plan Is Being Developed

It is essential to understand why the group incentive plan is being developed. The reasons need to be grounded in the strategy of the organization. Research indicates that for a group incentive plan to succeed, its primary purpose should be to align the organization's performance goals with the reward opportunities available to employees.[2] By aligning the organization's interests with the interests of employees, a mutual sharing of risks and rewards is achieved.

Reasons for the incentive plan should reflect the values and com-

214

mitment of senior managers. Group incentive plans can be used to achieve many different goals, including increased profitability or revenues, reduced expenses, and safety improvements. They can also improve employee morale, reduce employee turnover, polish a company's image, assist with employee recruiting and training, and provide a sustainable competitive advantage by creating a highly motivated workforce. The extent to which senior managers actively support the design process and implement the changes needed will reflect the true value of the program to them.

The group incentive plan should not, however, be considered a means to adjust employee pay to market levels. If competitive pay depends on payouts from an incentive plan, the plan will be under pressure to make payouts that are not truly contingent on performance. This pressure undermines the integrity of the incentive plan. Incentive plans can enable an organization to enhance the competitiveness of its total compensation package, but only when the base salary portion is already in line with what the competition is paying.

Balance Team Focus and Individual Focus

One of the critical issues in the design process is to determine the primary unit of focus: the overall organization, business units or teams, or the individual.

There are few absolutes in the design process. In most cases, organizations do not focus exclusively on any single organizational unit. The focus should depend on the way work is structured. If work requires a high degree of integration among individuals or work units, the incentive payouts should reflect the degree of integration. If individual competitiveness is desirable, as it is in many sales incentive plans, a more individual focus may be desirable.

The challenge is to create a balance between what the individual can affect and what the organization needs, because as plan design moves up to a larger, integrated organizational unit, the line of sight and control over performance determinants by individuals diminish.

Group rewards create certain risks and opportunities. One of the most important concerns when creating a group-oriented plan is that the impact of the individual will be lost if the focus is on the group. As individuals, we like to feel that we can make a difference. Group rewards can hide this impact, since in a pure group incentive plan, each member of the group receives the same reward. Performance-oriented organizations fear that as a result, their best performers will reduce their efforts, and the worst performers will let the others do the work.

Nevertheless, a properly structured group plan encourages collaboration between employees as no other system can. Individuals will often share the workload, increase communication, and cross-train each other. The performance of a well-integrated team is often far beyond the level of individuals working by themselves.

W. Edwards Deming taught American industry that performance improvements result from combined efforts, not individual heroism. Beyond performance, there are other good reasons for a broader focus. For example, it is much more cost-effective to measure the results of a business unit than the results of an individual. In addition, team members working as a group can often provide greater encouragement and reinforcement for peers than individual managers can provide. As anyone who has worked for long hours through tough times with a well-functioning team knows, being valued by peers is an especially satisfying reward.

The decision as to which unit should be the focus of the incentive plan—the overall organization, an organizational unit, work teams, or individuals—is often based on balancing the integration needed between people with the amount of influence individuals will have on the outcomes. The decision might lead to the adoption of multiple plans, each tied to performance at a specified level. Noncash rewards might also be used to offset possible limitations in the design of an incentive plan. For example, if the incentive plan is tied to company performance, then other noncash rewards, such as theater tickets, might be used to recognize individual achievements.

Identify the Right Performance Measures

To modify an old saying, "Be careful what you reward. You will surely get more of it." Performance goals should be chosen carefully, based on corporate strategy.

One important criterion of a successful performance measure is that it must be specific enough that all plan participants know exactly what is expected. For example, no organization can measure a positive attitude. Measures that cannot be translated into action often lead plan participants to wonder what was intended by the measure and to select actions that may be contrary to the objectives of the plan. Performance measures should focus on action rather than abstract performance concepts.

For example, a goal of reducing expenses by 10 percent should result in managers' reviewing expenses in key budget categories. A goal of 100 percent on-time delivery should compel employees to monitor product schedules and work to meet delivery dates. A goal of 15 percent growth in net revenues may encourage the sales force to increase sales and minimize any returns. A goal to improve customer satisfaction, as measured by specific surveys, should compel employees to listen carefully to customer needs and find ways to meet them effectively and expediently.

Exhibit 9-2 is an overview of measures that may be relative to group performance. When two or more measures are included, the bal-

Exhibit 9-2. Achieving a Balanced View of Performance.

Financial Focused	*Customer Focused*
Value Creation -- Revenue growth -- Revenues (product) mix -- Profit margins -- Economic value-added -- Cash flow return on investment **Shareholder Return** -- Return on equity/assets -- Return on invested capital -- Earnings per share -- Total shareholder return	**Time to Market** -- On-time delivery -- Cycle time -- New product development **Customer Satisfaction** -- Market share -- Customer feedback -- Account penetration/Number of services -- Customer retention -- Quality of customer treatment
Operational Focused	*Capabilities Focused*
Operational Efficiency -- Budget to actual expenses -- Product/process quality -- Reliability/rework -- Accuracy/error rates -- Safety rates **Resource Utilization** -- Process improvements -- Cost reduction -- Project/plan implementation	**Human Resource Capabilities** -- Employee satisfaction -- Turnover -- Percentage implementing PM process **Internal Effectiveness** -- Teamwork effectiveness -- Service/quality index -- Project/plan implementation -- Response time to resolve issues

ance should be consistent with the long-run financial health of the organization. For example, on-time delivery may be a key to success, but it should be balanced with a second (and possibly a third) measure so that employees do not forget product quality or costs.

It often makes sense to consider more complex measures, such as shareholder value, economic value-added, quality, customer focus, organizational excellence, and becoming the employer of choice. These concepts or principles are important to the mission of any organization, but they need to be translated into measures that guide people's actions and decisions. That means breaking them down into specific, verifiable measures that are intuitively linked to the more complex concept. For example, what do we mean by organizational excellence?

Measures do not need to be either financial or quantifiable. They do, however, need to be verifiable. That means that if a number of people observe an outcome, each will conclude that the task was accomplished. Data are often highly verifiable if they are based on objective events or the collection of a reliable set of outcomes, activities, or opinions, such as from a customer satisfaction survey.

Measures that are within the individual's influence, or line of sight, are normally more meaningful than those the employee cannot affect. Influence is not the same as control. There is little about the performance of an organization that a single employee truly controls, but there is much that a single employee can influence. Influence over measures is usually a question of degree and accountability, another reason that the primary unit of focus is so important.

Timing is another key element of an effective performance measure. The time frame between action and observable result must be reasonable. Individuals need feedback as quickly and frequently as possible so they can gauge whether their actions are leading to desired results. Should this feedback be on a daily, weekly, monthly, quarterly, or annual basis? Again, the answer depends on how work is structured and what measures are necessary for the organization to succeed.

Keep in mind that behaviors are what lead to results and that the purpose of an incentive plan is to influence behavior. Our experience has convinced us that a clear set of performance measures is needed to make the incentive plan effective, and that these measures need to be directly attributed to the strategy or key success factors of the organization. The closer the alignment is between measures and strategy, the more effective the incentive plan will be. The plan design needs to integrate the strategic drivers of an organization with the areas over which individuals have a high degree of influence. This enables the variable-pay program to have the desired impact on behaviors.

Plan design does not end with the identification of performance measures. The appropriate levels of performance also need to be determined. Performance goals need to be challenging but achievable. Although the organization wants to maximize performance, if employees fail to perceive the plan's performance goals as achievable, the plan will have no credibility.

Since every organization is different, it would be impossible to develop a process for setting performance levels that apply to most situations. However, there are common factors to consider when determining practical performance goals—for example:

- Historical performance levels
- Strategic requirements
- Comparator levels (how well others do)
- Best-practices levels (how well the best do)
- Recent investments in technology or new processes

Development of performance measures requires what is probably the most complex set of decisions to be made when designing an incentive plan.

Determine How Much Money Is Enough

Since it was uttered by football player Rod Tillman in the film *Jerry Maguire*, "Show me the money!" has perhaps become the slogan that best defines our times. We are all motivated to some degree by monetary interests; otherwise variable-pay plans and other group incentives would never work.

Once an organization has determined what to measure, it is ready to plan appropriate reward levels. Employees will want to see the money. The key for the organization is to determine how much it needs to show them to effect the desired behaviors. The incentive plan will work only if employees perceive the potential reward to be of greater value than the emotional and physical cost of changing their actions. This is a critical concept.

The opportunity for an award is based on the degree to which the employee understands what actions are needed to achieve the desired performance level and the degree of influence he or she has over the factors that will lead to achievement. Action taken to meet or exceed desired performance levels depends on the individual's believing that the desired level can be achieved. If the opportunity to achieve stated goals is small, the employee will make little effort to achieve the desired result.

The next element is the degree to which the award is worth the effort. This is a return-on-investment formula based on two different perspectives. First, from the organization's point of view, does the improved performance justify the additional compensation costs? Second, from the individual's perspective, is the amount of the award worth the effort?

There is much folklore about the amount of money it takes to motivate people. Some believe as little as 3 percent to 5 percent of salary is sufficient. Others believe it takes 15 percent to 20 percent of salary. Behavioral and incentive program research demonstrates that the organization can provide much less than what conventional wisdom suggests and still create a highly effective incentive plan.[3]

It is unlikely that the same incentive will be effective for all members of the organization. When determining the amount of money necessary to motivate an employee, the employee's current compensation should be a frame of reference. For employees who earn basic pay levels of under $30,000 annually, an opportunity to add 3 percent to 5 percent to their pay should be sufficient to motivate behavioral change, since that amount is typical for an annual pay raise. Those who are at higher levels of pay, perhaps over $100,000, will be motivated only if they have an opportunity to increase their income by 20 percent to 30 percent or more. For individuals in certain positions (e.g., executive or investment management positions), variable-pay opportunities often need to be at least 50 percent to 200 percent of pay to drive desired performance.

Individuals often compare their pay with that of their peers and what is reported in the media. However, market data are useful only if they validate the appropriate level of payout opportunity. Competitive practices are not as important as the impact the program has on the organization's own members.

An exponential relationship exists between an individual's compensation level and the amount of opportunity that is attractive enough to influence the individual's behavior. Incentive plan designers need to understand and determine how much is necessary to influence behavior based on the target population's unique frame of reference.

Finally, it is important to gauge the degree of change employees are likely to make based on the pay opportunity. Behavioral change that leads to desired performance is based on discretionary effort. Employees will choose the degree of extra effort they expend based on the value of the award.

Occasionally incentive systems attempt to compel people to act in specific ways that will enable them to get what they believe they deserve. This is essentially a negative reinforcement that is characteristic of performance systems in which pay at risk is the core principle. For example, some physician incentive plans withhold a portion of compensation and pay it out if the physician achieves a certain medical expense ratio or other objectives. There is seldom additional compensation for doing better than the preestablished performance level. This encourages individuals to achieve the target but not excel beyond it. In contrast, many sales incentive programs include an accelerator provision that provides a greater commission percentage of the sale for exceeding expected performance levels. In this case, there is a clear benefit for taking actions needed to exceed the established goals.

Whether an individual achieves a high level of performance depends on the plan's structure and his or her perception of the perceived opportunity it provides. Has the program been structured to provide the target group with a meaningful payout opportunity?

Define Participation Requirements

Determining which employees to include in the plan is easy when the plan is designed for a discrete unit with a low level of integration, such as a sales force. Often, though, determining participation raises some thorny issues. For example, should the group incentive plan include the business unit's senior managers? Supporting technical and professional staff? Administrative support staff? Sales and marketing staff? Labor union members? And, if they are included, do they receive the same payout as other employees?

When the organization is already using incentive plans, it may be more difficult to define whom to include in the new program. The organization may, for example, decide to exclude sales staff and senior managers if they already participate in an incentive plan. However, exclusion could present problems if these groups perceive the new plan as being superior to their incentive plan.

Should the new incentive plan replace a portion of or all of their existing incentives, or should it be added to their existing plan? To resolve this issue, consider whether their participation and commitment are needed to achieve the desired performance improvements. Also consider whether it is important to treat people consistently by allowing broad participation in the plan. If an employee who does not currently participate in an incentive program receives a payout, should employees who already participate in incentive programs receive the same payout from the new plan?

In addition to eligibility criteria, the organization needs to consider whether participation will require a modification to participants' current compensation structure. Should individuals take a reduction in pay to participate in the incentive plan? Should future raises be reduced or eliminated? Or should the plan simply supplement their existing pay program? There are reasonable arguments for each alternative, but the decision should be based on the desired impact on motivation and cost.

When employees are required to give up existing salary or future pay increases, they immediately wonder what they have to do to get it back. An organization can, of course, reduce pay, but few organizations do this except in extreme situations, since doing so can have a negative impact on morale and employee retention and may subvert the plan's goals.

A more common approach, illustrated in Exhibit 9-3, is to establish a two- to three-year transition phase, in which current salaries remain flat, but incentives increase. This transition strategy can be used to change the mix of base versus variable pay. With this approach, compensation stays aligned with the market levels, based on a total compen-

Exhibit 9-3. Impact of Implementation of a Variable-Pay Plan on Base Salary Increases.

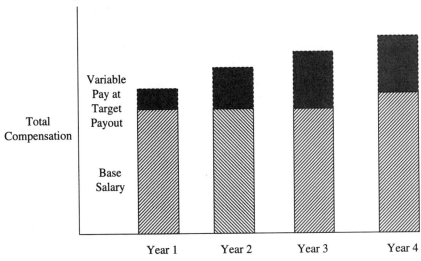

sation philosophy. The approach also enables an organization to hold down increases in base salary costs while increasing the competitiveness of its overall compensation levels.

Understanding the organization's desired position in the market-place is a helpful gauge for planning payout levels, but the real driver of these decisions should be the value of results attributable to adding incentives.

Many considerations are involved in determining the most appropriate course of action. The design team must examine the issues and create a reward strategy that sets appropriate pay levels. The strategy must reflect not only the participants, but the price of admission into the plan.

Determine Sources of Funding and Return on Investment

If the desired level of performance could be achieved without the cost of incentive plans, the organization would never implement them. Therefore, the cost considerations should be viewed as the investment necessary to gain the "return" of improved performance. This concept is critical to remember at the beginning of the design process and when the final plan is being reviewed for approval.

Cost depends on what is measured and how the program is structured. Costs are normally calculated as a percentage of the payroll of eligible participants or as a percentage of operating costs. When all incentives are pooled, cost is determined by the size of the pool. It is useful to review the range of potential payouts (i.e., from the payout threshold to the ceiling, if any), and compare the required funding with improved performance at each level.

Four principal funding sources exist. First, funding can be included in the plan documents as a specific formula or percentage at each performance level, which is known as being hard-wired, based on the measures used. If improved performance generates the ability to pay, the program can be self-funded. Second, funding may come from a decrease in compensation or a reduction of future pay raises. Third, funding, and improved productivity, may be the result of team members' sharing the workload when individuals leave and are not replaced. Finally, funding can be viewed as an investment to improve performance or the overall competitiveness of the organization's compensation structure.

Because the most successful incentive plans connect employees to the organization's outcomes, the cost of a plan should be evaluated in relation to the performance that is achieved. In other words, costs should be measured against the return on investment. Organizations that view costs outside this reference often fail to realize the full potential benefits of their incentive plans.

Research on variable-pay incentive plans shows that they usually do work. A common return on investment (ROI) is between three and five times the payout.[4] In other words, if the organization made incentive payments of $1 million, it should realize at least $3 million to $5 million in additional profits (or an equivalent return in revenues, reduced costs, or whatever else is measured). Many organizations realize even greater returns.

Determining the ROI is easiest when the primary measure is financial. But if the organization uses a variety of operational, satisfaction, or strategic measures, ROI cannot be based on dollar comparisons. A question to answer is: Does a substantial improvement in the critical measures justify the additional compensation costs? In many cases, it does.

ROI should not be simply a financial calculation, but a complete measure of achievement of desired performance improvements. Without the incentive plan, there would be less likelihood that the performance improvements could be achieved.

Involve Participants in Plan Design

Although external consultants or experts within the organization often play a critical role in guiding plan design, it is usually advisable for employees who will participate in the plan to be involved in its design as well.

Design team membership can be limited to managers, or it can include a wide range of employees. A desirable team size is usually eight to twelve people. Large teams can slow the process and transform it into a political forum. Small teams may lack sufficient participation and perspective from critical areas of the organization, and create insufficient support or commitment to the program.

If employees in nonexempt positions are part of the design team, it is important to limit the group to an advisory role rather than have it be part of the decision-making body. Court cases have resulted when nonexempt employees have helped determine compensation and workplace conditions, because the team was considered to be a company union and was therefore subject to National Labor Relations Board regulations.

Involving participants in the design process has many advantages and disadvantages. By involving them, the organization increases the likelihood of acceptance of the plan, because employees throughout the organization will know that peers participated in the design. Because the process is more open, it can strengthen the trust and confidence employees have in management. In addition, the realities of the organization will be integrated into the program's features. Factors such as performance measures, team makeup, and payout levels are likely to be based on accurate data if employees who will participate in the plan also participate in its design.

However, when the design team includes participants, senior management cannot dictate the design of the plan or its major provisions. The design team needs to have the freedom to do its work without undue constraint. When a team is designing the plan, the process takes longer than if it were designed solely by experts (internal or external). Once formed, internal teams will proceed through the traditional group development stages of "forming, storming, norming, and performing." (These words were coined by Bruce Tuckman in 1965, in his classic model of developmental sequence in small groups.) The group may become dysfunctional if it is not led effectively.

In addition, when people from different areas of the organization are part of the design team, they often are placed in the uncomfortable position of agreeing to plan provisions that may not be acceptable to their constituency group. They then become responsible for defending the provisions and convincing their constituents to agree with them. This is particularly difficult for individuals representing nonexempt positions, financial departments, and administrative support functions. The role of a design team member is challenging, but it can be a rewarding experience that adds to the individual's stature.

Introduce Incentives into a Culture of Entitlement Carefully

An incentive plan can help transform an organization with a culture of entitlement into an organization with a culture of achievement. A culture of entitlement has high stability and predictability, and employees have no incentive to alter their job performance.

Entitlement culture patterns often develop through years of internal protection and guarantees. But variable-pay programs and other incentive plans are by nature uncertain. If performance goals are achieved, payouts are made. If results are not achieved, payouts are not made. This inherent conflict can be managed if expectations are managed.

It may be desirable, for example, to have a payout after the first performance period, but the performance levels should not be too easy to achieve, and goals should not be retrofitted so that a payout can be made. To do so would undermine the integrity of the program and reinforce the idea that the program is not truly contingent on performance. In other words, employees would believe that the entitlement culture had not really changed. Rather than transforming the existing culture, the incentive plan in this case would reinforce the existing culture.[5]

Those who have experience with incentive plans recognize that the plans do not truly take effect until after the first checks are awarded. At that point, employees have tangible proof that management is serious about the program and that the incentive plan is real. Participants may be elated or disappointed, but they are certain to react. Their reaction will stimulate change in their performance and in the culture of the organization.

Some periods may pass without payouts. Does this mean that the incentive plan is not working? It could mean that the incentive plan is working very well, but that other circumstances caused the lackluster performance. The managers of the program need to understand this dynamic and provide employees with sufficient warning that organizational performance does not justify a payout. When this happens, it often shocks employees into taking action that can lead to future success. Management should focus on understanding the problems that led to a performance shortfall and on developing corrective action.

Know What Managers Need to Do Differently

Many organizations spend considerable time and energy designing incentive plans, and then promoting the plans and how they work—yet the plans still fail. Some companies develop glossy brochures and conduct presentations to all employees. Then they wait for the results.

The introduction of the incentive plan is just the beginning of the process. Cultural change does not come easily or quickly. The incentive program must be integrated into the process by which the organization manages performance. That may require extensive measurement and new information systems. Always remember that the success of the incentive plan is decided during the performance period. Designing the program is often the easy part of the process. The hard part is achieving the desired results.

Effective group incentive plans require some fundamentally different actions by managers. First, performance measures must be translated into specific actions that can be used to communicate and to educate staff members. Employees often become very creative once

227

they understand the actions they need to take to increase what they can receive.

Second, once people know what to do and receive specific education on how to do things differently, they need feedback. Feedback can be provided at the group and individual level, but it must be provided openly, often, and with passion. Consider the impact that feedback has at sporting events, and imagine how much more successful an organization could be if employees in the workplace had the enthusiasm of spectators at a sports arena. This lack of feedback in the workplace may account for major differences in energy and competitive spirit between the sports field and the business environment.

When success is recognized often, success becomes a habit. Managers need to become active in encouraging and reinforcing the action people can take to improve the performance of each work unit. Informally this can be accomplished simply by saying, "Thank you," when it is warranted, by taking an interest in an employee's work, and by responding quickly to the needs and ideas of performers. Formal recognition can be provided through special programs and events.[6]

A recognition process can encourage and reinforce the actions people need to take to succeed on an ongoing, real-time basis. The group incentive plan provides a limited motivational impact, but when it is combined with a process that reinforces progress, it can transform the workplace. Management of an incentive plan is an action sport, not a spectator sport.

Recognize When It Is Time to Modify or Terminate the Plan

Some believe it is time to end the incentive plan when it no longer makes payouts. They may be right, but there are other factors to consider. It may also be time to dismantle the plan when it becomes the target of negative conversation or widespread ridicule.

Sometimes the incentive plan needs to be restructured to adjust to a change in business strategy or in key success factors. Some plans, such as the often cited gain-sharing plan at Lincoln Electric Company, have existed for decades. But there are other times when the incentive plan should be terminated. It is important to know when and how to terminate the plan.

A company that is deciding whether to continue the group incentive plan should determine whether the program has run its useful course and what the organization will gain by continuing the program. It would be a challenge to find an organization that can no longer improve its competitiveness. Many programs are designed to reinforce continual change and improvement, not to reach some predetermined level of performance, then to stop and just maintain that level. The more likely case is that people no longer see any opportunity for a payout, and this expectation diminishes their commitment and involvement to making improvements. Performance charts should signal when the time to terminate the plan is approaching.

In addition, the plan should be modified or terminated if the organization changes its strategy, structure, or management philosophy. Incentive plans require a strong commitment by senior management and a clear alignment with the key success factors of the business. If either of these changes, the incentive plan needs to change too. In some cases, it is enough to upgrade the existing program. Assuming the incentive plan was a success, the same design team should be involved in the redesign process and in planning the transition to a revised plan. These changes demonstrate that senior managers value the program and want to upgrade it to reflect changes in the business.

If the program is terminated, the decision must be explained to employees. This communication will strengthen management's credibility. If management is silent on the subject, employees' trust in the organization's leadership will be reduced.

When the plan is terminated, the company needs to determine whether it will stop making payments or buy out participants by increasing their base pay. The action depends on the amount of pay involved in the program and its importance to employees. There are no correct answers, only warnings to handle this situation delicately.

The group incentive plan should be improved continually to enhance its positive impact on people and the business. Improvements may, for example, include how well the measures are understood and how well people are trained and guided to take the desired actions. Improvements may also be made in how performance feedback is presented, displayed, and discussed. Measures can be made more reliable over time. The feedback process can be more meaningful to the performers.

Finally, the performance levels can be adjusted upward periodically to reflect an increasingly competitive product or service market. The primary danger with continually increasing the levels of performance is that employees may come to believe that the thanks they receive for achieving the goals is to have their goals raised to the point where they are unachievable. This obviously backfires on the performance environment.

Gradual change is often better than drastic change. The program can be modified easily by increasing or decreasing the number of measures or changing the weighting or payout opportunities associated with them. If the changes are significant, communication and education will be key requirements for retaining commitment to high performance. Changes need to be made in a manner that builds confidence in the program and ensures that everyone affected by the program—participants, executives, customers, and suppliers—realizes meaningful benefits from its continuation.

Conclusions and Cautions

· ■ ·

Group incentive plans are not appropriate for every organization. Many factors determine their success or failure, including the design process and final design, the quality of management, and performance-tracking systems.

The organization can achieve a competitive advantage from its incentive plan only by incorporating the fundamental concepts of alignment, involvement, and reinforcement.

A carefully designed incentive plan does not, of course, guarantee marketplace success. However, organizations that are successful in the marketplace almost always have highly effective reward programs and recognize that group incentive plans provide a powerful incentive to enhance performance.

In another book, this chapter could be called, "Zen and the Art of

Group Incentive Design." The central theme would be that there is no perfect approach, but that every approach is not equally effective. Certain design principles can be learned and applied to enhance the probability of success. Each organization needs to find an approach that reflects its unique business, culture, systems, and management philosophy.

Discovery and development contribute greatly to a program's positive impact on the organization. Understanding these issues and addressing them effectively will enhance the organization's competitiveness and success in an increasingly complex marketplace.

Case Study: A Successful Group Incentive Plan

A national cable television company faced the situation of transforming the culture of the company from one characterized as a bureaucracy to one that would be highly competitive. The marketplace for television transmission systems is changing dramatically, and if the company did not respond, it would be out of business. The company, which had approximately thirty different systems around the country, wanted to implement a team-based incentive program for all the systems to support a variety of efforts to improve the performance and change the culture of the company. It had implemented various cost-reduction efforts in the past and now needed to get employees focused on customer service, revenue growth, and expense control.

The program, which came to be known as SPIRIT (for Superior Performance Increases Rewards and Improves Teamwork), was developed by a design team of senior managers and representatives from the field organization that was led by an external consultant. They reviewed many options for designing the plan and decided on a goal-sharing approach. This approach used a performance scorecard to display key performance measures and serve as the tool to determine incentive payout calculations. Each local system would have its own scorecard, and the same payout percentage would apply to all members of the system, except the general manager. An example of the scorecard is shown in Exhibit 9-4.

The same program was established at each location. Although

231

Exhibit 9-4. SPIRIT Performance Scorecard.

The SPIRIT Performance Scorecard

SYSTEM ______________

LOCATION ______________

PERFORMANCE PERIOD ______________

		Threshold		Budget/Plan			Target				Exceptional	
MEASURES	X Weight	50	60	70	80	90	100	110	120	130	140	Points
Customer Satisfaction Survey Score	20%	60	65	70	75	80	85	88	90	92	95	24
Service Reliability Score	15%	5 pts	8 pts	11 pts	14 pts	17 pts	20 pts	24 pts	27 pts	30 pts	35 pts	19
Customer Service Score (FCC Compliance)	20%	70	75	80	85	87	90	93	96	98	100	20
Net Revenue ($ Thousands)	15%	900	950	1000	1050	1100	1200	1300	1400	1500	1600	12
Controllable Expense to Budget (% to budget)	30%	110%	105%	100%	98%	95%	93%	90%	88%	85%	83%	30

Community Service and Contribution Extra Points:

• **Sponsoring Community Special Olympics**

5 Points

Payout Opportunity Table

0 - 69	0
70 - 79	2%
80 - 89	3%
90 - 99	4%
100 - 109	5%
110 - 119	6%
120 - 129	8%
130 - 140	10%

TOTAL SCORE

105
+ 5
110

the performance levels differed slightly for some systems, they all used the same measures:

- *Revenue growth*—nonprogramming revenues compared to budget
- *Expense to budget*—the actual controllable expenses compared to the system's budget (e.g., excluded programming costs)
- *Customer satisfaction*—the measurement of the service levels delivered to the customers, as determined by a telephone survey from the corporate marketing department within forty-eight hours of the service call
- *Customer service*—the degree the system met or exceeded selected Federal Communication Commission requirements for customer service
- *Service reliability*—the reliability service score that measured the timing and length of service outages for customers

As shown on the performance scorecard, the payout was based on the total score. The payouts ranged from 2 percent of 10 percent of one's total earnings. The funding was established through the measures and the performance levels. Historical or budget levels were set at the level of 70 performance points, but target payouts were set well above this level. If target payouts were made, then the plan would be self-funded through revenue growth or expenses to budget. Payouts were made on a quarterly basis, and each quarter stood on its own as a performance period. This decision stemmed from the fact that senior managers wanted employees to focus on immediate performance improvement issues and not be delayed in rewarding desired performance.

The plan was implemented in January, at the beginning of the company's fiscal year. After six payout periods, the company had achieved a payback of over 6.5 to 1, meaning that if the company had paid out $1 million in incentives, it had increased its profitability by $6.5 million. Senior managers and employees in the systems receiving payouts were very positive about the plan and knew that it had made a dramatic change in the organization's culture and per-

formance. After two years, the executives wanted to understand the differences between those systems whose performance was very high on the incentive program and those that fell below standard. The essential difference was in how the program was managed at the local system site.

The high-performing cable systems had continuous discussions and educational sessions with employees on how they could affect the overall metrics. The data were current and displayed prominently at the facility. When information came in regarding the financials, customer satisfaction, or engineering reports, groups of employees met to discuss the findings and develop specific, high-response strategies to make improvements. As ideas were developed and tested, they were implemented. As employees developed effective ideas, implemented changes, and performed at a high level, they were recognized often. At the end of each month, there was some form of celebration within the system, and often more recognition events occurred spontaneously during the month. The low-performing locations did none of these activities.

This company realized the impact of a well-designed, strongly supported, and actively managed group incentive plan. The results happened because people started working differently. Should they have always been acting as a high-performance organization? Yes. Did they? No. What was the difference? The group incentive plan served as a catalyst for change. The process focused people on clear measures, gave them frequent feedback, encouraged specific actions, and provided a stake in the success they created. Through this process, everyone was a winner: employees, managers, shareholders, and customers. The group incentive program made the difference.

Notes

· ■ ·

1. Thomas B. Wilson and Carol C. Phalen, *Rewarding Group Performance: An Approach to Designing and Implementing Incentive Pay Programs* (Scottsdale, Ariz.: American Compensation Association, 1996).

2. Jerry L. McAdams and Elizabeth J. Hawk, *Organizational Performance and Reward: 663 Experiences in Making the Link* (Scottsdale, Ariz.: American Compensation Association, 1994).

3. Ibid.; Thomas B. Wilson, *Innovative Reward Systems for the Changing Workplace* (New York: McGraw-Hill, 1995).

4. McAdams, *Organizational Performance*.

5. Wilson, *Innovative Rewards*.

6. Ibid.; Bob Nelson, *1001 Ways to Reward Employees* (New York: Workman Publishing, 1994).

10

Aligning Pay to Team Results

· ■ ·

Steven E. Gross
a principal in William M. Mercer Inc.

T eam-based pay has been a direct result of the new work
paradigm described in Chapter 1 of this book. Organizations are placing increasing emphasis on worker empowerment at all
levels and expecting employees to work together to achieve common
goals. Pay-for-performance has become the norm when designing compensation programs. This chapter focuses on how to pay for team performance, or rather, how to reward employees who are operating in
some capacity as a team.

Before discussing the team pay alternatives, I briefly set the framework by answering the following questions:

- What is a team?
- What are the different types of teams?
- When should team pay be implemented?

I then define the term *team pay*—its various components and how
it is used for different team types. Finally I explain a thirteen-step methodology that serves as a guide for implementing team pay. This methodology enables organizations to address the numerous issues that must
be considered when designing a team pay program: Should all team
members be paid equally? How should individuals be rewarded and
recognized on teams? What is the balance between base pay, recogni-

tion awards, and incentive compensation? How can an organization make team pay work?

What Is a Team?

· ■ ·

Although people tend to use the words *team* and *group* interchangeably, there is a distinct difference. *Group* may describe a department, a business unit, or a specific functional area; however, a team is best described as "a small number of people with complementary skills who are committed to a common purpose, set of performance goals, and approach for which they hold themselves mutually accountable."[1] A team therefore is smaller than a group; in fact, it should be small enough to support a common purpose and mutual accountability. In other words, the members should be able to make a significant contribution to the team's goals and see the impact of what they have done.

Most teams fail because they lack clear goals and objectives and mutual accountability. Lack of team-based pay tends to becomes a factor the longer a team is in place because the novelty of working on a team starts to wear off and members want to be paid for what is expected of them.[2]

Team Types

The most commonly used teams are parallel, process, and project teams. Organizations at any given time are often using some combination of these three main types. Five characteristics help distinguish among the different team types:

- *Commitment.* Are team members dedicated full or part time to the team?
- *Duration.* What is the intended life cycle of the team? Does it exist permanently or on a short- or long-term basis?
- *Emphasis.* Do team results depend on individual contributions or on a collective (the members are interchangeable) or collaborative (the members operate as experts) effort

237

- *Outcome.* Are team results shared or individual? In other words, who is to blame if the team fails: individual team members or the entire team?
- *Direction.* Do team members report to a team leader or to others outside the team, or both?

Exhibit 10-1 shows how the most common team types are defined by each attribute.

Using the attributes in Exhibit 10-1, each team type can be described in more detail. On *parallel teams*, employees representing different functional areas are brought together as a team. Some examples are a task force to scout out a new office location or shop for a new computer system. A parallel team is part time and temporary, meaning that members participate on the team and work in their regular jobs simultaneously.

On *process teams*, employees with similar backgrounds are brought together to form a full-time, permanent team dedicated to a common purpose. An example is a customer service unit of a telecommunications company using teams composed of administrative employees from sales, accounts receivable, and expediting.

On *project teams*, employees with compatible backgrounds are dedicated to the achievement of a specific objective. An example is a project team of designers, engineers, marketing experts, and manufacturing representatives working to develop a new car model. Members

Exhibit 10-1. Attributes of Common Team Types.

	Team Type		
Attribute	*Parallel*	*Process*	*Project*
Commitment	Part time	Full time	Full time
Duration	Short or long term	Permanent	Long term
Emphasis	Individual	Collective	Collaborative
Outcome	Individual	Shared	Shared
Direction	Multi	Single	Multi
Example	Office move committee	Customer services call center	Product development

participate on a project team full time but for a finite duration (short or long term depending on the project itself).

There are some other team types existing in organizations today, but team pay tends to be less of an issue for these types. On *partnership teams*, employees from different organizations work together on a project. In the filmmaking industry, for example, different independent parties (actors, directors, producers, and others) are brought together to make a movie. On *coordinating teams*, managers share information for a common purpose. For example, managers responsible for a common product in various countries work on a team to make decisions regarding product enhancements or marketing strategies. And on *ad hoc teams*, employees meet casually for a team objective, for example, to plan a company picnic or holiday party.

In this chapter, we concentrate on the more prevalent team types (parallel, process, and project) where team pay is an important part of the team infrastructure. It is important to recognize the differences among the team types because the pay approach varies with the type.

When to Introduce Team Pay

Only after a supportive team structure is in place should team pay be introduced. A supportive team structure has the following characteristics:

- Goals are clear, not vague.
- Accountability is mutual, not diffuse.
- Management support is strong, not random.
- Role clarity is defined, not ambiguous.
- Team leadership is effective, not inadequate.
- Team knowledge is complementary, not unrelated.
- Reward focus is team based, not individual.

This supportive structure is created during the four stages of team development: forming, storming, norming, and performing.[3] During the forming stage, team members must be aware of their common goals and the organization's commitment to the team concept. During the storming and norming stages, members start to define and accept their roles on the team and begin to hold themselves mutually accountable. In the last stage of performing, the members think in terms of "we" rather than "me" and focus on acquiring skills and competencies to improve their performance and share in the rewards.

The team structure becomes more stable during the norming stage, at which point team pay can be introduced to support the transition from norming to performing.

What Is Team Pay?

Every compensation structure has four reward components that should always be considered in creating the compensation architecture:

- How will the pay ranges be determined?
- How will base pay increases be administered?
- Will recognition awards be used?
- Will there be incentive compensation opportunity?

The reward challenge for teams is twofold. First, the proper balance between individual motivation and team goals must be maintained. As individuals, team members may think, "Where is my money?" But as team members, they need to change their thinking to, "We did it!" Second, but equally important, the reward structure should promote the best mix of competition and collaboration. For the base pay reward components (e.g., pay ranges and base pay increases), the focus is much more on the individual. However, for the variable-pay components (e.g., recognition awards and incentive compensation), the emphasis should be on collaboration.

How the four components are defined depends on the team type. Let us consider each component separately; then we will discuss the combination of the components for a team pay architecture.

240

Pay Ranges

Fair and *equitable* are the adjectives that should describe any base pay system. This is perhaps even more important when designing team pay structures since perceived inequity or unfairness among team members can be a significant obstacle to effective teamwork. But does "fair and equitable" mean all team members should be paid the same? The short answer is no. The long answer is that if team members are basically doing the same jobs, then they should have the same pay opportunity. That does not necessarily mean the same pay levels or increases, which should be based on other factors, such as skills and competencies.

Having the same base pay opportunity is more critical for process team members who have similar backgrounds and expertise and are typically cross-trained to perform the same tasks. Broad bands, or fewer and wider grades, tend to work well for process teams because a sense of equality is created from the employees' being in the same pay band or range. What their actual pay levels and increases are can be linked to their individual contributions.

For parallel teams, base pay opportunities should primarily depend on what the team members do in their regular jobs since their team involvement is on a part-time basis. For project teams, although the members are working full time on the team, each member is typically bringing a different skill and expertise to the team, and his or her base pay opportunity should reflect those differences.

Base Pay Increases

How employees move through their pay ranges sends a strong message to the individual regarding the organization's values. There are a variety of approaches to administering base pay increases (e.g., merit increases based on individual contributions, skill- or competency-based pay), but some are more appropriate than others depending on the specific team type, as shown in Exhibit 10-2.

For a parallel team, where individuals participate on the team part time while working in their regular job, base pay increases are typically tied to performance in their regular job and possibly their performance on the team. The message must be sent that performance on both the

Exhibit 10-2. Approaches to Administering Base Pay Increases.

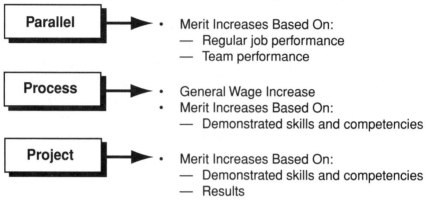

Parallel ──► • Merit Increases Based On:
— Regular job performance
— Team performance

Process ──► • General Wage Increase
• Merit Increases Based On:
— Demonstrated skills and competencies

Project ──► • Merit Increases Based On:
— Demonstrated skills and competencies
— Results

team and the regular job are important and that the employee's efforts and activities must be balanced between these two responsibilities.

For process teams where the individual's regular job is in fact being a full-time member of a permanent team, base pay increases should be tied to competencies and skills evaluated through multirater reviews in order to encourage teamwork and the acquisition of desirable skills and competencies.

For project teams where individuals participate on the team full time (but for a limited duration), base pay increases should be tied to results and/or skills and competencies.

Recognition Awards

Recognition is something that employees crave in general, and it is critical for team members in particular. It is important that the accomplishments of team members be recognized. In a team environment, individuals may feel as though they have lost their identity to the team, and therefore their individual contributions to the company are left unrecognized. If used properly, recognition awards can provide the necessary kudos without upsetting the team cohesiveness.

Recognition awards are used to recognize one-time events where the performance or achievements, or both, exceed expectations. Team and individual performance can be rewarded through recognition awards, although recognizing an individual's performance without re-warding the team's performance would send a contradictory message. Team members may feel as though the company places more value on their individual performance.

A *recognition award* is either cash or noncash given after the fact, meaning after the performance is known. In contrast, *incentive compensation* represents a before-the-fact arrangement, with award opportunities based on predetermined goals established before actual performance is known. Since recognition awards are not based on pre-established objectives, they tend to have less of a front-end motivational impact than incentives and for this reason should not be used as a replacement for incentive compensation.

Noncash awards such as gift certificates, movie tickets, and free dinners are meant to reward efforts and activities, while cash awards (typically $250 or more has the greatest impact) are meant to reward results.

Recognition awards can be used for all three team types, although process teams probably should place less emphasis on them since they may create a competitive atmosphere that conflicts with the daily collaboration required on a process team. In general, recognition awards can be introduced easily, quickly, and inexpensively without layers of approval and analysis. But to avoid being perceived as a favoritism program, the design should include the following elements:

- *Purpose.* State the program's purpose and communicate it to employees.
- *Eligibility.* Decide if certain groups are excluded.
- *Award levels.* Use a few to recognize different accomplishments and degrees of contribution.
- *Funding.* Budget the program expenses annually.
- *Types of awards.* Balance cash and noncash.
- *Nomination procedure.* Establish clear, simple procedures, although companywide rewards may be more elaborate.
- *Approval process.* Determine the process based on the size of the award (bigger awards need higher approval).
- *Timing.* Make awards as close as possible to the event.
- *Award presentation.* Publicize and personalize are the keys.

Incentive Compensation

Incentive compensation is compensation other than base wages or salaries. It fluctuates according to some level of performance, is typically meant to motivate individuals or teams, uses specific, preestablished goals, and is communicated before the start of the performance period.

Incentive compensation is considered a before-the-fact variable-pay technique. The link between pay and performance is established before the performance is known, and employees have a clear idea as to what performance level will yield what payout amount. Incentive compensation is best used for process and project teams where team members should know up front what is expected of them in order to motivate them to achieve higher performance levels and therefore higher award payouts.

The use of incentive compensation on a parallel team could create a conflict of interest for team members who also have their regular jobs to do. A higher incentive compensation opportunity for team performance could persuade some members to ignore their regular jobs in hopes of achieving a greater team incentive payout.

Organizations use incentive compensation for a number of reasons: to reinforce cultural change, align pay with business results, suppress entitlement mentality, encourage employee stakeholdership, communicate values to employees, and focus employees' activities.

The design of an incentive plan for a team takes into consideration the same issues that would be addressed in other incentive plans. (Those issues have been addressed in other chapters and are outlined in the checklist at the end of this chapter.) The payouts at the end of each performance period have to reinforce key measures related to team success, however that is defined. One of the important policy considerations is the precedent established by introducing an incentive plan that is limited to a small group of employees. Specific team-based plans go in a different direction than do gain sharing or profit sharing, which generally have broad participation.

Measurement is a critical aspect of incentive compensation and is often the element that organizations spend the most amount of time trying to define. According to a 1997 Mercer Survey of High-Performing Teams (101 Organizations), the top two performance measures on teams are productivity/efficiency and financial performance.[4] Other measures are cost control, customer satisfaction, cycle time and time to market, and quality. Teams typically use a combination of financial and operational measures.

Another element that organizations struggle to define is award determination. According to a 1996 ACA Team Research Study, 76 percent of survey respondents gave team members the same size reward, meaning either the same dollar amount or the same percentage of pay.[5] The same dollar amount tends to be more accepted on process teams, where team members are interchangeable and multiskilled. This is in contrast to a project team, where team members are bringing different skill and competency levels to the team, and awards based on the same percentage of pay would better reflect the varying contributions and support the differences in base pay.

Team Pay Architecture

· ■ ·

All four components—pay ranges, base pay increases, recognition awards, and incentive compensation—must be brought together to create a team pay architecture customized for each team type. The team pay architecture conveys a specific message to employees about what the organization values, reinforces the culture, and can either foster or hinder team effectiveness. Exhibit 10-3 shows the pay architecture that tends to work well within the different team environments. However, there are numerous options, and the architecture must be created to fit not only the team type but also the organization culture.

For parallel teams where members have divided loyalties and differing levels of contribution, an after-the-fact pay architecture works best when performance is known. Pay ranges should reflect the different skill levels brought to the team. Merit increases should be based on individual performance in a member's regular job as well as his or her contributions to the team. Recognition awards may be cash or noncash, although for parallel teams, noncash is the more appropriate vehicle to recognize efforts and activities, and cash awards should be reserved for recognizing tangible gains above expected performance.

245

Exhibit 10-3. Pay Architectures for Team Environments.

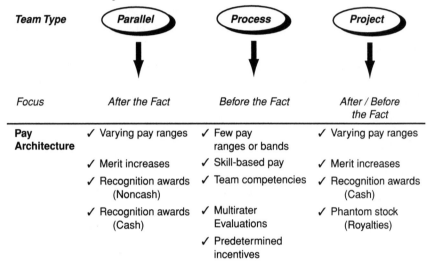

Team Type	Parallel	Process	Project
Focus	After the Fact	Before the Fact	After / Before the Fact
Pay Architecture	✓ Varying pay ranges	✓ Few pay ranges or bands	✓ Varying pay ranges
	✓ Merit increases	✓ Skill-based pay	✓ Merit increases
	✓ Recognition awards (Noncash)	✓ Team competencies	✓ Recognition awards (Cash)
	✓ Recognition awards (Cash)	✓ Multirater Evaluations	✓ Phantom stock (Royalties)
		✓ Predetermined incentives	

For process teams where members do similar work with comparable training and education, a before-the-fact pay approach is critical to motivating members. The regular job of process team members is in fact working on a team where rules and expectations are established up front. Pay ranges should be established using wide bands. Merit increases can be based on skills and competencies to encourage cross-training as well as multirater reviews (by team members and internal and external customers) to promote team members' interacting with one another. Incentive compensation can be used to establish specific goals within the team's control and reward the achievement of those goals. Recognition awards for individual performance are emphasized less in a process team's architecture because they can create a level of competitiveness that is detrimental to team cohesiveness.

On project teams where members represent different functions and levels within an organization, a mixture of before- and after-the-fact techniques can be used to create the pay architecture. Since participation on the team is temporary, pay ranges are usually not affected by team involvement. Merit increases can be based on a combination of skills, competencies, and team contributions. Cash awards are typically used to reward team achievements (usually financial) above expectations and significant individual contributions. Incentive compensation should be used only when clear goals can be preestablished and will not limit creative thinking. Phantom stock or royalties are best used for product development to create intrapreneurship, which is entrepreneurialism within an organization.

Team Pay Implementation

· ■ ·

An effective team pay program is established by following a three-phase approach of assessment, design, and delivery. Exhibit 10-4 shows the step-by-step approach to issues that must be addressed within each phase. Although certain issues may be more important than others given the specifics of a team, the organization, and the overall objectives, all of the issues need to be addressed at some level to ensure a thorough approach to creating a team pay program.

The purpose of the assessment phase is to determine the environmental factors that could affect the compensation strategy (e.g., organizational design, business goals, culture, workflow). The first step is to create a compensation design team composed of members from staff and line operations (e.g., human resources, operations, finance) who will bring the appropriate skills and knowledge to the process. The purpose of the team is to address each of the issues identified in Exhibit 10-4. The management interviews in Step 2 provide management's view of the current organization and culture and determine which types of behaviors are required for future success. Specific discussion issues typically include performance expectations and measures of success, how employee actions influence overall results, and the alignment of compensation and performance management systems.

The employee focus groups in Step 3 have the following goals:

- Documentation of the organization's culture
- Identification of work behaviors that lead to outstanding individual and team performance
- Clarity of individual jobs versus roles
- Understanding of the relationship between pay and performance

Exhibit 10-4. Step-by-Step Approach to Creating Effective Team Pay Programs.

Phase I: Assessment

1. **Planning**—Establish a compensation design team responsible for defining the program's purpose and managing the developmental and implementation process.
2. **Environmental diagnostic**—Conduct management interviews to identify the business characteristics and desired outcomes that affect pay.
3. **Readiness diagnostic**—Gather employee perceptions of current and ideal practices through employee focus groups to determine employees' readiness for team pay.
4. **Compensation strategy**—Define the compensation philosophy and strategy, including its linkage with the organization's overall goals.

Phase II: Design

5. **Design concept**—Draft an architectural framework that provides design guidelines for team pay.
6. **Design components**—Design a plan reflective of the compensation strategy and based on the design concept. This includes addressing the incentive pay components (eligibility, measurement criteria, goals, timing, payout formula, and award levels).
7. **Testing**—Test the initial design on a retrospective and prospective basis, and revise the elements as needed.
8. **Transition**—Integrate the recommended plan with existing human resources initiatives. This includes using pilots.
9. **Union participation-avoidance strategy**—Determine a union involvement-avoidance process that will promote long-term support for the plan.
10. **Administrative requirements**—Develop an administrative plan that covers record keeping, performance management, and plan documents.

Phase III: Delivery

11. **Education/communication strategy**—Develop a strategy for program introduction that strives for employee understanding and acceptance. Both are critical.
12. **Organizational integration**—Identify the human resources initiatives (e.g., training) that should be undertaken to support the new program.
13. **Ongoing monitoring**—Ensure ongoing program success.

- Issues with the existing programs
- Recommendations of various plan options
- Identification of any implementation obstacles.

Information gathered during the management interviews and employee focus groups should be used in Step 4 to develop the compensation philosophy and strategy. Specific attention should be paid to performance expectations and measurement, base pay opportunity and increase processes, recognition awards, and incentive compensation. Sample compensation philosophy and strategy statements are shown in Exhibit 10-5.

The purpose of the design phase is to develop a compensation program that is consistent with the assessment phase and pays for performance. Although organizations are tempted to jump over the assessment phase and start plan design, a plan's chances of success decline if the compensation philosophy and strategy have not been developed and agreed to by senior management. Otherwise a solution is created for a problem that has not been clearly defined. During Steps 5 and 6, design concept and design components, guidelines are established based on

Exhibit 10-5. Sample Compensation Philosophy and Strategy Statements.

Philosophy	Strategy
Base pay and total cash compensation will be at competitive levels in the marketplace. ➡	Base pay will be targeted at the fiftieth percentile with total cash (base pay plus incentive opportunity) targeted between the fiftieth and seventy-fifth percentile in the marketplace.
Compensation will help attract and retain high-quality employees. ➡	Base pay increases will be based on skills and competencies.
Pay will be aligned with business results and team performance. ➡	Incentive compensation awards will be based in individual and team performance measures.

the compensation philosophy developed in the assessment phase. The design concept addresses two basic issues: the mix of pay (e.g., 90 percent fixed and 10 percent variable) and the variation in pay among team members. The first issue includes the decision as to whether an incentive opportunity will be a straight add-on to existing base pay levels or instead will have an impact on future base pay increases (either reducing the increases or slowing their growth).

The second issue is really a function of the team type. With process teams striving for achieving a certain level of multiskilling among team members, significant variations in pay opportunity are not desirable. On the opposite end of the spectrum are project teams where members typically have the greatest variation in skills and competencies, and therefore pay differences are desirable. Parallel teams tend to fall somewhere in the middle of the spectrum. The design components step puts the detail into the plan based on the design concept. The key issues addressed are those described in Exhibit 10-3.

Step 7 in the design phase, testing, is actually done prior to piloting the design. It is critical that the plan design be tested with data from real or "live" situations on a prospective and retrospective basis. This means a lot of number crunching to determine what payouts would be made at what performance levels. Throughout the testing step, the plan variables will likely be modified to achieve the most effective design. For example, an incentive plan for a customer service team that includes a productivity and quality component may need to have the quality component weighted more heavily if test results show a significant decline.

After the testing step is complete, the compensation design team must decide how to make the transition into the new program—that is, roll it out companywide or in a few pilot locations. If an existing program has not been modified substantially, a companywide rollout may be the better approach. If the program includes a new or significantly modified incentive plan, then a few pilot locations with several teams would probably be the better choice.

Step 9, a union participation-avoidance strategy, is critical to the success of the program. If the organization is nonunionized, the plan design must consider the impact on any potential unionizing activities. If unions already exist, the compensation design team must consider when to involve the union; the optimal point is most likely when the team is addressing the specific design components. Although most companies prefer to wait until the plan has been developed, gathering union input and support upfront can help avoid a major obstacle in the future. The sooner the unions are involved with the design of any new program, the greater ownership they will have with the program and the greater likelihood that it will be accepted.

The last step in the design phase is to address the administrative requirements. If it is determined that a plan is overly complex or too costly to administer, it is not " well designed." Simplicity is key. The areas on which to concentrate include record keeping, performance appraisal systems, incentive payout issues (i.e., who cuts the check, and how it is issued), recognition award issues, and the plan document, which serves as the legal document for reference by management and employees.

The last phase of delivery, like the first phase, is often dismissed as having a lower level of importance. However, the best-designed plans will fail if the delivery strategy is overlooked. An education and communications strategy (Step 11) will maximize employees' immediate understanding of the new compensation program and create an atmosphere for acceptance. The communications strategy should specify how to deliver the plan's message to all affected audiences (e.g., through meetings, brochures, or videos). The goals of the strategy should be understanding and acceptance. To have one without the other defeats the purpose and will not garner the much-needed employee support.

During Step 12, organizational integration, the compensation design team identifies the management and employee initiatives that will further the new program's success—for example, the identification of training needs associated with the implementation of the new plan. The adoption of a new compensation plan generally requires a redefinition of roles and potentially an upgrading of managerial capabilities in order to realize the plan's potential. Specific types of training should be identified where warranted.

The last step to ensuring program success is monitoring after plan implementation. This is an ongoing effort to assess employees' understanding and acceptance of the program, as well as specific actions or activities taken as a result of the program. The plan's success should be determined by its impact on desired organizational changes such as culture, team members' behaviors, success measures, operations impact, and financial results.

Case Study: Trigon Blue Cross Blue Shield

Trigon Blue Cross Blue Shield, Virginia's largest managed health care company, based in Richmond, underwent an enormous reorganization in 1992 by changing its functional structure to a flatter, more flexible structure using teams. Process teams composed of exempt and nonexempt representatives from claims processing, customer service, marketing, and underwriting were created to leverage the skills of its 4,000-employee workforce, increase productivity, and maintain or reduce costs.

The team structure allowed the organization to respond to customers more quickly, increase productivity and business literacy, share knowledge instantly, and more easily spread work and resources. Following are some of the results from the team structure and team pay philosophy:

- *Increased service levels (reduced turnaround time, improved customer survey results)*
- *Reduced administrative expenses*
- *Improved business literacy among employees*

Trigon successfully implemented team pay because it recognized the importance of approaching the effort using the three-phase methodology of assessment, design, and delivery. The idea of incentive compensation was not discussed until the teams were operational for at least six to twelve months. As part of the assessment phase, team members had to complete a team incentive questionnaire, shown in Exhibit 10-6.

The purpose of the questionnaire was to determine a team's readiness for incentive compensation. The other important activities during the assessment phase were conducting employee focus groups and establishing a peer review process. The peer review process was developed separately from the salary adjustment process

Exhibit 10-6. Team Incentive Questionnaire.

True or False: Team incentives are designed to:

_____ Help focus individuals on the value of teaming up to get results.

_____ Simply pay out more money.

_____ Enable management to link strategy and rewards.

_____ Motivate teams to achieve more.

_____ Address employee relations issues.

_____ Demonstrate company commitment to team results by attaching dollars.

_____ Drive a new culture.

_____ Force reluctant employees to work together as a team.

_____ Promote incrementally improved business results by leveraging the power of team behavior.

_____ Prepare employees for the new work environment where they share more risk and return with their employer.

so that team members would become familiar and comfortable with reviewing their peers before linking the reviews with salary changes.

After a team was deemed ready for team incentives, the compensation architecture was designed. Team members' initial base pay was determined through individual position evaluations and adherence to internal and external equity. Base pay increases focused on what the individual achieved (results) and how (competencies). More recently, there has been a shift toward a broad-banding structure to allow for more flexibility in the pay administration and to encourage employees to acquire multiple skills.

The variable component was composed of both recognition awards and incentive compensation. The purpose of the recognition awards was to reward individual and team efforts and activities above expectations. For example, significant process improvements or break-through cost savings would warrant a recognition award. Non-cash awards such as entertainment tickets, recognition in the company newsletter, and letters from the manager were often used. Cash awards were used much less frequently, because Trigon believed they could erode the team incentive concept.

Trigon designed the team incentive plan based on a pay-at-risk concept: base salary ranges were reduced 5 percent and merit increases were reduced up to 1 percent for the opportunity to earn a team incentive ranging from 0 percent to 15 percent of base pay. Exhibit 10-7 presents the details of the incentive plan. Performance is measured and reported monthly, and incentives are paid out annually during the first eight weeks of the following year. Incentive payouts have averaged 8 percent of base pay since the team pay program was implemented in 1994. The incentive compensation program started as a few pilots and now encompasses nearly 30 percent of Trigon's total workforce.

Case Study: Unisys

In 1994 Unisys, the information management company providing solutions and systems integration for business and government, was relocating its back office accounting function to a new location. As part of this effort, Unisys designed the new location's organizational structure around process teams, believing that higher levels of per-

Exhibit 10-7. Trigon's Incentive Plan.

Incentive Plan Element	*Trigon BC BS Plan Design*
Eligibility	All full-time members
Measurement criteria	Financial (50 percent)—administrative expense reduction and enrollment growth Operational (30 percent)—customer response time Long-term objectives (20 percent)
Measurement period	Monthly
Funding	Pay at risk
Award distribution	0 percent–15 percent of earnings (base + overtime)
Payout formula	Financial measures × operational objectives
Payout period	Annual (twice a year under consideration)
Communications	Newsletters, meetings

formance and continuous improvement would be possible only through a different approach to managing and rewarding individuals and teams. Each team handles a different accounting activity, such as accounts payable, travel expenses, and fixed asset accounting.

Since this was a greenfield site, Unisys chose to implement team pay at the same time as the team structure. The unit was being built from the ground up with 140 new employees and only a few transferees. With this approach, employees would be receiving a consistent message from the very start: they were expected to work as a team and would be paid as a team. The teams originally ranged in size from two to twenty-three members, but more recently the maximum team size was set at fifteen to seventeen members. Members were grouped into four broad salary bands representing four job categories:

- Student, part time, temporary
- Account services associate (nonexempt)
- Account services analyst (exempt)
- Coach

The new team structure and team pay architecture contributed over the first four years to a 40 percent reduction in transaction costs, higher customer satisfaction ratings, further extension of best practices across functions, and lower rejection rates in the travel accounting unit.

For the base salary component of the team pay architecture, four salary bands were created without midpoints or midpoint control, and the band ranges were wider than normal ranges. Base salary increases were grounded on the development and demonstration of competencies (referred to as core behavioral attributes) and were administered within longer time periods (e.g., sixteen- to eighteen-month cycles). Superior performers received increases in twelve- to fifteen-month cycles. Exhibit 10-8 shows the different increase percentages and corresponding cycles for each performance rating.

The team pay architecture also included recognition awards and incentive compensation. Both cash ($150 to $10,000) and noncash

Exhibit 10-8. Increase Percentages and Cycles for Performance Rating.

Performance Rating	Increase Range	Months Since Last Increase	Target Average
Exceeded requirements	6–8%	12–15	7.0%
Met requirements	2–4	16–18	3.5
Did not fully meet requirements	0–2	19–24	1.0

(e.g., gift certificates, commendation letters) recognition awards were used to reward extraordinary achievement in a single event.

Incentive compensation was based on statistical, numerical, and project-oriented goals built around critical success factors, defined as key areas where "things must go right." These factors included customer delight, cost-effectiveness, and revenue growth. Each goal was weighted according to its importance to the overall strategy, and threshold, target, and maximum levels were established. For example, a statistical goal such as backlog could have a threshold level of four days and a maximum of one and a half days. The goal weighting was then multiplied by the result to determine the payout. Exhibit 10-9 shows further details of the incentive plan design.

Exhibit 10-9. Details of the Incentive Plan.

Incentive Plan Element	Unisys Plan Design
Eligibility	All team members
Measurement criteria	Productivity and quality
Measurement period	Quarterly and annually
Funding	Self-funded
Award distribution	20 percent of base pay (recently lowered to 10 percent)
Payout formula	Additive measures with different weightings
Payout period	Quarterly
Communications	Ongoing

Unisys faced some big challenges when developing the team pay program—for example:

- *Difficulty with team members' rating peers*
- *Significant time commitment required*
- *Some dislike of any pay at risk*
- *Some belief that teams should have the final determination of their goals*

Unisys was able to address these issues successfully and ultimately used its team pay model as a prototype for other units within the organization.

These issues are typical of many other organizations that are trying team pay for the first time. The real challenge is to educate and communicate with team members constantly while monitoring the team's progress in order to achieve the greatest level of success.

Checklist of Issues for Team Pay

Team Purpose

☐ What are the team objectives? Are they clear?
☐ Are results a collaborative effort?
☐ Is there a specific project or results to be accomplished? Are team roles full time?

Salary Management

☐ Should all team members be in the same salary range or band?
☐ Are increases tied to individual performance? Skills? Competencies?

Recognition awards

☐ What is our purpose?
☐ What alternative awards do we want to consider? Cash only? Non-cash?
☐ Is our process for nominations and approval clear?
☐ Do we want to budget for recognition awards?
☐ Who will make award decisions?

Incentive Compensation

☐ What is our purpose?
☐ Who is eligible? Part-time team members?
☐ What are the performance measurement criteria? Performance period?
☐ Who establishes performance goals?
☐ What is the payout formula? Are payouts self-funded?
☐ Are payouts at risk or add-ons?
☐ Are payouts determined as equal dollars? As a percentage of salary?

Notes

· ■ ·

1. Jon R. Katzenbach and Douglas K. Smith, *The Wisdom of Teams: Creating the High-Performance Organization* (New York: McGraw-Hill, 1992).
2. Steven E. Gross and Jacqueline L. Johnson, "Integrating Pay and HR Management Maximum Team Performance at Unisys," *ACA Journal* (Summer 1997), p. 68.
3. Jon Katzenbach and Douglas K. Smith, "The Discipline of Teams," *Harvard Business Review*, March/April 1993, p. 111.
4. Jacquelyn S. DeMatteo, Ph.D., Michael C. Rush, Ph.D., Eric Sundstrom, Ph.D., and Lillian T. Eby, Ph.D., "Factors Related to the Successful Implementation of Team-Based Rewards," *ACA Journal* (Winter 1997), p. 20.

11

Global Pay and Results

· ■ ·

Neil K. Coleman
a vice president at Organization Resources Counselors

The emergence of the global marketplace is having a profound impact on the traditional ways in which work is managed, as well as on how employees are compensated. The increasing emphasis on productivity and continuous improvement is a widely accepted value worldwide due largely to the economic impact of the global marketplace. However, in the rest of the world, when compared with the United States, the alignment of pay and results as a tool to improve performance is clearly lagging.

Who Is in the Global Workforce?

Until quite recently, it appeared that companies had few choices as to how employees around the world were to be compensated. These choices have traditionally been related to the classification of the employee. The three basic classifications are local employees, expatriate employees, and international cadre employees.

Local employees, defined as those hired and working in their home country, have typically been paid consistent with local practices on a country by country basis. Historically, pay practices have been viewed as the outgrowth of unique local circumstances. Each country developed its own practices which reflected cultural issues, governmental policies such as tax laws, and the unique relationships between employers and employees. In many cases, pay practices have been impacted by organized labor or industry associations. More recently, a person of any nationality might be hired on the same basis as other local nationals, though that person may be a citizen of a country other than the country of hire.

Expatriate employees are defined as employees working outside their home country on a short term assignment basis (typically one to five years). Upon completion of the assignment, these employees expect to return to the location of origin. Although expatriate employees may have several short term assignments outside their home country, they are not compensated according to local market pay practices. Typically, they are compensated in accordance with their home country pay policies. These employees are granted special allowances to maintain their purchasing power while on a foreign assignment. As a consequence, the base salary and variable pay, if any, are typically tied to the permanent location and are not generally tied to the productivity of the assignment location.

International cadre employees are defined as employees hired on the basis that their career would be composed of international assignments. Traditionally, these employees were compensated either according to a consistent policy linked to the country practices where the headquarters was located or to a specifically designated market. For example, Schlumberger is a French-based company, but its international cadre traditionally have been paid consistent with the United States compensation practices. On the other hand, Shell is a Dutch/English company and its expatriates are paid consistent with a Dutch compensation model. The unique aspect of the international cadre is that, by definition, the employees so classified expect to spend their careers on a global basis and are compensated in different ways than are expatriates or local national employees. Since assignment length may vary, the issue of pay being linked to productivity in the place of assignment is mixed. Usually, incentives are linked to headquarters or overall corporate performance rather than to the location of assignment.

Redefinition of the Marketplace

In the United States and in countries across the rest of the world, there has been a strong perception that the ways in which pay is determined and delivered constitutes a well-defined marketplace that reflects a common set of values unique to each country. This perception, however, has frequently not been based on reality since pay practices vary widely based on a number of variables, such as industry, geographical location, company size, location of the parent company (where applicable), where a company is in its growth cycle, and the degree of creativity or risk taking a company might exhibit in dealing with local traditional pay practices and response to statutory requirements.

In empirical studies of cultural values in many different countries, Geert Hofstede found several common cultural factors in every location, but how these issues were addressed varied widely by country. The clear message was that each country's compensation system needs to reflect those country values to be effective.[1] Said differently, the variation in values requires unique compensation programs for each country. The assumption has been that any attempts to establish single global pay systems or even regional systems are doomed to failure, since the country-to-country differences mean that conceptually, one size could not fit all. The common analogy is to state that one views the world from the height of 20,000 feet, thus seeing none of the local variations.

Hofstede's work, developed in 1980, became the generally accepted model until the mid-1990s, when its power began to wane. Two major and related forces have spearheaded this change: (1) the growth of the multinational corporation and its strong impact in the global marketplace and (2) the perception that the American business model has demonstrated its positive impact on productivity.

A number of progressive multinational corporations have started to view the global marketplace within the context of the corporation's own strategic plans and response to competition on a global scale. Rather than focus on each country individually, these organizations look at the global marketplace and seek to develop synergistic approaches that maximize the best practices and apply them to the highest degree possible in local markets. Quality of products and services, increasing market share, and sustaining a competitive edge are core goals that trigger a high level of interest in creative approaches to compensation.

The American economy and the underlying business models are frequently perceived as desirable in the marketplace. Because U.S. economic growth and economic stability are respected, U.S. business practices are of considerable interest on a global scale. U.S. business schools attract a global student body, and American business models are being emulated in many cultures. Nowhere is the trend more apparent than in the growing application of U.S. short- and long-term incentive systems in countries where traditional local approaches have prevailed.

Traditional Values Versus New Pay Practices

· ■ ·

Thus far, multinational companies have adopted only modest changes in the pay programs for local national employees outside the location of the company headquarters. In fact, most large companies have yet to globalize their compensation systems by establishing a common set of compensation-related values regarding how pay is to be targeted and determined in each country.

An interesting example of a leadership position has been established by Unilever N.V. This Dutch-British multinational has established a comprehensive and detailed global pay philosophy and policy. As part of the policy, variable pay and pay linked to performance are integral elements. Although the size of the award and the performance measures are determined locally, the concept represents a corporate core strategy. The policy has been implemented worldwide and applies to all employees, not just executives. In comparison, Motorola has established a global incentive management plan using a U.S. model in terms of overall global performance and applying the plan to its global managers.

Considering incentives (and bonuses linked to performance) as an example, the traditional practice has been to provide performance incentives in countries where there was a prevailing practice to do so and not to pay incentives in countries where it was not the local practice. The most obvious example is Japan, where the traditional nenko system generates little variance in pay that is not related to age, seniority, or family status. Studies of Japanese traditional manufacturing operations conducted in 1996 showed that the level of income has no real net effect on employee commitment and motivation.[2] In Japan, employee welfare issues, including perquisites, rather than pay appear to have the major influence on raising and sustaining employee commitment. This is a substantial contrast to the linkage believed to exist in the West.

In regard to expatriates, the practice has been to pay incentives that are consistent with their home countries, even when incentives are either not provided in the country of assignment or alternative pay delivery systems are used there. The obvious inequities caused by these practices are considered to be manageable since each class of employee (local national, expatriate, and international cadre) is managed separately but consistently.

These practices are more understandable when one views the different ways in which culture has an impact on individual and team motivations. In a recent study for Gemini Consulting, employees were surveyed in thirteen countries in regard to their core needs. Items identified include the ability to balance work and personal life, work that is truly enjoyable, jobs that are secure, jobs that offer good pay, and jobs that involved interacting with enjoyable co-workers. Among the four geographical regions of the world, pay was not a leading need; indeed, it ranked lower than many of the other needs employees expressed. According to the study, only in Russia did pay rank the highest. In essence, the study demonstrated that cultural values vary by location and that pay is not strongly linked as a motivator.[3] This may help explain why performance improvement is linked to factors of employee satisfaction other than solely based on linkages to pay.

Bob Nelson, president of Motivation, a consulting firm, observes that rewards and forms of recognition that appear to motivate American workers may not work for workers in Latin America or Asia. He further observes that the same action praised in the United States might be inappropriate and produce negative reactions from offended employees.[4] In Japan, for example, which is characterized by a traditional collectivist culture, linking individual pay to performance is considered potentially disruptive to the relationships among co-workers The preferred basis for pay delivery is linked to years of service, loyalty, and even an individual's family situation. In comparison, in South Korea pay is strongly linked to productivity and individual performance.

From a somewhat broader viewpoint, Jeffrey Pfiffer, a Stanford professor, argues that incentives linking individual performance to pay may be counterproductive. He makes a strong case for the use of group incentives because he believes that organizational results are due to collective behavior.[5]

For all of these reasons, there appears to be a lag in the effective use of incentives in many large multinational companies among local national employees, especially in Asia. However, among smaller companies, a number of creative approaches are emerging to integrate local market practice with pay practices linked to performance improvement. The use of pay incentives by a foreign company starting a local operation appears to be one of the many ways to attract local employees. As a result, the global marketplace as it relates to pay and results is in the early stages of change, slow in some locations and faster in others. The driver is the global economy, which makes it important to find ways to lower production costs, establish a competitive edge to attract customers, and increase operating efficiency.

Organization Resources Counselors Global Practices Survey

· ■ ·

In 1998, Organization Resources Counselors (ORC) conducted a study of pay practices among local nationals, expatriates, and international cadres and found substantial differences among countries. Annual incentive practices appear to be the best indicator of interest in using compensation to improve performance. The study gathered data from U.S.-based and non-U.S.-based multinational companies.[6]

For U.S.-based multinational companies, as Chart I shows, the local executives' compensation program is more highly leveraged toward variable pay than are the non-U.S. multinationals, with annual incentive targets for U.S. nationals typically 5 to 10 percent higher worldwide than for non-U.S. multinationals.

Chart I

ORC Survey of Global Incentives for Local National Executives
Highest Level Local Executive
Median Incentive Target %

Region	US Multinational	Non-US Multinational
US	65%	50%
Western Europe	44%	38%
Eastern Europe	32%	35%
Asia Pacific	30%	32%
Latin America	38%	32%

When target awards for second-level executives are compared, however, the non-U.S. multinationals tend to have a consistent level of incentive targets across all regions (except for their executives located in the United States, which are higher).

Chart II

Second Level Local Executive

Region	US Multinational	Non-US Multinational
US	48%	40%
West	30%	25%
East	22%	25%
Asia	20%	22%
Latin America	18%	22%

For both the U.S.- and non-U.S.-based multinationals' annual incentive plans, Exhibit 11-3 shows that over 70 percent of the respondents reported using a combination of performance criteria relating to local or regional business sectors or to global performance criteria. Fewer than 15 percent use totally global criteria, and even fewer use only local business unit criteria.

Chart III

ORC Survey of Global Incentives for Local National Executives

Performance Unit Basis	US Multinational	Non-US Multinational
Combined Local, Regional, Corporate Business Unit	83%	73%
Global only	10%	14%
Local only	7%	13%

In terms of the specific performance criteria, the survey data show that companies tend to use the same basic performance criteria globally, including profitability, earnings growth, return on investment, and other traditional measures. Naturally the criteria are industry specific. U.S. multinationals tend to keep the incentive payout targets rather consistent among the business units (71 percent), and only 29 percent vary them by business units, whereas the non-U.S. companies surveyed are equally divided.

Chart IV

ORC Survey of Global Incentives for Local National Executives

Target Payout	US Multinational	Non-US Multinational
Vary by Business Unit	71%	50%
Does not Vary by Business Unit	29%	50%

Focusing on long-term incentives, the U.S.-based multinationals use stock options almost exclusively, and the grants tend to be much larger than are found outside the United States. For the non-U.S. multinationals, long-term cash incentives and equity plans are used either independently or in combination. The link of long-term equity (stock) plans to actual performance levels is not direct, and many other market factors affect the stock price in addition to company performance.

The global pay practices among the largest global multinational companies reveal important patterns. If one assumes that incentive compensation is most effective when is it based on line-of-sight performance objectives, then the survey indicates that the tie of incentive pay to local performance for the majority of the large companies in the survey is rather weak. The data show that improved performance is only one of several criteria driving incentives payouts. The survey results lead to the conclusion that traditional values for local and expatriate executives remain alive and well and that innovative ways to link pay and performance are being introduced very slowly.

An important survey finding was that nearly two-thirds of participants recognized the need to redesign and realign annual incentives plans to support business goals, with a specific challenge in trying to recognize local market conditions within a consistent global framework of incentive programs. The actual implementation is obviously lagging.

Smaller or emerging global companies that do not have a tradition of following local practices have been more innovative in the use of incentives paid for the achievement of local business objectives. Most of this innovation appears to be by companies in the high-tech, electronic, or consumer products markets. In these industries, there is a greater emphasis on using pay as a motivator and reward mechanism. To improve recruiting, the smaller and lesser-known companies tend to use greater pay leveraging, with payouts tied to local or global results.

Another factor that is driving change from traditional local market practices is the pressure resulting from the high demand for local executives who have the skill and experience of working in a multinational work environment. In the People's Republic of China (PRC), for example, the overwhelming demand for local executives has created a marketplace in which creative approaches to compensation have been used to attract and retain these executives in the midst of a dynamic and volatile market.

ORC surveys indicate that local nationals are attracted and retained by a number of factors in addition to compensation, including status recognition, opportunities to be trained (particularly in the West), involvement in decision making, and the granting of perquisites. These trends are complicated by the fact that local compensation surveys do not provide the depth of data to have a stabilizing influence in compensation planning and management. There are numerous companies that have linked performance to pay in terms of short- and long-term bonuses. Although such practices have ties to company results, they are driven by the need to attract and retain executives rather than by performance issues.

Linking Pay to Performance for Nonexecutives

Three major factors affect the use of variable pay for nonexecutive and hourly paid employees. The first is that many countries have statutory requirements regarding mandatory profit sharing for all employees. Where this is a requirement, it creates a link to performance, but it also makes it difficult to justify additional plans that would provide for meaningful line-of-sight incentives. The second reason is the influence of organized labor, and the third is the societal cultural values that affect the safety net that employees have learned to expect.

Among the countries that have statutory requirements regarding profit sharing are Brazil, China (a payment of 5 percent of profits must be made to employees), France, Taiwan, and Venezuela. A formula such as 10 percent of profits allocated for employee distribution is common, with actual payments ranging from 3 to 10 percent of the employee's base pay.

In other countries, both statutory requirements and tradition mandate the use of the so-called thirteenth- (and up to an eighteenth-) month payment that are only tangentially related to performance, if at all. This type of bonus usually equals up to one month's pay. In most instances, these extra payments can simply be considered alternative forms for delivering salaries and wages. In such cases, the concept of a separate variable-pay plan linked to performance is not a viable option as long as the statutory or traditional practice remains.

Strong unions have traditionally opposed variable-pay plans (unless they were a clear add-on) on the basis that they could have a negative impact on union members, that productivity was a management responsibility and involved issues such as investment, and other factors not directly related to the conditions of employment. European trends are a case in point. In the European Community (EC), directives embrace the concept of employee involvement in management decisions that affect employees. The concept of codetermination in Germany is clearly the model. The unions have become the employee representatives in well over 90 percent of the cases. As a result, there is little interest in a direct tie of pay to performance.

This is not always the case, however, and some variable-pay plans have been implemented by European companies; frequently they provide for upside potential but limit the downside risk. For example, the United Kingdom-based company Guiness (now part of Diageo) bases increases in pay on a combination of market movement, individual contribution, and overall business performance. There is a clear reference to performance but not necessarily to issues of improved productivity. Another U.K. example is Woolwich Bank, which has installed a pay system based on competencies, but actual pay is also related to the results of those competencies. Although it is a complicated system of assigning points to results based on individual competencies, the end result is a pay-for-results program.

In Latin America, there is not a widespread tradition of directly linking pay to performance among factory workers. Although a few multinational companies are seeking to implement variable-pay plans, they are the exceptions. In Venezuela, for example, the large national oil company Petroleus de Venezuela (PDVSA) has recently established a global pay policy that encompasses the concept of variable pay, though it has yet to find expression at the lower levels of the organization, and there appears to be no support from the unions.

Team awards are used in many countries not so much as incentives, but as rewards for seniority, loyalty, and other nonperformance-type behaviors. For example, in Japan, awards have traditionally been granted on a group basis and may be either financial or nonfinancial in nature. The size or value of the award varies on the basis of group performance. The number of companies that are shifting toward pay plans based on meritocracy has increased dramatically since the mid-1990s. An interesting study conducted by Motorola regarding the linkage between pay and performance of teams in its global operations did not find a strong linkage. The study showed that performance was more strongly linked to a variety of factors and that pay was not the driving force in team performance.[7]

The third inhibitor to the development of linking pay to performance are the strong cultural values in many countries that provide a safety net to employees with regard to pay, benefits, and a number of social entitlements. In these situations, the concept of variable pay for executives is accepted, but it is not widely accepted with those lower in the organization. Japan has traditionally not had such plans, but evidence is emerging that some local companies are experimenting with the concept.

Although management expresses interest in the greater global utilization of pay for performance concepts, to date there is little evidence outside the United States and Western Europe that this trend has become widespread.

Trends and Issues for the Future

· ■ ·

The evidence suggests that the alignment of pay and results on a global basis is still in the early stages. In addition to governmental and union restraints, traditional local competitive practices, and organizational conservatism slow the spread of innovative ideas. Nevertheless, plans that link pay to performance are being established among smaller companies, those in high-growth industries, and companies that need to compete with innovative employment offers to help attract and retain employees whose talents are in short supply. In countries experiencing an economic downturn, employees frequently fear the concept of variable pay since it tends to remove a sense of security and stability of pay in a period of crisis.

In spite of these inhibiting factors, the economic realities of remaining competitive and finding ways to improve performance are likely to maintain the pressure on companies to strengthen the tie between pay and results. It is expected to be much more of a common practice in years to come.

The Process for Successful Plan Development and Implementation

· ■ ·

In almost every culture, there are a few basic guidelines for planning that should boost the prospects for success. Realistically the most effective planning process is essentially the same in every country. The guidelines fall into two categories: (1) identification of the basic process for developing and implementing such plans and (2) the identification of potential pitfalls.

How to Develop and Implement Pay Plans

■ *Create or highlight a need for change.* This element typically involves raising employees' awareness of the dynamics of the competitive marketplace and the need to improve performance. This element may be directly caused by a crisis, or it may be expressed as a longer-term strategy to make the operation more successful.

- *Analyze the compensation and productivity issues to create an economic case for the added value of variable pay.* Proving the efficacy of variable pay is much easier if the existing competitive level of pay is low or moderate when compared to the external market. It may also make sense to find the funds for payouts in improved performance. Economic support for variable pay is much more difficult if it increases operating costs.

- *Encourage employee involvement in the development of the pay plan.* This may include a multifunctional employee task force, focus groups, or matrixed organizational structures, which all give credibility to the process and ensure practical and realistic objectives. At a minimum this should improve the prospects for plan acceptance.

- *Specify an overall pay philosophy and establish clear plan objectives.* Prior to the actual plan design, the process of establishing the relationship among the various pay elements is critically important. In addition, it is essential to clarify the purposes and objectives of the variable pay plan.

- *Establish performance criteria in terms of measuring results.* Typically the performance metrics are quantifiable and, like any other incentive plan, they are established in advance of the performance period and are tracked and communicated to all plan participants. The metrics have to be both understandable and credible.

- *Thoroughly communicate the pay and productivity plan to employees who will be affected by the plan and ensure that employees understand and accept the plan.* Employee acceptance and commitment are essential to the success of the plan. Communication is necessarily an ongoing high priority.

- *Monitor the plan and provide informational feedback.* This is a key element to maintaining the plan's credibility.

Pitfalls to Avoid in Implementing Plans That Align Pay and Results

- *A new plan is installed but is neither accepted nor understood by employees.* The lack of understanding may be the result of a poorly designed plan, setting unrealistic performance goals, or employees' perceiving either that the plan is a form of management manipulation or that the unstated goal of management is to reduce employee compensation.

- *A plan is designed that may be effective in one part of the organization but is an imposition on another part of the organization.* In this case, the critical nature of the design and implementation process, which is so crucial in gaining employee acceptance, is ignored. The inflexibility of a design undermines the credibility of the design as well as employee acceptance.

- *A plan is designed that is rigid and difficult to adapt to changing business conditions and unforeseen circumstances.* This occurs when a plan design has objectives, performance targets, and performance measures that resist modification. The best plan is reviewed and modified frequently to ensure that it is aligned with realistic business expectations.

Conclusion

For companies that conclude employee compensation should be aligned with operational results, there are opportunities to implement policies and plans to achieve this reality. Even in the most traditional cultures, if the process to develop the plan is effective, the plan design is adaptive to business conditions, and employees understand and accept as credible the reasons for the change in compensation strategy, employees can and will accept and support creative approaches in which the employee and the company can both benefit. The hurdles are not insurmountable, and with adequate planning it is completely feasible to develop a global strategy that is responsive to local needs. Recent trends suggest this strategy will continue to grow in importance.

Notes

1. Hofstede Geert, *Cultural Consequences: International Differences in Work Related Values,* Beverly Hills: Sage Publications, 1980.

2. Arne L. Kallenberg and James R. Lincoln, "The Structure of Earning Inequities in the United States and Japan," *The American Journal of Sociology*, Vol. 94, 1996 Supplement, S121-S153.
3. Gemini Consulting, "Study of Worker Attitudes Across Cultures Around the World," study conducted by Yankelovich Partners, 1998.
4. Bob Nelson, *1001 Ways to Reward Employees*, 1994, New York: Workman Publishing.
5. Jeffrey Pfeffer, "Six Dangerous Myths About Pay," *Harvard Business Review*, May/June 1998, pp. 109–119.
6. Organization Resources Counselors, *Global Pay Practices Survey*, 1998.
7. David Goodall, "International Remuneration," presentation and unpublished manuscript for the 1998 American Compensation Association.

12

Communicating Pay
Using Marketing Principles to Sell Compensation

· ■ ·

Richard J. Anthony, Sr.
founder and president of Solutions Network

Before entering consulting, I wrote advertising copy and press releases for widgets that cranked the wheels of commerce and packaged goods that competed fiercely for front-and-center shelf space in grocery stores. My stint as a copywriter conditioned me to paint as vivid a mental picture as I could of my target audience.

When I traded the glitzy world of marketing communications for employee and organizational communication, it did not occur to me that what I had learned as a copywriter for print, broadcast, and direct mail would come in handy.

After more than twenty-six years as a counselor to senior management on organizational change and employee communication, I am grateful to some of the most creative purveyors of ideas I have ever known: award-winning copy chiefs and copywriters who tutored me in the art of persuasion and taught me how to load, aim, and fire marketing messages with precision.

Persuasion and precision are especially important when communicating with employees, particularly when the subject is their pay. The most expertly designed compensation program will fall short of management's expectations if it is not expertly communicated (marketed). Ask a union organizer when employees are usually most susceptible to the prospect of third-party representation. Ask a supervisor when productivity drops off and absenteeism picks up. Ask a disaffected employee why she does not have the same warm feeling about the company. These three scenarios often develop within a few days after management has announced a new compensation plan that sounded as though it was on target when the outside consultant presented it to the CEO, but lost something in the translation to the troops.

Breaking Through

Because employees are better educated, better informed, more sophisticated, and more cynical than in previous generations, mass communication techniques—the equivalent of dropping leaflets out of airplanes—do not work any more. Yet senior managers continue to delude themselves that issuing an announcement, holding a meeting, or publishing an article in the company newsletter constitutes effective communication, automatically resulting in employee understanding, acceptance, and commitment. It doesn't work that way.

In a presentation to senior management recently, the vice president of human resources of a client company stressed the importance of repeating key messages about a new competency-based reward system. He had read that messages must be repeated seven times to register and be remembered. To underscore his point, I reminded the group that in advertising, a flight is thirteen placements, not seven. In other words, advertising media analysts believe that an ad must run a minimum of thirteen times to begin to get through the noise level created by the thousands of other messages competing for the prospective buyer's attention.

Effective organizational communication, like effective marketing communication, is the product of a systematic approach to penetrating the defense mechanisms most people have built over the years to screen the barrage of messages that assault their senses. The approach begins with research, pauses with feedback, and then cycles back again.

Pay programs fail for one or both of two reasons: they are overdesigned by compensation engineers who lose sight of the people the programs are supposed to reward, and they are poorly communicated. Over the years, I have seen expensive examples of both—expensive in terms of the money wasted on good intentions and the resulting ill will among employees who did not understand how the programs worked and were therefore suspicious of the employer's motives.

- In upstate New York, a bank suffered the disruption and expense of a long union organizing campaign because the new compensation program was too complex for employees to understand and had been perfunctorily communicated. Following the election, which the bank narrowly won, the same program was reintroduced through extensive communication and was accepted by employees.

- Nurses in a Pennsylvania hospital rebelled when the administration announced a merit pay system linked with changes in how nurses were to provide patient care. Meetings were subsequently held to quell rumors and to explain the advantages of the new program. It was enthusiastically accepted.

- The faculty of a large northeastern university threatened third-party representation when the administration suggested that some measure of performance might be used to determine pay progression.

- Productivity among plant workers in a large Midwest manufacturing facility dropped precipitously when rumors about changes in the quarterly incentive program began circulating. Management, in its zeal to sell the new program, had failed to point out that the company reserved the right to modify the payout formula if business conditions warranted. Employees saw it as manipulation of the program to cut incentive payouts.

These examples illustrate that even the most expertly designed, well-intended compensation programs have a high risk of being misunderstood and undervalued by employees unless the programs are expertly communicated. The problem is that in too many cases, the communication process begins after the compensation program has been designed. Like an assembly line, the compensation specialist passes the program on to the communication specialist with instructions about how it should be "sold" to employees. This hand-off approach to compensation communication is a holdover from bygone days when the workforce was less inquisitive and more trusting.

Sophisticated Audiences

Surveys show that today's workforce is increasingly cynical, skeptical, and mistrusting. Workers of all ages, no matter how satisfied they may be with their jobs, are wary of placing too much trust in their employers. Career counselors, outplacement specialists, transition consultants, and other commentators on the vagaries of the twenty-first-century workplace agree that the employer-employee relationship has been irrevocably changed. Workers (anybody on somebody else's payroll) have been conditioned to accept that they are expendable; that they are becoming free agents in a global economy; that job mastery no longer equates to job security; that they are at risk of becoming casualties of the knowledge economy; and that they are ultimately responsible for themselves.

Workers in their late forties and fifties feel betrayed because the protection of the "head down, nose to the grindstone" has been ripped away. Workers in their early thirties and early forties are scrambling to adjust to the new "learn more, earn more" rules of the game. And under-thirty workers feel like migrants who sell their skills and temporary allegiance to the highest bidder.

Employers' expectations of the workforce are changing. The rate of change varies by industry and by company size. But that fundamental changes in performance standards are occurring is indisputable. In the wake of reengineering, continuous improvement, total quality management, and just-in-time everything, we are experiencing a crescendo of interest in work teams, competencies, continuous leaning, and employee involvement. Paradoxically, employees seem to be gaining influence over how they do their work and losing influence over whether they will have a job.

Compensation specialists who do not take a holistic approach to designing new reward systems are out of touch with today's reality. The holistic approach must include early consideration of the question, "Can this program be communicated [that is, sold] to employees, and will it drive the behaviors needed to succeed?"

I am not talking about the words and pictures that are crafted for folders, brochures, videos, and speeches. Those are simply the manifestations of a communication process that must be strategically driven and anchored in measurable results. My definition of effective communication goes far beyond the words and pictures.

Effective Communication

· ■ ·

Effective communication is the sharing of information in an environment of mutual trust and respect intended to change or reinforce attitudes, and ultimately behavior, in order to achieve specific desired outcomes. Applied to compensation communication, this definition has the following implications for management:

- *Sharing information* refers to management's willingness to share the power that comes from being aware, from understanding, and from the opportunity to question and expect honest answers. Too often management is unwilling to share financial or operating information with employees on the theory that "they won't understand," or "they'll start asking questions that are none of their business." The counterargument is that if employees are being forced to shoulder more of the risk of business, they have a need and a right to information they can use to improve their value and contribution to the enterprise they count on for a paycheck. So often in the past, management has taken the position that employees will "just have to trust us to do right by them." Managers who feel that way are grossly underestimating their employees' ability to understand and overestimating their credibility with employees.

- Creating an *environment of mutual trust and respect* means treating employees like adults in terms of involving them in the business of operating the business, being true to values that are promulgated within the organization, and giving good example in dealing with difficult situations and people. Over the past several years, surveys have shown a decline in employees' trust and confidence in senior management. Survey data also show that employees are dissatisfied with how they are paid; that is, they no longer docilely accept the "black box" approaches to compensation that are difficult to understand. If management is not completely forthcoming, employees assume the worst motives.

- *Changing or reinforcing attitudes and ultimately behavior* is based on a proved marketing adage that share of mind precedes share of market. Perhaps the adage should be modified to read, "heart and mind." Or, as Ben Franklin said, "To be effective in persuasion, appeal to emotion not to the intellect." Few other workplace issues are as emotionally volatile as pay. Conventional wisdom has maintained that how much a person is paid is emblematic of his or her worth. The typical pay structure has been a euphemism for the organization's social structure and established the dividing line for those who are, those who have, and those who are likely to succeed. Changing generations of opinions and perceptions about the symbolic and intrinsic value of pay require time, patience, and an appreciation of the complexity of the value systems associated with "what I'm paid."

- *Achieving desired outcomes* refers to predetermined levels of performance and contribution that warrant commensurate reward. For most employees, today's message is that increases in earnings will be tied to measurable, sustained improvements in performance and productivity. Reward systems are, by implication, results driven. The communication challenge is to ensure that results are translated into expectations and that the rewards for performance and contribution are understood and valued.

This definition of effective communication goes far beyond information dissemination. It involves risk and requires constant attention to ensure that all interests are balanced in deciding how much information to share.

Effective compensation communications begins and ends with research. In between are the critical steps required to gain the attention, trust, and acceptance of the audiences.

Prologue Research

· ■ ·

It is naive to think that you start with a clean slate when communicating anything with employees, especially when the subject is pay. From the first moment on the job, employees begin to develop opinions, biases, beliefs, and prejudices about the company, co-workers, working conditions, future prospects—and their pay. From the second moment, they become the nucleus of a new opinion group or a member of an existing group. In short order, employees become involved in a process that can quickly lead to their estrangement from the company. It is a natural phenomenon and should not be taken personally by a manager or supervisor. It is, however, a process that can be influenced and should be taken seriously by the professional communicator charged with getting into the hearts and minds of the workforce.

Today—in the wake of downsizing, rightsizing, and reengineering—communication about pay has to bridge a chasm of suspicion and mistrust among a majority of employees in most U.S. companies. Therefore, in planning a compensation communication strategy, companies begin with the proposition that their messages will likely encounter considerable resistance from the filters employees have created to rationalize unfavorable perceptions and beliefs about the company. This is not to say that employees are necessarily hostile toward the company. Rather, they are unwilling to turn themselves over without reservation to an organization that could decide they are expendable.

Prologue research, which is research that proceeds program changes, can take multiple forms.

■ Individual interviews with senior management to ascertain their interpretations of the communication environment and the potential obstacles that should be taken into account in developing a communication strategy. These discussion can be somewhat free flowing. A skillful interviewer will know which questions to ask, when to remain silent, and when to seek clarification or closure on relevant issues. Keep in mind, however, that most senior managers are insulated from the realities of life on the lower floors or the plant floor. They have a top-down perspective on the organization and probably can no longer relate to the worker whose understanding of the company's reward system does not go beyond the bimonthly paycheck. Nonetheless, their thoughts can be helpful in assessing potential obstacles and in developing key messages.

- Focus group discussions with homogeneous groups of middle managers, first-line supervisors, and exempt and nonexempt workers will invariably provide valuable insights into the company's culture and values. In these sessions, the facilitator will learn what people's perceptions are about behaviors that are rewarded and hear stories that are part of the company lore—about transgressions and broken promises, expectations and bruised egos, inequities and unfair treatment. The facilitator must resist the temptation to judge, lest he or she lose objectivity and impartiality. Instead, the facilitator must have the skill to manage the focus group members' need to ventilate and to get at the essential issues usually hidden in the subtext of the discussion.

- Communication audits usually take the form of a confidential questionnaire focusing on workers' satisfaction with existing communication policies and practices. Whether distributed to the entire workforce or a representative sample, the questionnaire is a channel for a quantifiable assessment of the communication environment. If the findings indicate a high level of distrust among respondents, the communication strategy must take that obstacle into account, or the results could be devastating. Questionnaires can be mailed to the homes of employees, administered on company time, or placed on the Intranet.

- A review of the communication archives can be revealing. The style and tone of formal communication can be indicative of the relationship between management and the workforce. The format, frequency, and media used to convey important messages can also illustrate the difference between mass information dissemination and purposeful, effective information sharing. Of course, the existence of quarterly video messages from the CEO on business prospects does not necessarily mean that management is doing a good job of information sharing. But it is an indication of a willingness to invest in communication, which is a prerequisite for effective information sharing.

This initial research step is an opportunity to assess the communication environment and postulate about the most appropriate communication plan and the likely outcome. Some general management consultants call it reconnaissance; others call it an environmental scan. No matter what it is called, the rigor with which this step is conducted can foretell the success of the communication campaign.

Let me share a story that is illustrative of many others with the same moral.

USING EMPLOYEE FEEDBACK TO DEVELOP A COMMUNICATIONS PLAN

My consulting colleagues had designed a form of gain-sharing program for the employees of a utility company. I was the lead communication consultant brought in with too little time to do any primary research. Faced with an imminent deadline, I accepted the client's assessment of the employee relations and communications environments. I was told there were no problems and that employees would react enthusiastically to the introduction of the new reward program.

Our experience proved otherwise. In employee meetings, reaction to the new program was incomprehensibly negative. The program should have gotten rave reviews from employees. Yet it seemed doomed to failure even before the effective date. Management seemed genuinely surprised and approved our recommendation to suspend the rollout of the new program in favor of focus groups to find out what the obstacle was.

The findings from several focus groups revealed a deep-seated distrust of senior management. As good as the new gain-sharing program appeared to be, employees suspected that the company would manipulate the financials to control the payout schedule. According to the long-service employees who participated in the focus groups, the new program seemed too good to be true. Therefore, they reasoned, management must be hiding something. To those employees, we were offering the Brooklyn Bridge, and they were not buying any of it.

Based on the findings of the focus groups, we modified the communication materials to deal head on with the issue of distrust. The approach disarmed the employees, who cautiously took a second look at the gain-sharing program and decided to give it a try, as long as management pledged full disclosure of relevant financial information.

Key Messages

Defining key messages—the words and phrases, simply and directly stated, designed to motivate people to action—can take a few hours, days, or weeks. Often the determinant is the number of people involved in the process and the number of people who feel they have a vested interest in the messages.

Most senior managers seem to believe that the more you tell them, the better the communication. In principle, they are right. In practice, they are usually wrong.

Contrary to popular wisdom, there is such a thing as overcommunicating—loading so much information into a single communication that employees cannot discriminate between what they need to know and what management believes they should know.

MAKE CERTAIN THE MESSAGE IS ONE THE AUDIENCE WANTS TO HEAR

The story is told of the vice president of corporate communication who was directed by the CEO to "get the word out that we have to improve profitability or we won't have an incentive plan payout." The vice president huddled with her staff and came up with a proposal for an aggressive print communication plan that hung from the slogan, "Profit Improvement Is Everybody's Job." (The human resources department could have told her that the plan favored high-paid employees, so most rank-and-file people probably would not get excited about the message.) A few supervisors could have told her that employees never did really understand what goes into profit improvement, nor were they particularly motivated to care to learn. And a sample of employees could have told her that they preferred face-to-face meetings on business issues, not two-page single-space letters from the CEO with the endearing salutation, "Dear Fellow Employee."

Eager to get the ball rolling, the CEO approved the communication campaign. It cost over $150,000 in hard and soft dollars. It failed. In fact, it antagonized many wage roll employees who concluded that senior management was interested only in protecting its own financial interests.

In addition to failing to conduct some basic research, the vice president of corporate communication did not develop a few relevant, well-honed messages. For starters, the appeal for profit improvement should not have been linked to the incentive plan. It sounded too much like a threat. It should have been tied to the company's ability to continue to pay competitive wages and benefits to a full complement of workers, to continue to train workers, and to continue to generate the sales revenue required to keep the company financially healthy.

The critical step in defining key messages is to put yourself in the shoes of the people you want to reach. Ask yourself, "If I were in their place, what would I want to know and understand to help me answer the fundamental question, What's in this for me?"

Often some of the key messages have to assure people of what will not happen. For example, the base pay program is not threatened and layoffs are not expected. Until employees have the answers to their primary security questions, they are not likely to pay much attention to management exhortations concerning performance incentives.

Frequency and Impact

Educators and politicians know that repetition is the key to learning, retention, and behavior modification. Teaching and persuading are iterative processes that usually begin with information dissemination and gradually advance to understanding and acceptance. When information becomes knowledge, relationships among factors and issues become more apparent—the relationship between compensation and benefits, between profit and success, and between performance and reward. Awareness and understanding of relationships, often the most obvious, occur as the result of multiple impressions on the emotions and the intellect.

Communication professionals talk about a "rollout," meaning a methodical introduction of a new product, service, idea, or concept. A rollout consists of multiple impressions, created by multiple experiences over time—for example, a direct mail piece distributed to employees, followed by a highlights folder, reinforced by group meeting, dramatized by a personalized statement, validated by a questionnaire. These five scheduled communication hits use different media to introduce and reinforce messages designed to influence attitudes and behavior. Add the Internet, CD-ROM, interactive telephone response, and you have the makings of a high-impact communication campaign that can be managed like any other management process—for results.

Most organizations create their own noise levels that tend to dull the impact of new information. Today most workers are assaulted by tens of thousands of messages each day. To maintain some level of equilibrium, people develop defense systems that filter incoming information. Breaking through the defense system requires frequency and impact.

Impact means capturing the attention of employees long enough for them to develop a self-interest in the message:

> "Tell me there will be changes in the compensation program, and I'll be somewhat attentive. Tell me my base pay is going to be market driven and that any future increases will depend on whether I develop new competencies and I'll give you my full attention, because you've just confused me. And you've threatened me with concepts that are alien to me, were developed by senior management or, worse, a consultant, neither of whom understands what I do or why what I do is important.

"Tell me that I can earn more if I learn more, that you are going to give me uncommon continuous learning opportunities, and that I will have the opportunity to make significantly more money without having to climb the corporate management ladder, and I am eager to learn more. Impact is hitting my buttons with relevant messages that address my interests and repeatedly answer the question, "What's in this for me?' "

Peer Communication

Most employees can hear what is coming at them from all directions, but they listen horizontally. That is, they pay special attention to what they hear from their co-workers, opinion leaders, and supervisors. Most of all, they are inclined to trust most of what they hear from people at their organizational level, including supervisors, who often relate more closely with their subordinates than with senior management.

Politicians know the power of grass-roots campaigning. Union organizers know the power of inside advocates. Senior management is just beginning to become aware of and understand the power of peer communication.

Several client companies I have worked with over the years developed and lived by a strict communication protocol when introducing change or conveying important information to the workforce. In most cases, the protocol included briefings for first-line supervisors and for groups of employee opinion leaders (often members of a communication committee), who were then expected to support the communication program and answer questions.

A current client assignment is a good example of effective peer communication. The client is introducing a competency-based compensation program as part of an organizational change campaign to accelerate profitable growth. The communication plan includes the staples—print, video, and employee meetings led by senior management. The communication strategy, however, depends heavily on gaining the understanding, acceptance, and support of first-line supervisors and groups of employees who will be equipped with the same information presented to management about the new compensation program. Effective peer communication is critical in this case because the new compensation program is fundamentally different from the old program and is certain to intimidate most employees at first, even though they can earn more under the new program.

Change, even beneficial change, is perceived as threatening at first. Receiving new information from a familiar face can lessen anxiety and facilitate acceptance by employees. Employee surveys consistently show that when asked about their preferred source of information, employees overwhelmingly select their supervisors or others with whom they feel they can more comfortably identify.

Leveraging peer communication requires that senior management share power (information) with supervisors and workers who are not part of the decision-making process and may succumb to the temptation to question the thinking that went into a new incentive compensation program, for example. Senior management must be willing to encourage participation in the form of questions and must be prepared to provide complete answers that may go beyond the traditional boundaries of disclosure.

Here are a few suggestions to help establish an effective peer communication network within an organization:

- *Develop a communication strategy* that specifically highlights the role of peer (horizontal) communication and a communication plan that outlines how supervisors and opinion leaders will be organized and equipped to play information-sharing, advocacy roles.

- *Develop a communication schedule that allows sufficient time to mobilize the peer communication network.* How much advance time is needed depends on the complexity of the topic and rollout timetable. If a new variable-compensation program is planned for a January 1 effective date, for example, the peer communication network should be mobilized in September to allow enough time to educate network members, equip them with the materials they need to be authoritative sources of information, and provide the opportunities (such as employee meetings) for them to play formal and informal roles in the overall communication process.

- *Use the peer communication network between major programs.* The complaint I have often heard from supervisors and employee opinion leaders is that management "uses" them when they need help, but otherwise pays no attention to them. Peer communication gets better with regular use for several reasons:

—Members of the network become recognized by their peers as reliable sources of information.

—Members eventually better understand the business and are able to present "subtext" messages about the company's need for performance improvement.

—Members develop dual (management and employee) perspectives on workplace issues that can provide management with valuable insight into effective people management.

—Members can be mobilized quickly and require less prep time if they have established a solid context or rationale for organizational change.

As companies rely more heavily on impersonal, electronic communication, the importance and value of peer communication will increase. Information technology is ideally suited for efficient information dissemination. Peer communication is better suited to effective information sharing.

Feedback

=== · ■ · ===

Consumer research is an integral part of marketing communications, before and after the launch of a communications campaign, to test the efficacy of the campaign. Did the messages get through? Did they register? Were they understood? Did they move target groups to action? Did the campaign produce "share of mind" for the product or service, a prelude to market share?

The same questions apply to internal communication. Did the

messages about the new compensation program get through the noise level that exists in every organization? Did the messages about how the new program will work register with those whose paychecks will be affected? Did they understand the rationale for the new compensation program and why the design of the program is good for them and the company? Is the new program likely to motivate them to behave differently in order to benefit from the program? Have employees bought in to the new program, and do they have confidence in it?

The answers to those questions determine the success of failure of the communication effort? If the answers are generally affirmative, the cost of the campaign was a good investment. If the answers are not generally affirmative, the cost was a bad investment, with low or no employee relations yield. In fact, negative feedback may indicate the need for further investment in remedial initiatives to address fundamental employee relations issues such as mistrust, confusion, or a weak sense of affiliation.

I would go so far as to contend that communication is the most important determinate of employee acceptance of a new pay program. Acceptance will depend in large part on the perception of the program, and that rides on communication. If the communications is ineffective, the new program could fail. That possibility makes feedback on essential step in the rollout of a new program.

The least effective and least useful feedback is indiscriminate hearsay that is normally based on extremes, both positive and negative. Even if there were a way to verify hearsay feedback, the validation would be of little value because it is not reflective of a representative group. The following approaches can be counted on to assess the overall effectiveness of the communication campaign against the criteria described earlier:

1. Meetings with first-line supervisors led by an impartial facilitator to determine the reactions of the supervisors and their perceptions of their subordinates' reactions.
2. Employee focus groups led by an impartial facilitator to elicit opinions and to test for understanding and acceptance.
3. A mini-questionnaire distributed to a sample group to elicit opinions and to test for understanding and acceptance.

4. Creation of a communication task group made up of employees from various organizational strata to examine the effectiveness of the communication campaign against the objectives that had been established.

Regardless of the approach used, the feedback should be examined carefully to evaluate the communication campaign and determine whether additional communication is necessary to correct misconceptions or to clarify key issues. Permitting misinformation to take root can be disruptive and expensive. If the feedback shows that additional communication is warranted, the specific messages should be crafted immediately and conveyed to employees in the most effective ways possible, ideally through the peer network.

Conclusion

Employees are sophisticated, discriminating consumers of information. One of the topics that invariably catches their attention is pay—how they are paid and how much they are paid. Communicating with employees about compensation can be perilous. A failure to communicate is even more perilous.

Effective compensation communication is based on researching the target audience(s), determining relevant key messages, repeating the messages frequently, engaging peer communication networks in the process, and systematically collecting and analyzing feedback to evaluate the efficacy of the communication campaign.

Even in the absence of federal or state regulations mandating full disclosure of compensation programs, employers are urged to pay closer attention to compensation communication for three reasons:

1. Employees' perception of the fairness and competitiveness of a pay program is becoming an increasingly important factor that affects their willingness to perform at satisfactory levels and to remain with the company. Pay is therefore very important to workforce retention.

2. The ratio of fixed to variable pay is gradually shifting to greater emphasis on variable compensation tied to individual and team performance. If employees do not understand the reward system and how it affects their pay, the result will be low morale, discontent, and defection.

3. The number of individual and class suits against employers alleging discrimination or improper administration is expected to double or triple over the next five to ten years. One of the first items of evidence that attorneys look at is the quality and accuracy of communications materials describing the compensation program.

Experts may argue about whether compensation is a satisfier or a disatisfier and whether pay really motivates employees. However, there can be no argument about the importance of communicating a compensation program to ensure that it is understood, supported, and accepted as fair and competitive.

SECTION IV

■

CONCLUSION

13

Using Pay as a Tool to Achieve Organizational Goals

· ■ ·

Howard Risher
a senior fellow in the Center for Human Resources,
Wharton School, University of Pennsylvania

Anyone who wants to understand the motivation that drives the success of the U.S. economy should plan a trip to San Jose and the Silicon Valley. Somehow a rumor in that area got started and now is accepted as fact that X number of millionaires are created every Y minutes. A few of those individuals are outside investors, but most are employees who have had the opportunity to participate in a company-sponsored stock ownership plan.

This country has seen other similar success stories in other industries and other areas. The media frequently carry stories of companies where a company's success made it possible for employees to generate significant personal wealth. That has been an important part of U.S. history. And it is common in those stories to focus on what those opportunities mean to the commitment and dedication of employees to their employer. Those opportunities are for the most part unique to the U.S. culture.

In a prosperous, thriving company, the sense of excitement is almost palpable. People are obviously caught up in the excitement and willing to work very hard to see that the success continues. At times it is surprising how willing people are to make sacrifices in their personal lives to make their employer successful. This commitment is shared to some degree by virtually every employee and is an important source of competitive advantage.

When we look into a corporate success story that was sustained over more than year or two, one of the common themes is the opportunity for employees to share in the financial rewards generated by that success. Only a few companies have created millionaires in the clerical and hourly ranks, but those stories receive a lot of attention. IBM did it, Wal-Mart did it, and now Microsoft is doing it. Those stories and others have become part of our folklore.

It seems as though we have always known that money is a motivator. If there is one theme that has been consistent in our cultural heritage, it is the ongoing importance of stories about people who became wealthy or about people who took considerable personal risk to improve their economic future. There are also stories of manual workers who made sacrifices to develop the skills or knowledge needed to earn higher wages and promotions. The importance of money as a motivator prompted many companies a century or more ago to introduce profit-sharing schemes and, in the first half of this century, piece-rate incentive systems. These plans may not have consistently produced the desired results, but the clear intent was to take advantage of the motivational power of money.

Beyond this there is a widely shared belief in the United States that good performance should be recognized and rewarded. The Girl Scouts reward the girl who sells the most cookies. The best students are rewarded with gold stars. Every sport, professional as well as amateur, hands out awards to its most valuable players (MVPs). The entertainment industry selects a few individuals for Oscars, Emmys, and other awards. Many other industries and occupations have created comparable awards to recognize outstanding performance.

Does Money Motivate?

There is no question that monetary incentives influence behavior and performance. Some people are motivated more than others, and there are, to be sure, people who would not be motivated by the prospect of additional income. It is probably true that some of the individuals who did not respond to the prospect of a 5 percent increase in pay might react very differently to a potential 25 or 50 percent increase.

But before a corporate executive is going to approve the addition of an incentive plan (for employees who did not participate in a prior plan), he or she has to be confident that it will prompt improved performance. In concept, the bottom-line improvement has to be greater than the increase in payroll expense. There are more than a few corporate executives who would not be willing to make that bet. There is no way to be sure a new plan is going to motivate employees to perform at higher levels.

Unfortunately the research on the motivational power of financial rewards is very limited and too often was done in artificial, laboratory settings rather than real work situations. The most prominent name is still Frederick Herzberg, who published his often referenced book, *The Motivation to Work*, forty years ago.[1] His conclusions were based largely on research that others did. When Herzberg is mentioned in an argument over pay, it is important to keep in mind that the factories of the 1950s and the labor-management climate were very different from the current industrial scene.

Herzberg's basic argument is that pay is more likely to make employees angry or frustrated; they become dissatisfied; pay by itself does not provide satisfaction. From that perspective, it is all too easy to make pay a demotivator. Anyone who has had a job would not find that surprising. The fact is that many workers do not believe they are paid what they are worth or that they have been treated fairly. They would like to be paid more, and, not surprisingly, they have a prepared argument that justifies paying them more.

If the goal is to generate true job satisfaction, so that employees walk away at the end of the workday with the sense that they had a satisfying day, that is not related to the way their base pay is managed or to their pay level. It is unrealistic to expect that from a pay program. That feeling comes from the work itself. Intrinsic satisfaction, as its called, can be a powerful motivator.

When employees become dissatisfied with the way they are paid, their malcontentment is commonly triggered by two possible problems:

they did not receive what they expected (that is related to what academics refer to as expectancy theory) or they perceive their pay as inequitable relative to their "value," their work effort, or to the pay of others. (That comes under the umbrella of equity theory.) These problems arise routinely. A key is that both are driven by perception, and that is often traceable to ineffective communications. If employees know the rules and know what they can expect, they are unlikely to become dissatisfied, unless, of course, management violates the decision-making rules. Poor decisions often make people angry.

The fact is that every organization has a pay program, and that program requires ongoing management decisions. The potential for perceived inequities is always present. Moreover, no matter what wage or salary program is used, some employees are always going to be less satisfied (or more dissatisfied) than others. To minimize the possible problems, management needs to make communications a high priority and carefully consider decisions. Management cannot do anything more.

Critics also argue that when pay is used as an incentive, it takes the focus away from the motivation derived from the work itself. The presence of financial incentives—"extrinsic" rewards—diminishes the impact of intrinsic rewards. Their argument is that pay gets in the way and causes more harm than good. In other words, if we could neutralize the impact of pay, and employees did not have reasons to think about it, they would be more satisfied with their jobs.

There is again a grain of truth in their argument. Pay, especially if it is poorly managed, can offset the satisfaction from doing a job well. However, the fact is that not every employee experiences job satisfaction. Even managers and professionals, and in every occupation, sometimes work in situations where there is little or no job satisfaction. On a related point, the reasons for the satisfaction are not going to be the same even for people working in the same occupation. Two nurses working in the same hospital unit, for example, could be motivated by somewhat different sources of job satisfaction. Even nurses may come to realize that they are not satisfied with their jobs.

A counterargument is that when employees are motivated by the satisfaction derived from the work, they may not perform their job in the way that is in the best interests of the organization. The nurses who find patient care satisfying may not have the hospital's goals in mind as they treat patients. Realistically, job satisfaction can be a powerful source of motivation, but it is impractical to rely on it as the only motivator. It is not a consistent motivator, nor does it necessarily lead to the achievement of organizational goals.

Despite the potential problems, it is probably safe to say that money always influences behavior. When wage and salary increases are across the board or in the form of longevity increases, the message is that performance is not important, and that affects the way people approach their jobs. When performance is not considered and everyone is treated the same, the high performers are the ones who are likely to be angry. Pay levels are also affected by promotional decisions, and in selecting someone for a promotion, employees see clearly what behavior is needed for them to move up the ladder. Money can never be completely neutral.

It follows, then, that it is always advantageous to align new pay programs with organizational goals. That contributes to a performance culture and sends the message to employees that performance is important. To paraphrase an old adage, "You get what you reward."

Surprisingly, perhaps, there is nothing in the research literature about how to maximize the effectiveness of employee pay programs. Is merit pay enough? Is a 5 percent increase half as effective as a 10 percent increase? What form of incentive is the most effective? The best we can do is to rely on common sense supported with personal experience and best practice feedback.

The experience in most organizations suggests that merit pay is seldom as effective as one might believe from textbooks. Merit pay is almost universal, but few would argue that it is very effective. At best it contributes to a performance culture, where performance is a shared priority and good performance is recognized and valued. If we want to determine how effective merit pay is, all we have to do is compare it with the alternatives.

At the other end of the spectrum, the anecdotal stories like the millionaires in the Silicon Valley usually involve megadollars (compared to the typical amounts in compensation programs). When opportunities of that magnitude are made available, it seems as though work and the drive for organizational and personal success can become all consuming.

Unfortunately, relatively few people have opportunities to work in an environment where they can become truly wealthy.

For most organizations, compensation is limited by the need to maintain a competitive cost structure. Stock options do not represent an accounting cost, but in broad-based option programs, the dilution effect is clearly a constraint. There is an obvious reason to view compensation as a cost, and that means it needs to be minimized and controlled. Rather than adopt a plan that is designed to pay, for example, 10 percent of base pay, it is usually easy to find support for cutting back the payouts to 8 percent or, better yet, to 5 percent.

How big do payouts have to be? We do not know. There are corporations where gain-sharing plans paying as little as 4 to 6 percent of base pay have a surprisingly positive impact. Payouts at that level are typical. However, the gain-sharing plan for employees of the city of Charlotte, North Carolina (one of the few in the public sector) typically pays in the $500 range. That is less than 2 percent to the typical employee, but in a conversation with Ken Wallace, the city's manager of compensation, says he "never ceases to be surprised by how excited employees are to receive their check." In the right circumstances, the amounts do not have to be large.

Maybe It's Not the Money

This is going out on a limb with no empirical support, but it may be that money itself is not the source of motivation. Herzberg is correct in arguing that pay is not a source of satisfaction. Actually, his second most important motivator, after intrinsic satisfaction from the work itself, is recognition. Everybody would like to have their "value" recognized, and when that happens, it is an incentive to replicate the behavior, so it happens again. Recognition is a key to any MVP award. It is also important in a school setting when the teacher hands out the gold stars. When someone does something good, he or she wants to be recognized for the accomplishment. Incentive plan payouts give recognition to an individual's contribution.

Incentive plan participation can enhance the stature of an employee's job. When a job is made bonus eligible, it usually signifies that the incumbent is expected to play a larger role in the organization, and more is expected of him or her. Generally bonus-eligible jobs have a higher status. This is another form of recognition, and it means something to everyone who becomes aware of the change. In that context, the additional income is the icing on the cake.

Incentive payments can also enhance an employee's stature with his or her spouse and family. The receipt of the payout is a time for family celebration, and that is another opportunity for recognition. This sense of celebration can even carry over to friends and neighbors.

It is significant to point out that promotions have a similar impact. The promotion involves additional compensation, but the amounts are typically not large. It is the recognition both within the organization and at home that makes people work very hard for a promotion.

Money to be sure affects an employee's lifestyle. The more he or she earns, the more affluent the lifestyle. The interest in a better life is certainly a motivator. There is a limit, however, to how much money is needed for lifestyle purposes. The acquisition of material possessions is presumably not the reason Bill Gates and Ted Turner continue to work.

For them and others, money is an indicator of success. It has been important throughout U.S. history and now is obviously important to the changes in Russia and Eastern Europe. Big salary increases or big bonuses seem to give people bragging rights. Somehow going from $20,000 to $25,000 can be just as symbolic as going from $200,000 to $250,000. Money makes people confirm an individual's importance. But again it is the recognition that is desired; the money is a measure of success.

From a different perspective, one of the intriguing aspects of group incentives is the enhanced motivation that comes from working with others. The old piece-rate incentives backfired. Employees resented the implicit control of their efforts and the competition among co-workers. With incentives like gain sharing, the idea that everyone shares in the payout seems to pull people together and makes it important not to let down co-workers. Employees like to feel they are succeeding as a group and will work hard to make that happen. The payouts also give them a reason to celebrate together.

The impact of incentives also needs to be considered in terms of expectancy theory and equity theory. Employees have to receive what they expected relative to their work effort. If the amounts are smaller than expected, it will be a problem. Surprisingly perhaps, if the amounts are too large, it will make employees uncomfortable and that can be a problem. That boils down to communicating the rules and living with them.

Equity theory demands that payouts reflect the individual's perception of his or her own work effort and results when compared with other employees. When people work hard and their efforts make the organization successful, equity theory suggests they share in that success. Moreover, if their employer is more successful than competitors, the employees should be better compensated.

Both theories, however, would work the same way if money were not involved. They are actually part of a broader concern with fairness. Pay is an important focus, but neither theory is limited to compensation. If the only expected reward is a pat on the back, an employee will be upset if it is not forthcoming.

This is not to suggest that money is not necessary. Pay is central to an employment relationship and, for better or worse, is a common scorecard to track one's success and personal value. The point, however, is that pay is symbolic, and its impact on motivation is complicated by organizational circumstances. There was a time when pay was viewed as the carrot, and it was assumed that employees were the donkey. Piece-rate incentives reflect this thinking. It is not that simple.

Pay and Organizational Change

· ■ ·

Traditionally organizations were viewed as machines, and management's goal was to make them operate efficiently. The piece-rate systems were focused on speed and on producing as much in an eight-hour shift as possible. That model was prevalent into the late 1980s.

Then the interest in total quality management exploded, and change became a way of life. The zeal of quality management was followed by an equally strong interest in reengineering.

Both of these initiatives involved significant organizational change, and both failed to live up to the announced expectations. The advocates of these initiatives approached the planned changes with zeal but were unable to develop the needed commitment to the new way of operating.

In hindsight, we now realize that too little attention was paid to the people issues. People resist change and are more comfortable with established ways of operating. It is particularly important to appreciate that in all but a few cases, the reward system was still reinforcing the old behaviors. Those organizations that changed their reward system, typically by introducing an incentive plan to reinforce the new goals, experienced less resistance. To use that adage again, "If you want quality, then you need to reward quality." Too many companies did not.

Organizational change by definition involves changes in the way jobs are defined, in the behaviors and skills required, and in the way employees interact. They need to understand that the expected changes are important to the organization, and they also need to understand the benefits to both the organization and themselves. Theirs is a voluntary decision to cooperate and jump on to the bandwagon. The reward system has to reinforce and facilitate this decision.

There can be a world of difference between a work group that drags its feet or silently resists change and one that embraces and commits to making change successful. The pay system is only one element in a change strategy, but it has everyone's attention and can be a powerful tool. Employees might say something about management's "putting its money where its mouth is."

Raising the Bar of Performance

· ■ ·

It seems at times that every organization is trying to raise the bar of performance. They are performing at one level and would like to raise the bar to a higher level. New technology and processes are in some cases required to reach the new level, but at its core this is a people management problem. The increases in productivity that Barry Macy found in his research—30 to 40 percent (see Chapter 1)—are attributable to a new work paradigm that enables people to perform at higher levels. Finding ways to raise the bar can be a decided competitive advantage.

Pay by itself is not going to accomplish this. If work processes are unchanged, a new reward system, such as a group incentive plan, may well generate better results, but it's likely to be limited. In the past that was a common strategy. Employees will work somewhat harder for at least some period of time, but the big increases in productivity are not attributable to speed or work effort. Working harder (i.e., increased effort) will not generate a 30 percent increase in productivity.

Furthermore, if the work unit has a history of poor employer-employee relations or simply poor management, it is unlikely that the employees will jump on the bandwagon simply because a new carrot is dangled in front of them. They may also lack the knowledge or skills to adapt their behavior to new work processes. They could also have inadequate equipment or resources available. To reiterate, Barry Macy identified a list of some sixty action levers that have been shown to affect productivity. Pay is only one of the levers.

Macy's research shows that the levers are more powerful when used in combination as the basis for an integrated change strategy. And that is the direction in which companies are heading. The changes related to this shift in strategy are documented in the 1998 State-of-the Art and Practice Council Report, a research project sponsored by the Human Resource Planning Society that looked at the thinking and practices in leading companies where human resources strategies and practices were acknowledged to provide competitive advantage. The researchers found that the focus on productivity had shifted to a broader definition of improved performance: increasing shareholder value. Significantly, the CEOs and COOs contacted for the study mentioned people as frequently as, if not more so than, the human resources executives when they outlined their major business priorities.

Those companies were redesigning their basic architectures to align strategy, structure, systems, processes, staffing, and culture to create an organization that is organized to succeed and that translates into increased shareholder value. A focal goal of their efforts was the creation of a performance culture that encourages leadership, teamwork, learning, and accountability.

People and their capabilities are central to this new way of managing an organization. This is the essence of the new work paradigm. The traditional emphasis on organization charts and job descriptions is being replaced by new beliefs about people and their contributions.

Attracting, developing, and retaining talent is a principal focus. Leading companies are looking into the future to identify the capabilities they need for continued success and then preparing staffing and development plans to make certain the people capabilities will be available when needed. The phrase *developmental organization* is now widely used to refer to a strategy to encourage and facilitate organizational and individual learning and development. Another phrase, *human capital*, signifies an important shift from thinking about employees as a cost to seeing them and managing them as a capital investment. These are profound changes in the management of people resources.

Among these leading companies, there has been a rapid shift to a new pay-for-performance philosophy. At the heart of the new reward systems is a belief that the organization benefits when employees are provided opportunities to share in the success. In other words, employees raise their level of performance to grab the opportunity. Sharing is seen as a win-win for both the organization and the employees. Those beliefs are the foundation for the new broad-based option programs. Those beliefs are also behind the decision by a growing number of companies, such as DuPont, to introduce incentive plans that cover every employee. The new employer-employee relationship includes higher performance expectations in exchange for a chance to benefit from the improved performance of their work units.

People want to work for a winner. They want to feel their contribution is recognized and valued. They can enjoy the challenge and feel comfortable making the commitment to their employer. It is very much the same as playing for a winning sports team. When that is an element of the employer-employee relationship, it can energize a group of employees.

This is a very different philosophy from the donkey-and-carrot orientation that is the basis for piece-rate systems. Those plans were designed to control employee behavior, and people resent attempts to control them. When employees learned how to perform their jobs in a manner that produced high pay levels, management commonly modified the output standards to control and reduce payout levels. Changing the standards is obviously not an effective way to win employee commitment.

In contrast, the new goal is to motivate employees to apply their full capabilities to the benefit of the organization. Toward this end, it would be decidedly advantageous to eliminate narrowly defined, mind-numbing jobs. The big increases in productivity come when employees are encouraged to use their capabilities and to think outside creatively. Working smarter is dramatically more important than working harder.

The new reward systems also reflect a willingness to use pay as a tool to achieve organizational goals. To reach the higher performance levels, companies are linking pay solidly to the achievement of desired results. If, for example, a goal is to improve quality or to increase customer satisfaction, incentives increasingly commonly are linked to those results. If we project the developments in compensation over the past few years into the future, the number of specific incentives for groups or teams is likely to mushroom.

Moving to a New Compensation Model

This book has focused on one aspect of a new compensation model that is rapidly unfolding: the use of pay as an incentive. The traditional model evolved from the methods industrial engineers and early personnel specialists developed to manage base pay. That model has the following characteristics:

- Wages and salaries have been closely controlled by human resources specialists. Line managers have had minimal input and little discretionary authority.
- Job information is documented in lengthy job descriptions that list assigned job duties. Whenever there is an alleged change in job duties, the change is supposed to be documented. Organizations are now changing too frequently to enable human resources staff to keep them up to date.
- The focus of base pay management has been the value of the

"job," which is determined by applying a job evaluation system. Relatively few people understand those systems, but these systems gained adequate acceptance to become part of corporate life.

- To reduce labor-management friction in the 1930s and 1940s, employers made internal equity a primary goal of wage and salary management. Internal equity was accepted as a pillar of a sound base pay program.
- Job evaluation systems were developed to maintain internal equity and align jobs in a hierarchy. That reinforced the importance of the hierarchy and perpetuated traditional organization structures.
- The concern with internal equity is also the reason that virtually all employers maintain one salary structure for all white-collar employees. The structures have been based on the same design principles from company to company.
- Merit pay was and continues to be virtually universal for all but blue-collar workers.
- The administrative procedures were designed for centralized control of base pay decisions.
- Incentive plans have been rare below the executive level, except for sales commission plans.

There has been a high level of interest in changing this model over the past few years. It is still easy to find leading corporations where the traditional model is strongly entrenched, but there is reason to believe that model is a dinosaur. The presentations at professional conferences and articles in human resources journals now explore the new concepts. The traditional model is no longer a topic for discussion.

The emerging model differs in several key respects. The job-based focus is being replaced by new ideas that focus on the value of the individual. Competency-based pay and skill-based pay are the primary alternatives in the new model. The emphasis on internal equity is shifting to make the alignment with prevailing market pay levels a more important consideration. The close centralized control is being replaced by much more flexible and decentralized decision making, with line managers assuming a broader role. The baton is being passed from personnel "police" to the line managers.

The last point is perhaps the most important because it means that managers have to accept the responsibility for managing the salaries of their people. It was easier when they could "blame it on Personnel." However, if they are to be accountable for results, then they have to accept responsibility for managing their people, and wage and salary decisions are central to that.

The transition to the new model has had more than a few bumps in the road. The management of people in the typical organization reflects a belief system that is widely shared at all levels. The importance of internal equity is an example of a basic belief. Another common belief is that incentive pay is unlikely to be successful for hourly and support personnel.

Those beliefs control or at least influence decision making . If senior management does not believe proposed changes are the "right" answer, they are likely to resist a proposal. At lower levels, they may not be asked for input when new programs are approved, but they will definitely react to a new program, and their reaction can effectively nullify any prospects that the program will be successful.

Companies that have introduced new pay systems that deviate from the traditional model have experienced problems that reflect the classic resistance to change. The problems are typically not related to design flaws. These are new concepts, and any changes will affect the way people are compensated. They are naturally very interested and frequently anxious about how changes might affect them. There is probably no organizational change that is as potentially disruptive as introducing a new pay system. These are of course pocketbook issues.

For these reasons, the transition to a new model is more likely to be successful if adequate attention is paid to the following issues:

- The articulation of the reasons for making the change and the goals in making the change. There have to be sound, credible business reasons for making the change. People have to understand why changes are necessary and how the changes will benefit the organization.

- An understanding of the beliefs that managers and employees hold. This can be secured in several ways, including focus groups and surveys. The beliefs need to considered in planning or steps taken to modify the beliefs. It would be a mistake to ignore the beliefs.

■ The development of a compensation strategy and program goals that have the full support of top management. This will be the foundation of any new program and the touchstone for evaluating the program's effectiveness over time.

■ The support of the organization's leaders. The sensitivity of the planned change makes top management support essential. It cannot be treated as "another personnel initiative." Ideally top management should play a prominent role in planning the change.

■ A strategy for securing input from the people who will be affected by a new program. A new compensation program needs broad-based support. The input could come in the form of a committee to guide the program design process or from focus groups reacting to ideas in the way that market researchers seek input.

■ A strategy for securing best-practice input from other employers that have recently adopted similar program concepts. The level of interest is high, but few companies have much of a track record. Those companies that have adopted new program concepts have learned valuable lessons that can help others to avoid the potholes.

■ A communications plan to keep people informed of what they can expect as the new program is planned. This is more than the dissemination of information. This is a marketing campaign to get people to accept the changes.

It is important to emphasize that these steps are only indirectly related to program design. The experts are needed, but the technical design considerations are overshadowed by process considerations. The new pay is part of a new work paradigm that is transforming the way work is organized and managed.

A Final Note

· ■ ·

The changes in the work paradigm and in compensation programs are driven by economic considerations. Every company is feeling the pressure to become more productive and more responsive. In that environment, the full utilization of resources is a high priority.

When we consider the pressures to improve performance, all too many employees have capabilities that have been underutilized in the old paradigm. That paradigm and the associated management practices have their origins in a different era. Corporations need the full commitment of their employees and all their capabilities. The compensation program should be the lever that makes that happen.

From the employees' perspective, the old paradigm has to be an albatross. Too many people have had the negative and wearisome experience of a career in boring, narrowly defined jobs. There are too many stories of people in those jobs who have significant accomplishments in their "after-hours" lives. People like to feel as if they are growing and realizing their potential, making a valued contribution, and working as part of a winning team. When they feel that way about their jobs and their careers, it carries over to the balance of their lives. When they do not feel that way, the less time they spend at work, the better. Too many jobs are like that.

As a consultant, I have gone in and out of hundreds of companies. In some a sense of excitement is in the air; in others the place is like a morgue. That does not happen by accident. The excitement generally means people are engaged in their work and committed to their employer's success. Companies have a choice.

Lester Thurow, in his 1992 best-selling book, *Head to Head*,[2] argues that workforce productivity is the only sustainable source of competitive advantage—the "key competitive weapon." Financial resources provided a competitive advantage in the past, but today investment funds are available to any company with a sound business plan. Thurow argues that technological resources can provide a short-term advantage, but it has become virtually impossible to rely on new products or scientific developments. It has become too easy to clone technology or products. His point is that organizations that get the most from their employees will prove to be the winners. An organization's people, their skills and their commitment, are the only sustainable source of competitive advantage.

The pay system is only a piece of the solution. The best pay system is not going to have much impact when other people management practices are ineffective or worse. In the right context, however, people can be excited by the prospect of coming to work and by the prospects present in the compensation program. Companies that are moving away from traditional compensation programs have an opportunity to significantly enhance career prospects in the organization. The linkage between pay and performance gives people the opportunity to benefit from their work efforts. That prospect can renew an employee's excitement about their jobs. This should be a focal issue in changing the work paradigm.

Notes

1. Frederick Herzberg, *The Motivation to Work* (2nd ed.) (New York: Wiley, 1959).
2. Lester Thurow, *Head to Head: The Coming Economic Battle Among Japan, Germany, Europe and America* (New York: Morrow, 1992).

About the Contributors

Howard Risher is a senior fellow in the Center for Human Resources, Wharton School, University of Pennsylvania and also works as a private consultant. He has over twenty-five years of experience in compensation, performance management, workforce management, and employee research. He previously managed compensation consulting practices for two international consulting firms. His clients have included a number of major corporations and health care organizations, federal and state agencies, and colleges and universities. He is the co-editor with Charles Fay of two previous books, *The Performance Imperative: Strategies for Enhancing Workforce Effectiveness* (Jossey Bass, 1995) and *New Strategies for Public Pay* (Jossey Bass, 1997). He serves on the Advisory Board of Compensation and Benefits Review. He has authored a number of articles on compensation and is a frequent speaker at professional meetings. He has a B.A. in psychology from Penn State and an M.B.A. and Ph.D. in economics and labor relations from the Wharton School.

Richard J. Anthony, Sr., is founder and president of the Solutions Network, a management consulting firm specializing in human resources, performance improvement, and organization effectiveness. He has twenty-seven years of experience as a counselor to senior management in the private, public, and not-for-profit sectors. One of his areas of specialization is organizational communications. He was previously chairman and CEO of the Alexander Consulting Group's U.S. human resources consulting unit, where he established the firm's global organization effectiveness practice. He was also a principal of Towers Perrin, where he was communications consulting practice leader. He is the founder and executive director of the Center for Privately Held Companies. He serves on the board of several not-for-profit organizations. He is a graduate of Villanova University and completed a Harvard Management Program. His office is in Radnor, Pa.

Richard J. Bannister, Jr., is a principal in Towers Perrin specializing in executive compensation. He co-leads the firm's value-based management practice, specializing in designing organization measurement management systems and compensation programs aligned with a company's values and business strategy. His clients include major corporations in a cross-section of industries. Bannister has published articles in leading academic journals and newspapers. He has a B.A. in Economics from Wharton and M.Sc. in Economics, with distinction, from the London School of Economics. He is working to become a Chartered Financial Analyst. His office is in Manhattan.

Neil K. Coleman is a vice president at Organization Resources Counselors, the leading consulting firm in the area of expatriate polices and practices, where he is responsible for the organization's global pay practices. He conducts compensation surveys and consults with client organizations regarding global pay policies. Prior to his consulting career, he held positions in global organizations, including Exxon, W. R. Grace, and the European American Bank. Dr. Coleman is also an Assistant Professor of Management at the University of Bridgeport, Graduate School of Business. He received his Ph.D. from New York University and holds a CCP from the American Compensation Association. His office is in Manhattan.

N. Fredric Crandall is a founding partner of the Center for Workforce Effectiveness in Northbrooke, Illinois, where he specializes in work design, reward systems, and organizational change management. He has extensive consulting experience in compensation planning, evaluation, incentive plans, and human resources and organizational effectiveness. He is a frequent speaker for groups such as the American Management Association and the American Compensation Association and has served as a course developer for the ACA. He is the coauthor of the recently published *Work and Rewards in the Virtual Workplace: A "New Deal" for Organizations and Employees* (AMACOM, 1998). He has a doctorate in Industrial Relations from the University of Minnesota, a master's degree from UCLA, and a bachelor's degree in economics from the University of California—Berkeley.

William Gentry is a consultant in Towers Perrin's compensation line of business, where he specializes in performance measurement and incentive plan design. Before joining Towers Perrin, he worked for a benefits consulting firm specializing in Section 125 plans. Mr. Gentry has an M.B.A. from the College of William and Mary, a B.A. in History from Virginia Commonwealth University, and a B.A. in Economics and Business from Randolph-Macon University.

Steven E. Gross is a principal in the Philadelphia and New York offices of William M. Mercer Inc. and national practice director for employee compensation. He is responsible for directing Mercer's activities in the design and implementation of innovative compensation programs for all levels of employee. Prior to joining Mercer, he was vice president and managing director of Hay Management Consultant's Northeast Region and leader of the workforce variable compensation practice. He is the author of *Compensation for Teams: How to Design and Implement Team-Based Reward Programs* (AMACOM, 1995). Mr. Gross has been quoted in a number of business publications, including *The Wall Street Journal, The New York Times, Fortune, Business Week, Time,* and *American Banker.* He has an M.B.A. from Wharton and a B.S. in Industrial Engineering from State University of New York at Buffalo.

James T. Kochanski is a principal of Sibson & Company, an international management consulting firm specializing in organizational effectiveness and compensation issues. His area of expertise is competency-based human resources programs, large-scale organizational redesign, and compensation plans. He was the editor of a special issue of *Human Resource Management* on human resources competencies and has published other articles on competency management. Prior to joining Sibson, Kochanski held human resources positions at Northern Telecom, Quaker Oats, and Kellogg. He is a graduate of the University of Maryland (B.S. in personnel and labor relations) and American Institute/ NTL Institute (M.S. in human resources development). Kochanski is based in Sibson's Raleigh, N.C., office.

Eric P. Marquardt is a senior vice president of Compensation Resource Group (CRG) and the manager of the firm's Midwest consulting practice. He specializes in executive and management compensation and focuses on the human resources issues related to mergers, acquisitions, and joint ventures. Prior to joining CRG he was the director of executive compensation and management programs at Merck & Co. He also served as a regional practice director for the Wyatt Company in San Francisco and previously worked for PepsiCo and Texas Instruments. He has published articles in a number of professional journals and speaks at conferences on executive compensation topics. Eric is a graduate of the University of Michigan and received a Masters of Labor and Industrial Relations from Michigan State University. He lives in St. Louis.

Pearl Meyer is president of Pearl Meyer & Partners, a Manhattan-based consulting firm that specializes in executive compensation, performance, organization, and selection. After founding and leading the executive compensation practice of another organization for over twenty years, she and a group of colleagues formed a new firm dedicated solely to compensation. She has long been an expert in the development and negotiation of senior executive employment contracts and agreements and in directors' compensation. She has been featured in *Fortune, The Wall Street Journal,* and *Business Week.* She has been published in major business media including *Harvard Business Review* and *The New York Times.* She is a cum laude graduate in mathematics and economics with Ph.D. studies at New York University.

Jude T. Rich is chairman of Sibson & Company, an international management consulting firm that helps clients improve performance through effective use of their employees. He has extensive experience in all aspects of human resources and organization effectiveness. His primary focus is executive compensation and specifically the linkage of short- and long-term incentive plans to company strategy and economic value creation. Prior to joining Sibson, he spent ten years at McKinsey & Company, where he was a partner and leader of the firm's human resources management practice. He has also held human resources and line management positions in several leading corporations. He is a fre-

quent speaker before such groups as the Conference Board's CEO fo-
rums. He has an M.B.A. and a bachelors degree, both with honors, from
Rutgers University. His office is in Princeton.

Edward Sullivan retired recently from DuPont, where he was a corporate compensation consultant and one of the principal architects of the
organization's transition to variable compensation. In his career with
DuPont, he played a lead role in the design of more than sixty incentive
plans. In the 1980s Sullivan was responsible for a major study of the
future of incentive compensation that led to a decision, announced in
1998, to introduce incentive plans covering employees at all levels and
in all DuPont business units. He has been a frequent guest speaker at
business conferences and has chaired or hosted a number of industrial
meetings dedicated to the use of incentive compensation He now works
as a private consultant. Ed has a B.S. from Quinnipac College.

Marc J. Wallace, Jr., is a founding partner of the Center for Workforce
Effectiveness, Northbrooke, Illinois. He is an internationally recognized
expert and consultant on rewards and human resources strategy on
compensation, and he is a highly regarded speaker and researcher. His
experience has led to the publication of over sixty articles and papers
and several books, including the recently published *Work and Rewards
in the Virtual Workplace: A "New Deal" for Organizations and Employees* (AMACOM, 1998). In 1995 the American Compensation Association honored Wallace with the Keystone Contribution Award,
recognizing his lifetime contributions to the fields of compensation and
human resources. He holds the B.A. degree from Cornell and the M.A.
and Ph.D. degrees in Industrial Relations from the University of Minnesota.

Thomas B. Wilson is president of the Wilson Group. Concord, Massa-
chusetts, which assists clients in improving their competitive advantage
by designing and implementing performance-based reward systems that
are aligned with the strategy and core values of the organization. He
has worked as a consultant for over eighteen years and has over twenty-
five years of business experience. Prior to forming the Wilson Group,
he was the vice president of reward systems for Aubrey Daniels and

Associates and a vice president and general manager for Hay Management Associates. He is the author of *Rewards That Drive Performance: Success Stories from Leading Organizations* (AMACOM, 1999) and *Innovative Reward Systems for the Changing Workplace* (McGraw-Hill, 1995). He has a Masters in Management from Vanderbilt and a bachelors in finance and political science from Southern Methodist University.

Index